The Landscape of Absence

EMILY DICKINSON'S POETRY

Inder Nath Kher

New Haven and London, Yale University Press, 1974

Published with assistance from the
Kingsley Trust Association Publication Fund
established by the Scroll and Key Society
of Yale College.

Designed by Sally Sullivan
and set in Baskerville type.
Printed in the United States of America by
Vail-Ballou Press, Inc., Binghamton, N.Y.

Published in Great Britian, Europe, and Africa by
Yale University Press, Ltd., London.
Distributed in Latin America by Kaiman & Polon,
Inc., New York City; in Australasia and Southeast
Asia by John Wiley & Sons Australasia Pty. Ltd.,
Sydney; in India by UBS Publishers' Distributors Pvt.,
Ltd., Delhi; in Japan by John Weatherhill, Inc., Tokyo.

Acknowledgment is made for permission to quote the poems and letters of Emily Dickinson from:

Thomas H. Johnson, editor. *The Poems of Emily Dickinson.* Cambridge, Mass.: The Belknap Press of Harvard University Press. Copyright 1951, 1955 by The President and Fellows of Harvard College. Reprinted by permission of the publishers and the Trustees of Amherst College.

Thomas H. Johnson, editor. *The Letters of Emily Dickinson.* Cambridge, Mass.: The Belknap Press of Harvard University Press. Copyright 1958 by The President and Fellows of Harvard College. Reprinted by permission of the publishers.

Thomas H. Johnson, editor. *The Complete Poems of Emily Dickinson.* Boston, Mass.: Little, Brown and Company. Copyright 1914, 1935, 1942 by Martha Dickinson Bianchi. Copyright 1929, © 1957, 1963 by Mary L. Hampson. Reprinted by permission of the publishers.

The Landscape of Absence

Dedicated
to the memory of my father
Gopal Dass Kher
and my mother
Kaushalya Devi Kher

CONTENTS

ACKNOWLEDGMENTS

I wish to express my gratitude to those who have encouraged
and helped me in various ways in the completion of this study.
I am especially grateful to Edward J. Rose of the University of
Alberta, who taught me the way of perception and inspired
me to undertake the exacting job of dealing with the whole of
Emily Dickinson's poetic vision. Professor Rose gave most gen-
erously of his time and energy to answer my questions, and I
benefited greatly from his broad learning, critical acumen,
and imaginative insights. John F. Lauber of the University of
Alberta also deserves special mention here: it was under his
supervison that this study was first undertaken as a doctoral
dissertation. My sincere thanks go to E. D. Blodgett, from
whom I borrowed the phrase "the landscape of absence" for
use as the title of this study. I owe a special debt to my former
teacher and guide, Frank Norman Shrive of McMaster University, who initiated me into the study of American literature,
and who introduced me to Emily Dickinson's poetry in the fall
of 1965.

I consider myself fortunate indeed to have discussed personally with Richard B. Sewall, Charles R. Anderson,
Northrop Frye, Henry W. Wells, Glauco Cambon, and
Douglas Duncan the salient features of my approach to Dickinson's poetry. Their perceptive criticism and appreciation of
my ideas were a constant source of encouragement and chal-

lenge to me. I deeply valued their suggestions and admonishments. I am particularly indebted to Professor Sewall of Yale whose continued interest in my work has been of the greatest value to me; without the benefit of my encounter with him, this study would not have been possible in its present form. I must also record here my deep sense of gratitude to Millicent Todd Bingham, who welcomed me to her home in Washington, D.C., in the fall of 1968, only two months before her death, and who enlightened me greatly about the state of Dickinson criticism, as well as about the poet's mind and art.

I acknowledge too the courtesy and valuable assistance of the librarians in charge of Emily Dickinson manuscripts: J. Richard Phillips, the Frost Library, Amherst College; W. H. Bond, the Houghton Library, Harvard University; Winifred D. Sayer, the Jones Library, Amherst. Mr. Phillips and Professor Bond were particularly helpful in making it possible for me to examine personally their collections of Dickinson materials, during the years 1968–70.

My sincere thanks are also due to the Social Sciences and Humanities Division of the Canada Council for a research grant in 1970; to the University of Calgary Grants Committee for a research grant in 1971; and to the Folger Shakespeare Library, Washington, D.C., for a grant-in-aid toward the purchase of a Xerox Copyflo of Emily Dickinson manuscripts at Amherst College, Amherst, Massachusetts. To the Canada Council, I am most particularly grateful for generous assistance.

My gratitude goes also to the editorial staff and readers of the Yale University Press for their careful and constructive criticisms of the manuscript. I am particularly indebted to Ellen Graham, Merle Spiegel, and Wayland W. Schmitt for their considerable assistance.

Finally, my warmest thanks go to my wife, Salochna, who endured so much; to my daughter, Rshmi, who comforted me; and to my brother, Narinder Nath Kher, who has always been a source of spiritual strength to me.

In quoting Emily Dickinson, I have used the Belknap Press editions, as acknowledged above on the copyright page. The parenthetical source citations following quotations refer to the numbers assigned by Thomas Johnson to the poems, letters, or prose fragments; L indicates a letter; PF indicates a prose fragment. To avoid typographical distraction, I have omitted quotation marks and the original capitalization in many short phrases from Dickinson, but in each case the source is given.

. . . oh what a torture are all these great artists and altogether these higher beings, what a torture to him who has guessed their true nature.

—Nietzsche, *Beyond Good and Evil*

With nothing can one approach a work of art so little as with critical words: they always come down to more or less happy misunderstandings. Things are not all so comprehensible and expressible as one would mostly have us believe; most events are inexpressible, taking place in a realm which no word has ever entered, and more inexpressible than all else are works of art, mysterious existences, the life of which, while ours passes away, endures.

—Rilke, *Letters to a Young Poet*

The poet has his own meaning for reality, and the painter has, and the musician has; and besides what it means to the intelligence and to the senses, it means something to everyone, so to speak. . . . The subject-matter of poetry is not that "collection of solid, static objects extended in space" but the life that is lived in the scene that it composes; and so reality is not that external scene but the life that is lived in it. Reality is things as they are.

—Wallace Stevens, "The Noble Rider and the Sound of
Words"

INTRODUCTION

The wisest of the Ancients consider'd what is not too Explicit as the fittest for Instruction, because it rouzes the faculties to act.

—William Blake, *The Letters*

In his *Emily Dickinson's Poetry: Stairway of Surprise,* Charles R. Anderson remarked: "To give her poetry the serious attention it deserves is the real task that remains. To study it intensively, to stare a hole in the page until these apparently cryptic notations yield their full meanings—this is the great challenge to modern readers." [1] Among more recent studies of Dickinson's mind and art, I feel indebted to Albert J. Gelpi's *Emily Dickinson: The Mind of the Poet,* Ruth Miller's *The Poetry of Emily Dickinson,* and Brita Lindberg-Seyersted's *The Voice of the Poet: Aspects of Style in the Poetry of Emily Dickinson.* But the challenge, as I see it, still remains to be met. In the present study, I hope to meet it by addressing myself exclusively to Dickinson's poetry and by exploring the metaphoric-metamorphic structures of her art. In order to accomplish this task, I think it is necessary to pay attention to "the larger structure of her imagination," to use Northrop Frye's words [2] and to come to grips with the *whole* of her poetic vision. In this direction, as far as possible, I will attempt to study Dickinson's poetry as a whole. I will also observe what constitutes the "terror" in her spiritual biography, and its relation to her poetry and her theory of

1

perception.[3] The detailed analysis will be based almost entirely on her poetry, and the meanings will be discovered through a close examination of poetic structure, imagery, and symbolism.

In an organic sense, Dickinson's poetry can be regarded as one long poem of multidimensional reality, each dimension presenting a certain deep and penetrating mood, a certain phase, a certain stage of that reality, and yet the whole of reality. It is unwise to assume an easy distribution of Dickinson's poems into various thematic concerns, because her themes invariably overlap and eventually merge with the fundamental concern for existence itself as seen through the power of the creative imagination. To put it briefly, I intend to show that Emily Dickinson's poetry concerns itself with the human predicament and destiny; that it builds interchangeable and interpenetrating symbolic structures on such perennial themes as life, love, despair, ecstasy, death, immortality, and self; that it embodies fully the cosmic theme of life and art as a continuous process; that it contains its own poetics or aesthetic theory; and that it is simultaneously concrete and intangible, present and absent. In essence, I wish to provide a comprehensive view of Dickinson's creative mind, her way of perception with which is linked the philosophy of the poetic process.

Emily Dickinson creates her own poetic mythology. She shows a remarkable ability to pierce the material world and discover in it the symbols of a spiritual reality. Therefore, this study will not overemphasize Dickinson's intellectual sources, her external biography, and the cultural history of her immediate ethos. To discover a certain likemindedness or resemblance of ideas between different writers is always possible. But to explain a literary genius in terms of the books he or she might have read is simply inconceivable.[4] Dickinson's poetry is born out of an active consecration to the call of her own mind, its creative terror, and its "polar privacy" (1695). Of course, she tells us of her intense reading of Shakespeare, the Bible (especially Revelations), Sir Thomas Browne, Keats, the Brontës, the Brownings, George Eliot, Dickens, Emerson, Thoreau, Hawthorne, and several others. But she does not make any attempt to arrive at a body of knowledge or system outside her own immediate perceptions. In a letter to Higginson, Dickinson reveals how her unique and independently creative mind works:

> I had no Monarch in my life, and cannot rule myself, and when I try to organize – my little Force explodes – and leaves me bare and charred – . . . . I marked a line in One Verse – because I met it after I made it – and never consciously touch a paint, mixed by another person – [L271]

In order to achieve a proper appreciation of Dickinson's poetry, we should guard against the tendency to psychologize and to draw inferences of a purely physico-biographical nature. We should keep our eyes steady on the text because our responsibility is to interpret poetry and not the person. Dickinson writes to Higginson: "When I state myself, as the Representative of the Verse – it does not mean – me – but a supposed person" (L268). The "supposed person" is the creative *I* of the poem. This creative *I* is the personality which the poet realizes as she creates it and realizes it persistently. This personality is not the ordinary individual; rather, it is a type which represents one's creative existence. C. G. Jung has aptly observed:

> The personal life of the poet cannot be held essential to his art—but at most a help or a hindrance to his creative task. He may go the way of a Philistine, a good citizen, a neurotic, a fool or a criminal. His personal career may be inevitable and interesting, but it does not explain the poet.[5]

In his brilliant essay on Emily Dickinson, Northrop Frye strongly suggests that "we shall find Emily Dickinson most rewarding if we look in her poems for what her imagination has created, not for what event may have suggested it." [6] Frye further remarks:

A poet is entitled to speak in many voices, male, female, or childlike, to express many different moods and to develop an experience in reading or life into an imaginative form that has no resemblance whatever to the original experience. Just as she made the whole of her conception of nature out of the bees and bobolinks and roses of her garden, so she constructed her drama of life, death and immortality, of love and renunciation, ecstasy and suffering, out of tiny incidents in her life. But to read biographical allegory where we ought to be reading poetry is precisely the kind of vulgarity that made her dread publication and describe it as a foul thing.[7]

Throughout this study, then, the object of my attention will be Dickinson's poetry and not Dickinson herself. The events which are directly related to her creative life and which help to illuminate her spiritual biography will be treated as integral to the process of Dickinson's poetic career. In this case too, the emphasis will be on the personality from within, the personality which cannot be studied without the framework of its creative reference.[8]

Emily Dickinson has often been considered as belonging to the mainstream of American culture, beginning with the Calvinism of Jonathan Edwards and culminating in the transcendentalism of Emerson. The American culture or psyche is a complex phenomenon. It has always manifested itself in the intricate pattern of clash between idealism and opportunity, spiritualism and materialism, intuition and rationality, romanticism and matter-of-factness, individual conscience and the orthodox Christian ideal of grace, private initiative and collective enterprise, transcendentalism and the purely pragmatic way, reverence for life and freedom and a certain delight in killing and human slavery. Both the extremes have been essentially ever-present and fairly mixed. Dickinson shows perfect awareness of her cultural milieu, and she occupies a unique position in the literary history of America. But, to study Dickinson's poetry within the confines of American history and culture only is to minimize the range of her poetic sensibility. The literary historians render her as a nineteenth-century American first and a poet second. I suggest that her art should not continue to be tested with reference to the limits of one particular literary ethos or climate. Being an existentialist-romanticist, Dickinson can be studied in the context of a vast literary tradition which starts with Gulliver's flight from Laputa, to use William Barrett's expression.[9] Dickinson's poetic insights can be compared quite favorably with those of writers such as Rimbaud, Mallarmé, Kafka, Sartre, Hesse, Dostoevsky, Nietzsche, and Kierkegaard, to mention only a few. In her sense of the tragic in existence, she anticipates Rilke, and in her daring search for the poetic word, she matches Hölderlin.[10] In short, Dickinson's poetry can be read and enjoyed in any part of the English-speaking world, and through translation anywhere in the world, because its primary concern is with the existential being. It is in this broad sense of the literary tradition that I intend to explore her poetry. My critical approach, however, will remain essentially centrifugal; that is to say, the emphasis will be on the work itself, and the reading will "proceed inductively through infinite adjustments of the stored energy of the text." [11]

For Emily Dickinson's poetry, I am using the 1955 variorum edition.[12] But I am suspicious of the dating of Dickinson's poems because there is no way to ascertain the actual time of their composition. Chronology, however tentative or approximate it may be, leads to the supposition that Dickinson's poetic career can be studied period by period or "developmentally." [13] Critics like Charles Anderson and Austin Warren are agreed, and rightly so, that there are no definite periods in Dickinson's poetic life indicating any significant curve of development in her artistic power. Warren observes that "Emily added to her styles without subtracting; and in maturity she wrote a new kind of poetry without relinquishing the liberty of slipping back into her earlier modes." [14] At any rate, in Dickinson's creative life "There is no first, or last, in Forever – It is Centre, there, all the time" (L288). Since Dickinson sees backward and forward simultaneously, and perceives as she creates, I intend to read her poetry backward and forward, in order to "get a panoramic view of her work." [15]

1

Center of the Sea

THE AESTHETICS OF TERROR

> That is my venture:
> dedicated to yearning,
> to rove through all days.
> Then, sturdily and amply
> with a thousand fibrous roots,
> to penetrate deep into life—
> and through suffering
> to mature far beyond life,
> far beyond time.
>
> —Rainer Maria Rilke, *Advent*

The poetry of Emily Dickinson may be viewed as a primordial metaphor, unique in the fecundity of its meaning and perplexing in the range of its vision. Such a metaphor invites each reader to participate in a creative experience which increases his awareness of the very basis of existence. Embodying both mythic and existential reality, it points to the center in which the concrete and the intangible meet, in which contraries exist side by side, and in which all the doublenesses of life are encompassed. Its metaphoric structure of reality contains both encounter and resolution, quest and fulfillment, suffering and exhilaration. The poetry is an emblem of a continuous process, representing a movement toward the inscrutable center of stillness.

Dickinson's genius unfolds itself within an oscillating pat-

7

tern which is essential to her art. Images of silence, death, and tomb do not refer to the negation of life; on the contrary, they affirm life. Movement and stillness, process and stasis are always reversible, and contraries lend meaning to each other as they intensify the central paradox which moves, beyond its own completion, in never-ending circularity. Her poetry makes resonant a world of tension between man's tragic sense of suffering and dissolution and his longing for repose, which is possible only through and in suffering. Its form and underlying meaning suggest T. S. Eliot's Chinese jar which "Moves perpetually in its stillness," [1] or Keats's Grecian urn whose silent form teases "us out of thought / As doth eternity."

It is especially at the moment of reversal, of rebirth, that man gains such a timeless perspective:

> Just lost, when I was saved!
> Just felt the world go by!
> Just girt me for the onset with Eternity,
> When breath blew back,
> And on the other side
> I heard recede the disappointed tide!
>
> Therefore, as One returned, I feel,
> Odd secrets of the line to tell!
> Some Sailor, skirting foreign shores –
> Some pale Reporter, from the awful doors
> Before the Seal!
>
> Next time, to stay!
> Next time, the things to see
> By Ear unheard,
> Unscrutinized by Eye –
>
> Next time, to tarry,
> While the Ages steal –
> Slow tramp the Centuries,
> And the Cycles wheel!   [160]

This poem is a dramatization of the moment of perception in which one perceives the secrets of life and death. Though the

poet is still existent in time, temporality no longer disturbs
her: the ages will steal, the centuries tramp, and the cycles
wheel by her once she has achieved timelessness through her
own dissolution and creation.

Emily Dickinson enacts this endless process of her myth of
the eternal return through interacting images and symbols
such as spring and winter, summer and autumn, sunrise and
sunset, light and dark, green and white, morn and night,
dawn and dusk, east and west. In her poetic vision, the acts of
dying and reviving take place simultaneously:

> The Dandelion's pallid tube
> Astonishes the Grass,
> And Winter instantly becomes
> An infinite Alas –
> The tube uplifts a signal Bud
> And then a shouting Flower, –
> The Proclamation of the Suns
> That sepulture is o'er. [1519]

Even in the heart of snowy, frosty winter, she visualizes her
bumblebees (86), April woods (179), and harvest all the year
(1025).[2] Her eschatology implies a new Creation: "Nicodemus'
Mystery" (140), which is also the mystery of being (1274), can
be resolved only in the spirit, in the regenerated self, or in the
imagination where alone can one be born again (see John 3:3).
It is *repetition*, the endeavoring again, which makes possible the
center to which each life converges (680). But this endeavoring
is full of despair and frustration; it is beset with fears and
temptations, afflictions and horrors. And Emily Dickinson's
acquaintance with despair is of the nature of the permanent
commitment:

> While we were fearing it, it came –
> But came with less of fear
> Because that fearing it so long
> Had almost made it fair –
>
> There is a Fitting – a Dismay –
> A Fitting – a Despair –

'T is harder knowing it is Due
Than knowing it is Here.

The Trying on the Utmost
The Morning it is new
Is Terribler than wearing it
A whole existence through.   [1277]

She looks at despair in a variety of ways: it is at once the drop
of anguish (193), the seal despair (258), the instant of a wreck
(305), a goalless road (477), a sumptuous despair (505),
"Chaos – Stopless – cool" (510), confident despair (522), a cavern's mouth (590), white sustenance (640), a perfect paralyzing bliss (756), and safe despair (1243). But her emphasis falls
on *experience,* because "Affliction feels impalpable / Until
Ourselves are struck" (799). The usefulness of despair lies in
passing through it:

Despair's advantage is achieved
By suffering – Despair –
To be assisted of Reverse
One must Reverse have bore –
The Worthiness of Suffering like
The Worthiness of Death
Is ascertained by tasting –   [799]

Intensely aware of the human predicament, Emily Dickinson is fully prepared to meet the dangers and horrors that life
is exposed to. The point of fascination for us is that she never
tries to escape dangers, rather she meets them face to face and
fits them into the fearful symmetry of her mind:

I lived on Dread –
To Those who know
The Stimulus there is
In Danger – Other impetus
Is numb – and Vitalless –

As 't were a Spur – upon the Soul –
A Fear will urge it where
To go without the Spectre's aid
Were Challenging Despair.   [770]

Through her demonic mastery of dread, danger, and despair, she seems to challenge even the fear and crisis of personal death:

> I made my soul familiar – with her extremity –
> That at the last, it should not be a novel Agony –
> But she, and Death, acquainted –
> Meet tranquilly, as friends –
> Salute, and pass, without a Hint –
> And there, the Matter ends –   [412]

The existential anguish and the spiritual tranquillity are instantaneously present in the structure of her imagination, and there is no easy sense of security in her poetic vision. Experiencing existence at the extremity, she refers to both the final inch and the precarious gait (875); and the necessity which impels her to measure every grief she meets with narrow, probing eyes (561) lends meaning to an art which embodies the imperative of existential danger:

> The Province of the Saved
> Should be the Art – To save –
> Through Skill obtained in Themselves –
> The Science of the Grave
>
> *No Man can understand*
> *But He that hath endured*
> *The Dissolution – in Himself –*
> *That Man – be qualified*
>
> To qualify Despair
> To Those who failing new –
> Mistake Defeat for Death – Each time –
> Till acclimated – to –   [539; italics mine]

Suffering presses upon her with tremendous inexorability, and affliction ranges boundlessness (963). But she has an equally awful capacity to "learn the Transport by the Pain – / As Blind Men learn the sun!" (167):

> The Soul's distinct connection
> With immortality

> Is best disclosed by Danger
> Or quick Calamity –
>
> As lightning on a Landscape
> Exhibits Sheets of Place –
> Not yet suspected – but for Flash –
> And Click – and Suddenness.   [974]

When darkness and anguish descend upon her, she mitigates their influence by proposing: "Transporting must the moment be – / Brewed from decades of Agony!" (207). She is used to wading "Grief – / Whole Pools of it" (252). She makes a certain conscious choice to play with danger, the secret of power and life that she calls a still volcano, or a quiet earthquake, or the solemn torrid symbol (601). The deliberate choice of danger is manifest in her letter to Abiah Root: "The shore is safer, Abiah, but I love to buffet the sea – I can count the bitter wrecks here in these pleasant waters, and hear the murmuring winds, but oh, I love the danger!" (L39).[3] Or when she writes:

> We like a Hairbreadth 'scape
> It tingles in the Mind
> Far after Act or Accident
> Like paragraphs of Wind
>
> If we had ventured less
> The Gale were not so fine
> That reaches to our utmost Hair
> It's Tentacles divine.   [1175]

It should be emphasized that Dickinson's symbolism concerning suffering, awe, danger, and despair is not generic but minutely particular. Her metaphors embody concrete experiential reality which can be felt and realized within the human heart:

> Peril as a Possession
> 'T is Good to bear
> Danger disintegrates Satiety

> There's Basis there –
> Begets an awe
> That searches Human Nature's creases
> As clean as Fire   [1678]

Her experience of pain is acutely personal:

> It ceased to hurt me, though so slow
> I could not see the trouble go –
> But only knew by looking back –
> That something – had obscured the Track –
>
> Nor when it altered, I could say,
> For I had worn it, every day,
> As constant as the Childish frock –
> I hung upon the Peg, at night.   [584]

This pain is eternally present:

> It has no Future – but itself –
> It's Infinite contain
> It's Past – enlightened to perceive
> New Periods – of Pain.   [650]

It is not *caused,* and, therefore, it cannot be allayed. It is the utter and absolute imperative that one has no choice but to choose:

> Experience is the Angled Road
> Preferred against the Mind
> By – Paradox – the Mind itself –
> Presuming it to lead
>
> Quite Opposite – How Complicate
> The Discipline of Man –
> Compelling Him to Choose Himself
> His Preappointed Pain –   [910]

All mortal suffering fades in comparison with the pain of such choosing, and no intellectual idea can equal this angled road of experience. Existence must be faced in all its concretenesses and not through abstract idealism:

> Ideals are the Fairy Oil
> With which we help the Wheel
> But when the Vital Axle turns
> The Eye rejects the Oil.   [983]

One must make several choices before the final choice, and make them deliberately; suffer the pathos inherent in them; and eventually go beyond them. Emily Dickinson knows all the vacillations involved in the process, but she sees them as resolved in the spontaneity of her being where the ingredients of a total experience shine simultaneously and not sequentially.[4] She realizes fully that

> For each extatic instant
> We must an anguish pay
> In keen and quivering ratio
> To the extasy.   [125]

In her solemn engagement with life she envisions:

> The Dying, is a trifle, past,
> But living, this include
> The dying multifold – without
> The Respite to be dead.   [1013]

The heart which is ordained to suffering (405) experiences the dying multifold. Living is a deadly serious business with her:

> I never hear that one is dead
> Without the chance of Life
> Afresh annihilating me
> That mightiest Belief,
>
> Too mighty for the Daily mind
> That tilling it's abyss,
> Had Madness, had it once or twice
> The yawning Consciousness,
>
> Beliefs are Bandaged, like the Tongue
> When Terror were it told

> In any Tone commensurate
> Would strike us instant Dead
>
> I do not know the man so bold
> He dare in lonely Place
> That awful stranger Consciousness
> Deliberately face –   [1323]

Participating in life rather than contemplating it from without, Emily Dickinson finds that the chance of life is the mightiest belief which overpowers her afresh every moment. It has an abysmal face which the ordinary human mind cannot fathom, or even be casually conscious of, without losing sanity. The madness, however, is paradoxical: by losing ordinary sanity one becomes sane in the real and divine sense. Such beliefs remain bandaged and sealed; the tongue cannot communicate their secret, for their terror is so pervasive that any attempt to make them vocal would be ineffective, deathlike. Since the challenge of life consists precisely in its terror and silence, it needs a bold person to face what Dickinson calls "That awful stranger Consciousness." The encounter must be deliberate, and such an encounter is the culminating point of Dickinson's spiritual biography. She realizes her destiny and vocation from within herself by means of an encounter in which the trivialities of existence fall off, and in which the seeming or real contradictions of life find a fitting place. It is from this perspective that I hope to show the real significance or import of her overnoted but not adequately explored statement: "I had a terror – since September – I could tell to none – and so I sing, as the Boy does by the Burying Ground – because I am afraid" (L261).

Critics have suggested various factors leading to the moment of terror in Dickinson's life. The major causes mentioned are the loss of a lover, the possible loss of her eyesight, and the fear of death. (A psychologist would not hesitate to trace it back to some sexual aberration, which was too embarrassing for her to discuss with anyone.) While these hypothe-

ses are not improbable, they fail to be convincing; Emily Dickinson does not offer any outward clue to the nature of the
terror. Nameless yet ever-present in the human psyche, the
discovery or realization, which is the most stupendous event of
one's life or being, is uncaused, like the preappointed pain
(910) in which Dickinson sees the chart of her vocation as a
poet-singer. She does not communicate her discovery to anyone, realizing that no one can share wholly the burden of a
destiny with others, but is moved only to become the *medium*
itself, the song that she sings, as the boy does by the burying
ground. The mythic boy seems to know the secret of existence, which includes the dying multifold without the respite
to be dead (1013), and he sings in order to cope with the terror of *living*. So does she. But in her case, the terror of being
is also the terror of her vocation. She must remain in awe of
her destiny in order to be fully consecrated to it. Fear urges
her to go without the specter's aid (770). Dickinson's terror of
vocation—which is poetry—is consistent with her idea of what
poetry is:

> To pile like Thunder to it's close
> Then crumble grand away
> While Everything created hid
> This – would be Poetry –
>
> Or Love – the two coeval come –
> We both and neither prove –
> Experience either and consume –
> For None see God and live –   [1247]

One always fears what one truly loves. One is struck with
wonder in its presence. Emily Dickinson's love is poetry; therefore she fears poetry. It is in this sense that she appears to me
to be afraid. Ruth Miller's suggestion that Emily Dickinson was
fearful of death and wrote poetry to ease her fear is a fairly
limited view because it does not represent either Dickinson's
idea of the function of a poet's art or her total experience of
the reality of death.[5] Fear of physical death is simply one of
the several postures in which Dickinson experiences the total-

ity of death; it is not the whole. If the poet sings to keep the
dark away (850), the same poet sings that we grow accustomed
to the dark in which

> A Moment – We uncertain step –
> For newness of the night –
> Then – fit our Vision to the Dark –
> And meet the Road – erect –   [419]

Emily Dickinson's appointment with poetry is so complete
that even a slight hint of the probable loss of poetic power is
bound to upset her immensely. Fortunately, it did not happen,
though she seems to be dramatizing such a loss in "It would
never be Common – more – I said" (430) with splendid poetic
energy. Paradoxically, what looks like the loss is actually the
gain in poetic vigor:

> I walked – as wings – my body bore –
> The feet – I former used –
> Unnescessary – now to me –
> As boots – would be – to Birds –
>
> I put my pleasure all abroad –
> I dealt a word of Gold
> To every Creature – that I met –
> And Dowered – all the World –
>
> When – suddenly – my Riches shrank –
> A Goblin – drank my Dew –
> My Palaces – dropped tenantless –
> Myself – was beggared – too –
>
> I clutched at sounds –
> I groped at shapes –
> I touched the tops of Films –
> I felt the Wilderness roll back
> Along my Golden lines –
>
> The Sackcloth – hangs upon the nail –
> The Frock I used to wear –
> But where my moment of Brocade –
> My – drop – of India?   [430]

At any rate, the problem of terror is not connected with any
loss of poetic power because then the *singing* would be impossible. Terror is rather the sharp point of her aesthetics:

> 'Tis so appalling – it exhilirates –
> So over Horror, it half Captivates –
> The Soul stares after it, secure –
> To know the worst, leaves no dread more –
>
> To scan a Ghost, is faint –
> But grappling, conquers it –
> How easy, Torment, now –
> Suspense kept sawing so –
>
> The Truth, is Bald, and Cold –
> But that will hold –
> If any are not sure –
> We show them – prayer –
> But we, who know,
> Stop hoping, now –
>
> Looking at Death, is Dying –
> Just let go the Breath –
> And now the pillow at your Cheek
> So Slumbereth –
>
> Others, Can wrestle –
> Your's, is done –
> And so of Wo, bleak dreaded – come,
> It sets the Fright at liberty –
> And Terror's free –
> Gay, Ghastly, Holiday!   [281]

Terror enlivens Emily Dickinson by dismaying her; its cap-
tivation lies precisely in its horror. By grappling it one conquers it. Its bald, cold truth relieves one from the snare of
false hopes. It teaches one the art of dying in which one can
stare at death. It is dreadful, but it is welcome because it liberates one from fright. Terror is freedom, a gay, ghastly hol-
iday—a vacation which is also a *vocation*. It is this vision which
is the one imperial thunderbolt (315) of the poet.[6] The power

of poetry shatters him with eternal dawn (323). The birth of a
poet is occasioned by the lightning and fire which enkindle the
spark of poetry (362). Dickinson makes poetry her right—a
"Right of the White Election" confirmed "in Vision – and in
Veto," and she calls this the delirious charter (528) which is
also her sacrament of the air (535). Though she is painfully
aware that "The Poets light but Lamps – / Themselves – go
out" (883), that they are the martyr poets who are fated to
write their pang in syllable (544), and that they are engaged in
the most difficult task of justifying the dream (569), she takes
upon herself the chosen fate of being a redeemer, a balm-
giver:

> If I can stop one Heart from breaking
> I shall not live in vain
> If I can ease one Life the Aching
> Or cool one Pain
>
> Or help one fainting Robin
> Unto his Nest again
> I shall not live in Vain.   [919]

But this role of the poet-redeemer and of the sacrificial hero
is undertaken with all its intrinsic humility and self-effacement
though its other features such as offense and self-assertiveness
are not unknown to the world. In one of her poems, Emily
Dickinson strikes a point of view, in perfect humility, that it is
perhaps more worthy to be able to admire the artist, and to
wonder at his creation, than to become the artist, though there
seems to be a thin line between the artist and his admirer:

> I would not paint – a picture –
> I'd rather be the One
> It's bright impossibility
> To dwell – delicious – on –
> And wonder how the fingers feel
> Whose rare – celestial – stir –
> Evokes so sweet a Torment –
> Such sumptuous – Despair –

I would not talk, like Cornets –
I'd rather be the One
Raised softly to the Ceilings –
And out, and easy on –
Through Villages of Ether –
Myself endued Balloon
By but a lip of Metal –
The pier to my Pontoon –

Nor would I be a Poet –
It's finer – own the Ear –
Enamored – impotent – content –
The License to revere,
A privilege so awful
What would the Dower be,
Had I the Art to stun myself
With Bolts of Melody!   [505]

In this triadic structure of painting, music, and poetry, the "I" of the poem, while remaining as a bright impossibility or a never-ending possibility of being a picture, wants to wonder and to apprehend sensuously the feeling-fingers of the painter whose creation "Evokes so sweet a Torment – / Such sumptuous – Despair." Instead of being the musician, the "I" chooses to be lifted to the horizons, and to pass through them with the elevating power of music. The "I" does not need any support for the journey but "a lip of Metal" created by itself. In the realm of poetry, the "I" looks for only one privilege, the awful privilege of the ear, the auditory power with which it can revere the poet, be contented with and enamored of him, and be the passive recipient of the bolts of melody, the art with which the poet stuns himself. In other words, the "I" seeks to appropriate the fingers of the painter, the metal-lip of the musician, and the ear of the poet, in order to be close to the artist in spirit.

In "I would not paint a picture," the hard-soft images of sweet torment, sumptuous despair, lip of metal, and bolts of melody once again confirm my view of Emily Dickinson as a

poet who creates the landscape of beauty out of her own landscape of terror, or for whom terror and beauty are one. In her
poetic world, the agreeable and harsh edges of existence in-
termingle freely: to her life is the most profound revelation of
harmonious dissonance, rich poverty, comforting danger,
joyous grief, luminous darkness, and peaceful tempest.[7] She
measures victory by defeat:

> Success is counted sweetest
> By those who ne'er succeed.
> To comprehend a nectar
> Requires sorest need.
>
> Not one of all the purple Host
> Who took the Flag today
> Can tell the definition
> So clear of Victory
>
> As he defeated – dying –
> On whose forbidden ear
> The distant strains of triumph
> Burst agonized and clear!   [67]

Life's triumph is always in proportion to our awareness of its
defeat. Our harbor lies in our consciousness of shipwreck, to
use Ortega y Gasset's favorite phrase.[8] This sense of security
vitalized by a sense of danger constitutes the ripeness or pre-
paredness which enables man to meet the stress and storm of
existence with cheer. It is so true that

> Water, is taught by thirst.
> Land – by the Oceans passed.
> Transport – by throe –
> Peace – by it's battles told –
> Love, by Memorial Mold –
> Birds, by the Snow.   [135]

Existence poses a constant threat, but this threat is the high-
water mark of any culture. Emily Dickinson shows a rare
"courage to be" in this ever recurring danger and finds her

identity or freedom in the fluxional paradox of liberty-cap-
tivity, or captive-liberty:

> No Rack can torture me –
> My Soul – at Liberty –
> Behind this mortal Bone
> There knits a bolder One –
>
> You Cannot prick with saw –
> Nor pierce with Cimitar –
> Two Bodies – therefore be –
> Bind One – The Other fly –
>
> The Eagle of his Nest
> No easier divest –
> And gain the Sky
> Than mayest Thou –
>
> Except Thyself may be
> Thine Enemy –
> Captivity is Consciousness –
> So's Liberty.   [384]

The danger implied in the images of rack, torture, mortal
bone, prick, saw, pierce, cimitar, and bind is reversed in the
counter images of liberty, "a bolder One," "The Other fly,"
and "gain the Sky." The soul at liberty of the first stanza becomes the eagle of the third stanza, who gains the sky, the
spiritual height, by diving into it. The act of diving involves a
downward plunge. But, paradoxically speaking, one can
achieve the height by diving into the earth's abyss, by going
down into one's self. This dive is certainly not an easy one; it
requires more than mortal courage and imagination to accomplish the flight. Only then is it possible for man to experience true liberty or emancipation within the paradox of
freedom-bondage. Freedom and bondage are moods or
aspects of consciousness or, as a Blakean would say, they are
contrary states of mind, which are equally true in the human
imagination, and man cannot rid himself of them without
peril to his very being. How can one run from the bondage of

being free? The metaphor of two bodies or bones, the mortal and the bolder, enhances the relation between mortality and freedom. The mortal bone or body is subject to torture and binding, but the "bolder" bone which is "behind" the mortal is free from suffering. And both bones are not only linked with each other but also contained in the "me" of the poem. The sense of mortality activates the inner world, which in turn casts its reflection upon the outer—a reflection in which the eagle of being soars in the full freedom of authentic living. The vision of life consists precisely in the quality of one's gaze at mortality. If the gaze is pure, mortality becomes freedom, and no rack can torture the gazer.

It is on the plane of the bolder bone that the drama of Emily Dickinson's contemplative thought takes place. Her manner of apprehension is revelatory of the process in which the temporal world loses its temporality without losing itself. Without concerning myself here at any length with the modes and theory of Dickinson's perception, to which I shall return in chapters two and three, I wish to stress the point that there is no real scope for exploring the traditional mystical, esoteric, or occult in her poetry, though it might seem easy to do so. Her poetry proposes the mystery of existence in its most concrete and sensuous forms. Her images and symbols are rooted in the body which can be realized only in the *here* and *now* of our being.[9] In the fullness of the moment she writes to Mrs. J. G. Holland: "if God had been here this summer, and seen the things that *I* have seen—I guess that He would think His Paradise superfluous" (L185). "Contained in this short Life / Are magical extents" (1165), but only if the earth is freed from its earthliness, the world from its worldliness, and the *moment* from its transitoriness. They must be seen as they are:

> Who has not found the Heaven – below –
> Will fail of it above –
> For Angels rent the House next our's,
> Wherever we remove –   [1544]

Since Emily Dickinson believes "The Fact that Earth is
Heaven," it does not concern her "Whether Heaven is Heaven
or not" (1408). She writes in her letter to Susan: "Oh Match-
less Earth – We underrate the chance to dwell in Thee"
(L347).[10] She resembles Blake in her treatment of time,[11]
though her manner is entirely her own:

> Forever – is composed of Nows –
> 'Tis not a different time –
> Except for Infiniteness –
> And Latitude of Home –
>
> From this – experienced Here –
> Remove the Dates – to These –
> Let Months dissolve in further Months –
> And Years – exhale in Years –
>
> Without Debate – or Pause –
> Or Celebrated Days –
> No different Our Years would be –
> From Anno Dominies   [624]

The imaginative experience of "nows" constitutes experience of the eternal time, the mythic *moment,* the dateless realm
of consciousness in which linear months and years evaporate
like fumes in the atmosphere of perpetual sunshine:

> There is a Zone whose even Years
> No Solstice interrupt –
> Whose Sun constructs perpetual Noon
> Whose perfect Seasons wait –
>
> Whose Summer set in Summer, till
> The Centuries of June
> And Centuries of August cease
> And Consciousness – is Noon.   [1056]

Dickinson's penetrating sense of earth, time, and body gives
her an awesome control over life in spite of, or even because
of, its mortality. She writes to Maria Whitney: "I fear we think

too lightly of the gift of mortality, which, too gigantic to comprehend, certainly cannot be estimated" (L524):

> To be alive – is Power –
> Existence – in itself –
> Without a further function –
> Omnipotence – Enough –
>
> To be alive – and Will!
> 'Tis able as a God –
> The Maker – of Ourselves – be what –
> Such being Finitude! [677]

The very act of living constitutes power, which is comparable to the creative energy of God, the maker of ourselves, even
though we are made in a finite mold. In a sense, our finitude
becomes our omnipotence because that is *all* we have. "I find
ecstasy in living – the mere sense of living is joy enough," says
Emily Dickinson (L342a).

But the act of living involves much more than the fact of
having been born. Existence is not a mere survival but a
challenging experiment with the forms that life reveals. Dickinson meets the challenge of existence in the most sensuous
and fearless manner:

> Between the form of Life and Life
> The difference is as big
> As Liquor at the Lip between
> And Liquor in the Jug
> The latter – excellent to keep –
> But for extatic need
> The corkless is superior –
> I know for I have tried [1101]

Only by plunging into life can one experience its power and
sway. The liquor in the jug is excellent to keep because it represents the possibility of being tasted, but it does not carry any
impact unless it is taken in. Dickinson performs the ritual of
drinking with utter solemnity:

> I took one Draught of Life –
> I'll tell you what I paid –
> Precisely an existence –
> The market price, they said.
>
> They weighed me, Dust by Dust –
> They balanced Film with Film,
> Then handed me my Being's worth –
> A single Dram of Heaven!   [1725]

The mystery of existence is revealed only to a person who passes through the low arch of flesh (616), who considers life's little acts as infinite and keeps his senses on (443), and who knows the art of *banishing* his egotistical self from his essential self (642). The exhilaration of this discovery makes earth an enchanted ground (1118) in which the smallest thing expands into infinity:

> The Life we have is very great.
> The Life that we shall see
> Surpasses it, we know, because
> It is Infinity.
> But when all Space has been beheld
> And all Dominion shown
> The smallest Human Heart's extent
> Reduces it to none.   [1162]

Emily Dickinson writes to Mrs. James S. Cooper: "Nothing inclusive of a human Heart could be 'trivial.' That appalling Boon makes all things paltry but itself" (L970). The human heart is the center of simultaneous growth and decay, creation and destruction. Dickinson knows well that within the interior land of being there is no place for the egocentric self, though egoism continuously assaults the harmony of the inner being, which must guard itself persistently against the onslaughts of the external reality. The fight seems perpetual, and both the loss and recovery of identity remain always within sight. The irony is that we shudder at the prospect of *knowing* ourselves, though we clamor to find the truth about ourselves. It is because we are caught up in a pattern of contradictions that the journey into the region of one's "withinness" demands such courage: "Paradise (is) no Journey because it (he) is within – but for that very cause though – it is the most Arduous of Journeys – because as the Servant Conscientiously says at the Door We are (always – invariably –) out" (PF99).

The arduousness of the journey is quite consistent with its ontological necessity; by encountering its inner horror and ex-periencing its ghostly power, we suddenly become aware of ourselves:

> One need not be a Chamber – to be Haunted –
> One need not be a House –
> The Brain has Corridors – surpassing
> Material Place –
>
> Far safer, of a Midnight Meeting
> External Ghost
> Than it's interior Confronting –
> That Cooler Host.
>
> Far safer, through an Abbey gallop,
> The Stones a'chase –
> Than Unarmed, one's a'self encounter –
> In lonesome Place –
>
> Ourself behind ourself, concealed –
> Should startle most –
> Assassin hid in our Apartment
> Be Horror's least.
>
> The Body – borrows a Revolver –
> He bolts the Door –
> O'erlooking a superior spectre –
> Or More –   [670]

The passages of human mind surpass all the corporeal places in the quality of being haunted. They are the incessant haunts of the spiritual bodies or thoughts in their pure spontaneity, irrationality, and darkness that sheds light. Ironically, al-though our being resides in these corridors, it is regarded as safer to meet the external ghost in the darkness of the night than to confront the inner, tranquil host of the mind. "The Stones a'chase" on a galloping horse is considered safer than "one's a'self encounter" in some lonely spot. If we are not fully prepared, the startling discovery of ourself behind ourself can cause us the horror that we normally experience on discovering an assassin hid in our apartment. As a threat to our material, vegetative existence, the "superior spectre" of our inner reality vanquishes our external reality. Notwithstanding the horror and danger involved in the discovery, the interior confronting seems to be an everlasting necessity. This inner need has been expressed by Dickinson in terms of the inevitability of an aesthetic structure within which the pain and horror of finding our *being* are transformed into delight and exultation. Her vision recalls Shelley's "A Defence of Poetry":

> Poetry defeats the curse which binds us to be subjected to the accident of surrounding impressions. And whether it speads its own figured curtain, or withdraws life's dark veil from before the scene of things, it equally creates for us a being within our being. It makes us the inhabitants of a world to which the familiar world is a chaos. It reproduces the common universe of which we are portions and percipients, and it purges from our inward sight the film of familiarity which obscures from us the wonder of our being. It compels us to feel that which we perceive, and to imagine that which we know. It creates anew the universe, after it has been annihilated in our minds by the recurrence of impressions blunted by reiteration.[12]

Highlighting, by implication, the experiential pain and suspense involved in our encounter with our being, Dickinson reveals what constitutes a state of wonder: [13]

> Wonder – is not precisely Knowing
> And not precisely Knowing not –
> A beautiful but bleak condition
> He has not lived who has not felt –
>
> Suspense – is his maturer Sister –
> Whether Adult Delight is Pain

> Or of itself a new misgiving –
> This is the Gnat that mangles men –   [1331]

Ambivalence is integral to poetic creation which enables man to endure the laceration of everlasting questions. The wonder of our being is a "beautiful but bleak condition" which we must experience by *feeling* and not by debate.

Emily Dickinson's intense awareness of the horror of an ontological discovery of ourself behind ourself, her total, and therefore dangerous, response to existence, the completeness of her poetic vision insofar as she is committed to, and possessed by, its creative power, and her single-minded devotion to her art compel one to observe that her whole life is a fully realized paradigm of poetic possibility. Life prompts her to write poetry of open form with perfect consciousness of the ironies and tensions involved in the creative process itself, which includes the *making* of a poem. She delineates the nature of her commitment to poetry in these words:

> Perhaps you laugh at me! Perhaps the whole United States are laughing at me too! *I* can't stop for that! *My* business is to love. I found a bird, this morning, down – down – on a little bush at the foot of the garden, and wherefore sing, I said, since nobody *hears?*
>
> One sob in the throat, one flutter of bosom – "*My* business is to *sing*" – and away she rose! [L269]

Since to love means to create, Dickinson's "My business is to love" is identical with Blake's "my business is to Create." [14] When the poet is a singer too, *love* is a metaphor for poetry. The business of poetry is tragic insofar as tragedy is a vision conveying the despair of vegetative existence when, for the first time, life is seen as a revelation of the divine spirit. The bird-poet sings even when nobody *hears.* The "sob in the throat" and "flutter of bosom" are integral to the creative-singing process, and the imperative voice in "My business is to sing" is no less than the demand of *destiny* which unfolds itself to man in his utter aloneness. [15]

In Emily Dickinson's poetics the symbolic structures are interchangeable and interpenetrating. Her poetry defies any neat categorization. A sense of unity pervades the perennial and existential themes of life, love, despair, ecstasy, death, immortality, and self, but permutations of themes render repetitions in interpretation unavoidable. It is in fact the network of themes which intensifies the meaning of her poetry, giving it depth rather than range. To those who regard her world as limited she says, "Area – no test of depth" (L811). It is by plunging beneath the waters that she finds her poetic vision: "How deep this Lifetime is – One guess at the Waters, and we are plunged beneath!" (L822). She grasps life's beliefs and doubts, certainties and uncertainties, facts and conjectures, realities and dreams with an uncanny vigorousness.[16] She considers life itself as a great vision. She writes to Maria Whitney: "You speak of 'disillusion.' That is one of the few subjects on which I am an infidel. Life is so strong a vision, not one of it shall fail. Not what the stars have done, but what they are to do, is what detains the sky" (L860).

Emily Dickinson's poetry is profusely mythic and religious in its soul-scathing challenge to break through the surface of existence. She shows no faith in an established, institutionalized form of *prayer,* and has no respect for doctrines and dogmas (L200). She writes to Susan Gilbert:

> The bells are ringing, Susie, north, and east, and south, and *your own* village bell, and the people who love God, are expecting to go to meeting; don't *you* go Susie, not to *their* meeting, but come with me this morning to the church within our hearts, where the bells are always ringing, and the preacher whose name is Love – shall intercede there for us! [L77]

Her use of the Bible, particularly Revelations, is not orthodox but aesthetical. The biblical revelation is transmuted into a poetic apocalypse in which she finds the sources "of the permanence and the mystery of human suffering," to use Richard Sewall's phrase,[17] and of the greatness of man who discovers his *reality,* his identity, his being through suffering. Her awareness of the human situation is rooted in her creative imagination, and not in any system of philosophical or theological thought. It is significant that her themes, images, and symbols evince a profound concern for the existential depths of man. Charles Anderson says that in her "explorations of the self and external nature" Dickinson often begins "with Biblical language and metaphor" but transmutes "these into new forms through the creative power of words, to render her experience of what it means to be human." [18]

"To be human," says Emily Dickinson, "is more than to be divine, for when Christ was divine, he was uncontented till he had been human" (L519). Her treatment of Christ is far from traditional; in several of her poems she identifies herself with Christ and his crucifixion,[19] and she knows Christ mainly through his humanity, his suffering. She writes to Mrs. Henry Hills: "When Jesus tells us about his Father, we distrust him. When he shows us his Home, we turn away, but when he confides to us that he is 'acquainted with Grief,' we listen, for that also is an Acquaintance of our own" (L932). By appropriating Christ's acquaintance with grief, Emily Dickinson, like Kierkegaard, makes Christ contemporaneous. The realization that suffering and crucifixion belong perennially in the center of one's being relieves Christ's crucifixion of the burden of temporal history:

> One Crucifixion is recorded – only –
> How many be
> Is not affirmed of Mathematics –
> Or History –
>
> One Calvary – exhibited to Stranger –
> As many be
> As Persons – or Peninsulas –
> Gethsemane –
>
> Is but a Province – in the Being's Centre –
> Judea –
> For Journey – or Crusade's Achieving –
> Too near –

> Our Lord – indeed – made Compound Witness –
> And yet –
> There's newer – nearer Crucifixion
> Than That –   [553]

"Crucifixion" is a daily occurrence; it happens in the being's center, which history cannot record. Within the framework of aesthetics, then, Christ becomes a "type" of suffering which is realized only within the human heart. And Christ's resurrection serves as a typology of expanded perception:

> Obtaining but our own Extent
> In whatsoever Realm –
> 'Twas Christ's own personal Expanse
> That bore him from the Tomb –   [1543]

Dramatizing her inner world through her poetry, Emily Dickinson *thinks* her objects and *sees* her thoughts. Yet she is never partisan in her way of seeing, for she seeks the balm of that religion that doubts as fervently as it believes (1144). Sermons on unbelief always attract her (L176). Such poems as "The Sweetest Heresy received" (387), "Only God – detect the Sorrow" (626), "Given in Marriage unto Thee" (817), "Far from Love the Heavenly Father" (1021), "God made no act without a cause" (1163), and "The grave my little cottage is" (1743) indicate Dickinson's idea of Christian trinity and her belief in the Christian notions of grace, election, and causality. She also betrays interest in a somewhat pantheistic but "illegible" God:

> All Circumstances are the Frame
> In which His Face is set –
> All Latitudes exist for His
> Sufficient Continent –
>
> The Light His Action, and the Dark
> The Leisure of His Will –
> In Him Existence serve or set
> A Force illegible.   [820]

But even a most casual reading of "Papa above!" (61), "I have a King, who does not speak" (103), "I had some things that I called mine" (116), "Should you but fail at – Sea" (226), "You're right – 'the way *is* narrow'" (234), "Why – do they shut Me out of Heaven?" (248), "Of Course – I prayed" (376), "I never felt at Home – Below" (413), "I meant to have but modest needs" (476), "I prayed, at first, a little Girl" (576), "It's easy to invent a Life" (724), "The Devil – had he fidelity" (1479), and several other poems will convince one of the mockingly humorous, skeptical, and sarcastic manner in which Dickinson treats the themes involving conventional religious motifs.[20] Her attitude toward the forbidden fruit can be construed by some as shocking and irreverent:

> Forbidden Fruit a flavor has
> That lawful Orchards mocks –
> How luscious lies within the Pod
> The Pea that Duty locks – [1377]

Her notion of a jealous God can be considered as opposing the all-loving God of Pauline theology:

> God is indeed a jealous God –
> He cannot bear to see
> That we had rather not with Him
> But with each other play. [1719]

Her treatment of the theme of baptism is very daring:

> I'm ceded – I've stopped being Their's –
> The name They dropped upon my face
> With water, in the country church
> Is finished using, now,
> And They can put it with my Dolls,
> My childhood, and the string of spools,
> I've finished threading – too –
>
> Baptized, before, without the choice,
> But this time, consciously, of Grace –
> Unto supremest name –

> Called to my Full – The Crescent dropped –
> Existence's Whole Arc, filled up,
> With one small Diadem.
>
> My second Rank – too small the first –
> Crowned – Crowing – on my Father's breast –
> A half unconscious Queen –
> But this time – Adequate – Erect,
> With Will to choose, or to reject,
> And I choose, just a Crown –   [508]

The external event or ritual of baptism is meaningless because it cannot guarantee that the baptized child will become a Christian.[21] Emily Dickinson relegates this event of her childhood to the world of her toys that she no longer plays with. There is no choice involved in the childhood baptism, and the real baptism takes place in the conscious, inner experience, in the fullness of one's being. The sexual symbolism of "Existence's Whole Arc, filled up, / With one small Diadem," suggests the fertilization of the experience in which one matures to true baptism. Only baptism which grants one the will to choose or to reject is the "crown" of one's freedom.

By approaching the sacred themes in her own creative way, Emily Dickinson gives them a new life. Charles Anderson has rightly pointed out that "she poked the Scriptures to make them come alive. The Bible was one of her chief sources of imagery and of truth but, as with all original religious thinkers, only when she could test it against her own experience and rewrite it in her own language." [22] Her "Bible" poem reveals this double-edged activity:

> The Bible is an antique Volume –
> Written by faded Men
> At the suggestion of Holy Spectres –
> Subjects – Bethlehem –
> Eden – the ancient Homestead –
> Satan – the Brigadier –
> Judas – the Great Defaulter –
> David – the Troubadour –

> Sin – a distinguished Precipice
> Others must resist –
> Boys that "believe" are very lonesome –
> Other Boys are "lost" –
> Had but the Tale a warbling Teller –
> All the Boys would come –
> Orpheus' Sermon captivated –
> It did not condemn – [1545]

The Bible, especially the Old Testament, is an old-fashioned document by uninspiring men. Since there is no "warbling Teller" of the story of man, the events, characters, and locales of the Bible do not transcend their historic-geographic dimension. When the poet sets out to create new dimensions and to relate them to man in all his predicament and glory, Bethlehem becomes the divine body, the inner Jerusalem, and the road leading to it is a rugged billion miles long (1487). True Eden is not found by dwelling in Eden, but by facing the experience of having been removed from there:

> Eden is that old-fashioned House
> We dwell in every day
> Without suspecting our abode
> Until we drive away
>
> How fair on looking back the Day
> We sauntered from the Door
> Unconscious our returning,
> But discover it no more [1657]

Paradise is regained only if it is lost. The awareness of having lost it gives us a new perspective of its immensity and worth, which in itself is a *discovery*.

In one of the moods of sarcasm, Emily Dickinson conveys her pithy emotion about a god of flint (1076) who deals in deprivation and denial:

> I asked no other thing –
> No other – was denied –

> I offered Being – for it –
> The Mighty Merchant sneered –
>
> Brazil? He twirled a Button –
> Without a glance my way –
> "But – Madam – is there nothing else –
> That We can show – Today?"   [621]

This consummate piece of irony portrays God's indifference to human aspirations. The mighty merchant sneers at his customers without even a glance at them. This attitude on the part of God perhaps constitutes a punishment of Man: punishment for having lost Eden, for having fallen from paradise in search of knowledge or identity.

Like Jacob, Emily Dickinson wrestles with religious questions in "A little East of Jordan" (59). She sees Satan as the brigadier and a personage of ability. If Satan had fidelity and not perfidy as his virtue, "The Devil – without question / Were throughly divine," says Dickinson (1479). Judas, the great defaulter, incites the rebel-poet in her, and David, the troubadour, inspires the lyrical quality of her poetry. Sin, seen as a distinguished precipice because it afflicts all men, is an archetype of the eternal ignorance of man. We must resist the consciousness of sin by a constant drive toward the awareness of our own existence, which we can reach only by *participating* in life, and not by watching it go by through the dim light of some perverse idealism. Those who believe in the Scriptures without testing them against their own spiritual experience and without recreating them according to their own existential needs are very lonesome. The other boys who do not show any faith at all are lost, from a spiritual viewpoint. Enacting her own creative version of the Bible, Emily Dickinson does not abide by the version of faded men. She becomes its warbling teller and captivates as Orpheus' song does. Like the mythical poet-singer, she sings her songs without implying any moral judgment or condemnation. In this way she tries to restore "the Circumference" to the Bible, which she thinks deals only "with the Centre" (L950). Since there is no center without circumference, Dickinson makes it her business to deal with the circumference (L268), or with the center of many circumferences, to use Melville's phrase in *Mardi,* in order to encompass both the inner and outer limits of man's being.

It should be obvious by now that, even though every poem dealt with in this section has an integrity of its own, it is unwise to read each one in isolation. Treated as clusters which oppose one another in the manner of handling the religious motifs, the poems illuminate Dickinson's aesthetic strategy in dealing with the religious themes. But the reader remains perfectly free either to seek the existential-aesthetic answers which are implied in the questions themselves or to face courageously the questions as questions.

Emily Dickinson can be labeled a poet of the sacred only if one recognizes that her sense of religion is seething with her sense of life in all its startling concretenesses and evanescences. She writes to Mrs. J. G. Holland: "There is not so much Life as *talk* of Life, as a general thing. Had we the first intimation of the Definition of Life, the calmest of us would be Lunatics!" (L492). Her experience of life as an "exquisite spell" "that everything conspires to break," or as being "so rotatory" "that the wilderness falls to each, sometime," reveals the precise quality of her commitment to existence itself, beyond which there is no religious reality.[23]

The abstract terms *mythopoeic, ontological, tragic,* and *existential* can all be applied to Dickinson, and they are not mutually exclusive; instead, they complement each other. She is mythopoeic in that she explores the primal reality of man who, while enduring the tensions and ironies of ordinary, mundane existence, strives, consciously or unconsciously, to discover the island of his dream—a dream which is *the* reality, spontaneity, and creative continuity. She is ontological in that her perception, which is both reception and creation, tries to reveal the mystery of being in the concrete though ambivalent symbolic structures; her mythic-symbolic constructs always reveal as much as they hide (indeed, reveal by hiding, or perhaps, hide by revealing). She is a poet of the tragic vision insofar as the sense of terror remains pervasive in her poetry. And, finally, in existential terms, she attempts to *know* the spiritual reality of her own life, and by implication all lives, through yearning, love, suffering, death, freedom, and creativity.

My purpose is not to provide any definitive system of values through which one might presume to understand Dickinson's poetic world. My chief endeavor is to create a basis for an encounter and dialogue with the creative mind of Dickinson, her particular way of perception and poetizing. That *dialogue* can never be closed in a world where nothing is absolutely certain and everything is in flux; and the major concern of the remaining chapters of this study is, by carrying on the dialogue, to provide a comprehensive but open-ended interpretation of the overlapping themes of absence-presence, perception, love, death, and self, as they become the recurrent concerns of Dickinson's poetry. Since the themes are interpenetrating, the chapters will not remain within conventional boundaries, nor will they indicate any hard and fast categorizations. Insofar as possible, I am attempting to study Dickinson's poetry as a *whole*. The dialogue, therefore, will be a continuous one. All along the way, auxiliary matters concerning the poet and her art will receive due attention.

But before moving on to the paradoxical theme of absence-presence in Dickinson's poetry, which I shall take up in chapter two, it seems appropriate to deal first with her network of nature symbolism. Since that network includes her other symbolic structures, it can provide some rare insights into her anagogic way of perception and her creative process.

"NATURE IS A HAUNTED HOUSE"

Dickinson's treatment of nature brings into focus the problems of the interrelationship of various existential themes, the mystery and ambivalence of reality, the inadequacy of linear language to cope with the poetic vision, and the implicit social function of the artist. Nature, like life, fills her with a sense of awe and wonder. She is sometimes baffled at the speaking silences of nature, but she never abandons her effort to probe its layers in order to find its roots. Several poems illustrate this quest, but one illuminates both quest and fulfillment simultaneously. It reads:

What mystery pervades a well!
The water lives so far –
A neighbor from another world
Residing in a jar

Whose limit none have ever seen,
But just his lid of glass –
Like looking every time you please
In an abyss's face!

The grass does not appear afraid,
I often wonder he
Can stand so close and look so bold
At what is awe to me.

Related somehow they may be,
The sedge stands next the sea –
Where he is floorless
And does no timidity betray

But nature is a stranger yet;
The ones that cite her most
Have never passed her haunted house,
Nor simplified her ghost.

To pity those that know her not
Is helped by the regret
That those who know her, know her less
The nearer her they get.   [1400]

A full-length interpretation of "What mystery pervades a well!" demands a simultaneous treatment of several other poems, related through their patterns of imagery and symbolism. The poem is unique in its portrayal of the process by which the subject-object relationship is perceived—is, in fact, created in the moment of perception. Every image is fused with the central feeling or idea: the human dilemma of being surrounded and engulfed by a sense of reality which is at once so close and so remote. Like Thoreau's Walden Pond the whole external world is also internal because "The Outer— from the Inner / Derives it's Magnitude" (451). This paradox is embodied in the haunting image of a well, which is enclosed by man's comprehension like water in a jar and yet eludes intellectual grasp.

Insofar as water symbolism refers to destruction and chaos, and a consequent new creation of the world, its aura of mystery is understandable. The mystery of that great water in the west which is termed immortality (726) resides in its unbounded limit none have ever seen. In the face of such ontological mystery, all the rest is perjury (1768). But unless the lid of glass is pierced through with the imagination, any self-conscious attempt to fathom its depths will result in nothing; every time one tries deliberately to penetrate it, one is confronted with an abyss's face. Since " 'Nothing' is the force / That renovates the World" (1563), however, we must come to terms with the abyss. We should not seek the rope which will save us from an abyss (1322), nor can the abyss be soldered (546). The bliss consists precisely in an existential plunge into the abyss (340). Dickinson writes that "emerging from an Abyss and entering it again – that is Life – is it not?" (PF32 and L1024). The abyss, she thinks, is its own apology (L968), and one must have the *courage* to accept its challenge. Only then can it become a concrete reality in the imagination which Blake calls the human existence (*Milton* 32, 32). The function of the mythic image is to compel the reader to encounter this reality.

The nature which is represented in this poem through the images of water, grass, sedge, and sea is embodied in the wholeness of the root metaphor of the poem. Just as the grass is so close to the waters of the well that it does not betray any fear and trembling, so the sedge assumes a similar relationship with the sea—the basic symbolic construct—which is floorless. The nature of this relationship is awe-inspiring, and the poet demands that the reader become humble and free and bold like the grass and understand the nature of the well, which is a miniature sea. The fundamental human problem, that of the right relationship and dialogue with the depth of life, is expressed metaphorically in the relationship between the grass and the well, the sedge and the sea. Man must come out of his puny self, which is a jar, and become a well, which is a form of awakened consciousness, in order to reach the dimension of the sea which is his real self, his freedom. As vast as humanity, the sea is, paradoxically, the real harbor of our existence in time (825).

The last two stanzas complete the open form of the poem by extending the scope and mood of mystery prevailing over the whole structure. The "haunted house" or the "ghost" of nature cannot be understood by the pragmatists who talk so much about her. Baffling and haunting ordinary human sensibility, nature wills silence everywhere (790); her ruthless "imposing negative" of death nulls opportunity of life (1673). Nature and God are the executors of one's identity (835). "Nature's Experience would make / Our Reddest Second pale" (841). Nature may appear to be a juggler because of the quick change in her moods (1170), but she is also the gentlest mother (790), the infinite aurora (925), and a sweet wonder (977). These variations reveal the lack of any rational order in nature, despite its essential unity. The ghostlike terrors inherent in the cosmic schema or the archetype of nature can never be simplified by deductive or inductive methods. The more man knows of it, the less he can communicate its final reality:

> "Nature" is what we see –
> The Hill – the Afternoon –
> Squirrel – Eclipse – the Bumble bee –
> Nay – Nature is Heaven –
> Nature is what we hear –
> The Bobolink – the Sea –

> Thunder – the Cricket
> Nay – Nature is Harmony –
> Nature is what we know –
> Yet have no art to say –
> So impotent Our Wisdom is
> To her Simplicity.   [668]

Silence overpowers a man who grasps the reality of the universe and his own precise relationship with it. But silence is the only medium in which to tell of the encounter and of the symbolic constructs it creates:

> There is no Silence in the Earth – so silent
> As that endured
> Which uttered, would discourage Nature
> And haunt the World.   [1004]

It should be clear that when Dickinson writes, "nature is a stranger yet," she does not imply that nature is wholly hostile to man. Hostility, wrath, and indifference are certainly some of the moods of nature, but they are mixed with the moods of tenderness, love, compassion, charity, and harmony. The simultaneous presence of these characteristics enhances nature's ambivalence and her haunting character. Nor does she mean that nature is completely unknown to her. In spite of nature's mystery, it is as concrete as a well or as close as a jar of water. Her intimacy with nature is further manifested in "The Bee is not afraid of me" (111), "The Grass so little has to do" (333), "My Garden – like the Beach" (484), "I know where Wells grow – Droughtless Wells" (460), "The Well upon the Brook" (1091), "Nature rarer uses Yellow" (1045), "The Sky is low – the Clouds are mean" (1075), "These are the Signs to Nature's Inns" (1077), "After the Sun comes out" (1148), "Of Nature I shall have enough" (1220), and "Touch lightly Nature's sweet Guitar" (1389), to mention only a few poems.[24]

"What mystery pervades a well!" has a significant place in the Emily Dickinson corpus. It presents the entirety of her poetic thought and sensibility in a symbolic structure which encompasses the scope as well as the depth of her experience. The deep sense of mystery that pervades the well is in fact the ultimate secret of life and cannot be the subject of literal communication: "Life is the finest secret. So long as that remains, we must all whisper" (L354). On another level, the well represents love in its depth and in its unbounded relationship with the grass. Death is implied in the jar, which is still, and in the abyss's face, which projects on human consciousness a fearful sense of inevitability:

> Declaiming Waters none may dread –
> But Waters that are still
> Are so for that most fatal cause
> In Nature – they are full.   [1595]

Yet immortality is indicated in the reflection of another world beyond its lid of glass. The well's mystery speaks directly to the essential self or being whose spiritual terror (ghost) cannot be simplified without violence to the very meaning of existence which encompasses all ambivalences. As a means of ontological perception, the well yields Being, free and bold, untouched by the practical and theoretical concerns of everyday, mundane existence. Hence it conveys the presence of the aesthetic-existential landscape by initially communicating an awareness of its absence—the absurd state in which the vision is not possible.

Finally, the well represents poetry not only in that its churning waters create their own music from the silence of the *deep* but also insofar as all its haunting shapes and forms echo the human voice with a finer tone. As a haunted house of nature, it becomes a metaphor for art. Emily Dickinson writes to Higginson: "Nature is a Haunted House – but Art – a House that tries to be haunted" (L459a). In other words, a work of art is an attempt to appropriate or reach the condition of nature in which, to quote Goethe, "we never see anything isolated, but everything in connection with something else which is before it, beside it, under it and over it." [25] Appropriation is not imitation. A work of art, in this case, becomes nature embodying all the terror and tenderness inherent in nature. As a reflection of the puzzling clarity of the artist's being, his "haunted house," it invites the reader to dive into his or her own abyss in order to find the existential truth concretely yet perpetually. Such a fully realized metaphor becomes its own poetics by expressing the chronic inability of linear language to portray or communicate the poetic experience.

Poetic language of this sort, like the well, creates its own limitless peripheries. When words are released from their denotative and scientistic bondage, language becomes a living act, a truly original utterance.[26] Metaphor is the incarnation of such freedom and spontaneity, and Emily Dickinson shows a keen awareness of the life-giving power of words.[27] She is equally sensitive to the dangerously elemental forces of language:

> Could mortal lip divine
> The undeveloped Freight
> Of a delivered syllable
> 'Twould crumble with the weight.   [1409]

However, the poet is concerned with the freedom which the delivered word enjoys by becoming the moving spirit of the creative act embodied in the poetry. Dickinson bluntly puts it elsewhere:

> A word is dead
> When it is said,
> Some say.
> I say it just
> Begins to live
> That day.   [1212 and L374]

She knew both the agonized search through word after word to match her vision and the sudden and spontaneous appearance of the "right" word in poetic creation:

> Shall I take thee, the Poet said
> To the propounded word?

> Be stationed with the Candidates
> Till I have finer tried –

> The Poet searched Philology
> And was about to ring
> For the suspended Candidate
> There came unsummoned in –

> That portion of the Vision
> The Word applied to fill
> Not unto nomination
> The Cherubim reveal –   [1126]

Here the word comes forth as an angelic being in a vision which carries within itself its own medium of free expression. But of course all poets complain that their inner comprehension is never completely transmitted in their works, that the accomplishment of the created object is something other than the inexpressible energy of the creative vision. While they believe in the power of words, there always lurks a painful feeling that they cannot, somehow, tell the ultimate of talk (407).[28] Hence Dickinson confesses:

> I found the words to every thought
> I ever had – but One –
> And that – defies me –
> As a Hand did try to chalk the Sun

> To Races – nurtured in the Dark –
> How would your own – begin?
> Can Blaze be shown in Cochineal –
> Or Noon – in Mazarin?   [581]

And, on the gap between poetry printed on paper and poetry as original perception, she writes:

> To see the Summer Sky
> Is Poetry, though never in a Book it lie –
> True Poems flee –   [1472]

This familiar problem extends far beyond the limits of mere vocabulary to the central problems of poetic vision.[29] Con-

fronting all the terror, freedom, and beauty of creation, the
poet stands in awe and wonders at its haunting immensity.
Even as he comprehends it, he is also comprehended by it.
Since he cannot simply utter this relationship, he must enact it
in his own creativity, so far as such an enactment is possible.
But each enactment involves a new creation, with a new terror
partaking of the first but not necessarily identical with it. The
fear inherent in playing the role of a god may make the poet
modest enough, insofar as he does not claim the full realization of his inner power in the objectivized form of his art. But,
paradoxically, the poet may sound offensive and pretentious
in explaining that his art, however glorious it may be, is proba-
bly a feeble shadow of the original that he contains within his
being.

Emily Dickinson avoids this difficulty by embodying the
paradox in works which define her vision not only in terms of
her language but also with proper recognition of its silence.
When she fails to find the word to contain her syllableless sea,
she does not regret the loss. On the contrary, she seems to
exult over the fact that her inner reality exists and can be felt
by itself, without any outward expression, and yet still be expressed in so many words:

> To tell the Beauty would decrease
> To state the Spell demean
> There is a syllable-less Sea
> Of which it is the sign
> My will endeavors for it's word
> And fails, but entertains
> A Rapture as of Legacies –
> Of introspective Mines –   [1700]

This bottomless awareness of both the boundless freedom of
words and the ultimate necessity for silence enabled her to
portray in language what I have termed the landscape of absence.

2

The Landscape of Absence

MANSIONS OF MIRAGE

> In placid hours well-pleased we dream
> Of many a brave unbodied scheme.
> But form to lend, pulsed life create,
> What unlike things must meet and mate:
> A flame to melt—a wind to freeze;
> Sad patience—joyous energies;
> Humility—yet pride and scorn;
> Instinct and study; love and hate;
> Audacity—reverence. These must mate,
> And fuse with Jacob's mystic heart,
> To wrestle with the angel—Art.
>
> —Herman Melville, "Art"

Existential aesthetics presents the domains of the visible and the invisible, the known and the unknown, being and nonbeing as one. There is always the inner layer—whether we are conscious of it or not—to almost every object which we perceive in the form of a concrete manifestation. The ratiocinative mind functions on the surface of the concrete phenomena as projected into time and space. But the poetic mind fructifies by moving on both planes, the outward and the inward, simultaneously, and thereby transcends the merely spatio-temporal dimension of things. The poet, then, sees the invisible in its visibility and the visible in its invisibility. What remains absent to the eyesight becomes present to the insight. The con-

47

creteness of what is absent is self-evident to one who sees creatively, one who transforms the opacity of objects into transparency. This inner-outer movement is fully embodied in Dickinson's poetry and suggests a constant relationship and metamorphosis between the poet and the world which stands before her.[1] In this interaction, the absence is felt as most intense presence. In the language of paradox, however, the presence is presence only insofar as it is absence, because it is beyond scientific verification. The complexity and richness of this presence have induced me to call Emily Dickinson's poetry the landscape of absence: the phrase itself is paradoxical and suggests something tangibly intangible, concrete yet vanishing, near and remote, apprehensible and elusive:

> A something in a summer's Day
> As slow her flambeaux burn away
> Which solemnizes me.
>
> A something in a summer's noon –
> A depth – an Azure – a perfume –
> Transcending extasy.
>
> And still within a summer's night
> A something so transporting bright
> I clap my hands to see –
>
> Then vail my too inspecting face
> Lest such a subtle – shimmering grace
> Flutter too far for me –
>
> The wizard fingers never rest –
> The purple brook within the breast
> Still chafes it's narrow bed –
>
> Still rears the East her amber Flag –
> Guides still the Sun along the Crag
> His Caravan of Red –
>
> So looking on – the night – the morn
> Conclude the wonder gay –
> And I meet, coming thro' the dews
> Another summer's Day!   [122]

The total impact of the poem is consonant with the mystery and wonder of existence. The feminine-creative flame of a summer's day solemnizes the poet. But the ambivalence of "something" remains pervasive. The poet hints at "A depth – an Azure – a perfume" as characteristics of a something in a summer's noon, and thereby suggests the inner-outer movement of the creative mind through the images of depth and azure. But the image of perfume makes that "something" out of one's grasp, like the source of light in the heart of a summer's night. The poet finally gives up the posture of inquiry and veils her face, as the polite archangels do in meeting God (65), so that the subtle-shimmering grace of a summer's day may not be withdrawn from her. The human heart continues to contain the magic of the wizard fingers that move "the night–the morn" in an endless, cyclic pattern. The wonder of life cannot be resolved by mediation; it has to be encountered directly in order to be realized as a concrete presence.

In the above interpretation, the landscape of absence has been considered as wonder or mystery. Mystery epitomizes a fundamental condition of absence which is "condensed presence" (L587). Dickinson shows a deep sense of creative fidelity to the essential mystery of being, which is also the mystery of her art. Even her personal relationships derive force from within the realm of the mysterious. She writes to Austin Dickinson: "It is a comfort to know that you are here – that your whole soul is here, and tho' apparently absent, yet present in the highest, and the truest sense" (L72). On another occasion she states: "Were Departure Separation, there would be neither Nature nor Art, for there would be no World" (PF52).

Within the context of aesthetic creativeness, the true scope of mystery or absence is limitless. Absence can be considered in many ways. I can consider it as *experience* which can be defined only through silence, stillness, and the darkness of the human heart. I can view it as *being* which embodies the primeval magic and terror of existence. I can look at it as *distance* or *beyond* which metaphorically represents inwardness, and which highlights the notions of instress and inscape. I can regard it as *withdrawal* from the world, which carries its own mode of encounter with the world. I can treat it as *deception* which affirms reality as dream and dream as reality. I can contemplate it as *perception* which is the angle of vision, and which reveals an instant relationship between the perceiver and the perceived in the act of creation. I can feel it as *love* which increases one's capacity to annihilate one's self and the ability to remain in uncertainties. I can apprehend it as *death* which negates and intensifies life at once. And I can identify it as *time* and *deity* which remain ever present, though ever hid. But all these forms are metaphoric and ambivalent and, therefore, refer to the condition of creation in which all the contradictions of life meet.

In the following pages of this chapter, I shall elucidate each one of the above-mentioned modes of looking at absence separately, while implying their integration from the viewpoint of aesthetic creation. Absence as *experience* implies a creative ability to go through existence, especially through the regions of stillness, silence, and darkness, which do not oppose but contain their counterparts—motion, sound, and light. Dickinson's poetic experience constantly reminds us of the stillness of the landscape in which movement has been perfectly harmonized:

> And yet, how still the Landscape stands!
> How nonchalant the Hedge!
> As if the "Resurrection"
> Were nothing very strange!   [74]

The motion involved in the resurrection is an unfathomable enigma of nature and its eschatology, which means revival or the eternal return:

> There are that resting, rise,
> Can I expound the skies?
> How still the Riddle lies!   [89]

Nature abides and creates and federates without a syllable (811). But her speechlessness or silence is integral to her infinite sounds. The bird-bard does not contradict the essential silence of creation by singing; rather, he creates the depth dimension of silence by singing what is silent or what is out of plumb of speech (989). The poet tells us about things which are mute and which speak only through and in their muteness:

> A House upon the Hight –
> That Wagon never reached –
> No Dead, were ever carried down –
> No Peddler's Cart – approached –
>
> Whose Chimney never smoked –
> Whose Windows – Night and Morn –
> Caught Sunrise first – and Sunset – last
> Then – held an Empty Pane –
>
> Whose fate – Conjecture knew –
> No other neighbor – did –
> And what it was – we never lisped –
> Because He – never told –   [399]

Dickinson's "House upon the Hight" is an autonomous symbolic construct. It is self-contained and has no transaction with the outside world of peddler's cart and wagon. There is no report of death from this house. Death seems to have been interfused with life. But, then, there is no life that one can see, for instance in chimney smoke, a sign of human habitation. Life seems to have been merged with death. In its windows or the doors of perception, which contain empty, unreflecting panes, is celebrated the aesthetic marriage of morn and night, sunrise and sunset, life and death, waking and sleeping, light and dark, voice and silence, presence and absence. The house is a metaphor for art. The poet brings out the ambivalent character of her creation; she leaves it in silence, only to be known through imaginative conjecture and not through intellectual effort. Even when the silence is transformed into sound, its music falls not on the sensual ear but on the spirit which resides in the inwardness of being. Music, in this sense, is silence speaking to silence:

I've heard an Organ talk, sometimes –
In a Cathedral Aisle,
And understood no word it said –
Yet held my breath, the while –

And risen up – and gone away,
A more Bernardine Girl –
Yet – know not what was done to me
In that old Chapel Aisle.   [183]

Listening to music which is *silence* is essentially a religious experience, and therefore, has all the undertones and overtones of awe. "Yet held my breath, the while" and "Yet – know not what was done to me," reveal the precise nature of the experience and the spiritual conversion which takes place in the human heart and is beyond rational knowledge. Sound is only the external manifestation of the internal silence which is, paradoxically, the profusion of sound:

When Bells stop ringing – Church – begins –
The Positive – of Bells –
When Cogs – stop – that's Circumference –
The Ultimate – of Wheels.   [633]

In Emily Dickinson's poetic vocabulary, church is interchangeable with the human heart. It is the temple where bells ring eternally. It is the center and circumference of reality. It represents the wheel in which the external cogs do not function.[2] It is the tree on which the bird-bard perches to sing his song "for nothing scrutable / But intimate Delight" (1265). The intimate delight is also intimate pain. The human heart, thus, becomes the reservoir of constant growth, spontaneity, light and darkness. From it emanate the still, tranquil mountains and the devouring volcanoes. It is the seat of creativity, which is reflected in the face of a man who is growing inwardly because "Growth of Man – like Growth of Nature – / Gravitates within" (750). In aesthetic creativity, man sees light by the dark and dark by the light, and sees it whole. This seeing or experience constitutes man's reality and is embodied in the human heart which measures like the sea (928).

In its most palpable form, the human heart becomes the inner theater in which the tragedy and romance of existence are enacted infinitely. Emily Dickinson juxtaposes the inner theater with the outer theater in these lines:

> Drama's Vitallest Expression is the Common Day
> That arise and set about Us –
> Other Tragedy
>
> Perish in the Recitation –
> This – the best enact
> When the Audience is scattered
> And the Boxes shut –
>
> "Hamlet" to Himself were Hamlet –
> Had not Shakespeare wrote –
> Though the "Romeo" left no Record
> Of his Juliet,
>
> It were infinite enacted
> In the Human Heart
> Only Theatre recorded –
> Owner cannot shut –   [741]

The most powerful expression of the human drama is embodied in the symbolic recurrence of the common day which rises and sets about us. Our birth and our death are dramatized every day. The vision of tragedy is best enacted when the participants are scattered, when each individual is alone and immersed in the silence of his own solitude. In recitation the tragedy perishes. The point is that the real drama of the lives of Hamlet, or of Romeo and Juliet, is played within themselves. Hamlet has "that within which passes show" (*Hamlet* 1.2.85). Juliet wears "the mask of night," and her love is "as boundless as the sea." Romeo's love is "blind" and "best befits the dark." [3] Although Shakespeare has disclosed a reality already existing in the hearts of Hamlet and of Romeo and Juliet, the infinity and darkness of their souls cannot be fully transcribed. The outer theater only reveals the secrets of the human heart, but the inner theater enacts them constantly. True experience occurs within, and it can be delineated only through the symbols of silence, stillness, and the dark—the symbols which convert absence into presence.

Absence as *being* carries all the dread and terror of existence, because it remains unfathomable, appareled in its own mystery. It cannot be wholly objectivized, though it has myriad forms which appear and disappear. It is like the *thought* which cannot be crystalized in the human intellect:

> A Thought went up my mind today –
> That I have had before –
> But did not finish – some way back –
> I could not fix the Year –
>
> Nor where it went – nor why it came
> The second time to me –
> Nor definitely, what it was –
> Have I the Art to say –
>
> But somewhere – in my Soul – I know –
> I've met the Thing before –
> It just reminded me – 'twas all –
> And came my way no more –   [701]

The invisible presence of being can be encountered in the human spirit in the form of "the Thing." Its concreteness can be experienced only in the full experience of existence itself. In the aesthetic sense, being is realized, paradoxically, in the awareness of nonbeing, in the very act of living in which both being and nonbeing assert themselves simultaneously. "And came my way no more" does not mean the negation of being; rather, it indicates the veil of being in the nonbeing.[4]

The concepts of process and becoming are basic to the understanding of being as well as nonbeing. Emily Dickinson regards being as a continuous process, and relates it to the creative power of anguish and terror:

One Anguish – in a Crowd –
A Minor thing – it sounds –
And yet, unto the single Doe
Attempted of the Hounds

'Tis Terror as consummate
As Legions of Alarm
Did leap, full flanked, upon the Host –
'Tis Units – make the Swarm –

A Small Leech – on the Vitals –
The sliver, in the Lung –
The Bung out – of an Artery –
Are scarce accounted – Harms –

Yet mighty – by relation
To that Repealless thing –
A Being – impotent to end –
When once it has begun –   [565]

The existential anguish which seems less important for a while becomes interminably noticeable by its relation to being, which is repealless. It assumes the form of a consummate terror which is integral to one's being. Its impact can be felt by empathy with the single doe chased by a crowd of wild dogs. The imagery of "leech on the vitals," "sliver in the lung," and "bung out of an artery" also suggest the presence of pain and danger as the necessary conditions in which one comes close to realizing being. And yet the terror of being is something much more subtle than physical crises. It cannot be seen:

No man saw awe, nor to his house
Admitted he a man
Though by his awful residence
Has human nature been.   [1733]

The primeval magic and the mystery of existence can be fathomed only through the excess of mystery itself. We should remain "Immured the whole of Life / Within a magic Prison" (1601), so that we may know the secret of true freedom. We

should be able to perceive more clearly by the dark what we
see by the light:

> Sunset that screens, reveals –
> Enhancing what we see
> By menaces of Amethyst
> And Moats of Mystery.   [1609]

Being is thus understood in terms of becoming through the
anguish, terror, awe, and mystery of the whole of existence.
Like Heidegger, Emily Dickinson also refers to the being of
the existent involved in the concrete human experience of existence itself.[5] But there is no place for a rational or philosophical system of ideas in Dickinson. She lingers on the ambiguous and loves to raise questions about the hidden in the
manner of a Kafka:

> What Inn is this
> Where for the night
> Peculiar Traveller comes?
> Who is the Landlord?
> Where the maids?
> Behold, what curious rooms!
> No ruddy fires on the hearth –
> No brimming Tankards flow –
> Necromancer! Landlord!
> Who are these below?   [115]

The dimensions of life or being are curiously linked with the
weird and cold atmosphere of the inn which is being run by a
magician who deals in the dead. But the grave or human finitude does not stop man from fulfilling his existence. Simone
de Beauvoir reminds us that "the individual alone has the
power of laying the foundations of his own existence."[6] Existence can be fulfilled in each moment of one's life. "Life is
what we make it," says Dickinson (698).

Absence as *distance* or *beyond* represents, paradoxically, what
is so close, within the grasp of the human psyche. It is an
inwardness which cannot be rendered directly. As the *experi-*

ence is made concrete through the symbolism of stillness, silence, and the dark, and as *being* is made manifest through nonbeing, the closeness and withinness of absence is projected through the indirect symbolism of distance or beyond. Whatever might be the content of distance, it is always felt and experienced as a concrete presence:

> Undue Significance a starving man attaches
> To Food –
> Far off – He sighs – and therefore – Hopeless –
> And therefore – Good –
>
> Partaken – it relieves – indeed –
> But proves us
> That Spices fly
> In the Receipt – It was the Distance –
> Was Savory –   [439]

Apart from the implication that expectation is contentment and gain is satiety (807), the poem presents the paradox that the real savor of food consists in its absence. Its flavor vanishes as soon as hunger is relieved. It is the absence or the distance of food which makes a starving man unduly conscious of it; he feels its absence as a most concrete presence.

Dickinson believes that "Wisdom is more becoming viewed / At distance than at hand" (1269). The closeness of human reality becomes plastic when seen through its remoteness and negatives:

> Delight – becomes pictorial –
> When viewed through Pain –
> More fair – because impossible
> That any gain –
>
> The Mountain – at a given distance –
> In Amber – lies –
> Approached – the Amber flits – a little –
> And That's – the Skies –   [572]

In aesthetic terms, distance is situated by the human will and not by the equator (863). Distance defines the relationship between ourselves and the dead (949). It can be overcome by love:

> Distance – is not the Realm of Fox
> Nor by Relay of Bird
> Abated – Distance is
> Until thyself, Beloved.   [1155]

The expression of *beyond* does not indicate any other worldliness. Its consciousness refers to an immediate reality, though it seems to wear the garb of mystery and remoteness:

> If I should cease to bring a Rose
> Upon a festal day,
> Twill be because *beyond* the Rose
> I have been called away –
>
> If I should cease to take the names
> My buds commemorate –
> Twill be because *Death's* finger
> Claps my murmuring lip!   [56]

The consciousness of one's accomplishments, conveyed here in the symbol of the rose and the sense of celebration are intermingled with the awareness of the moment *beyond* life's festivities. All acts of commemoration cease when death's icy hand touches and joins together the murmuring lips. Even though death's enigma is beyond man's reach, it always remains tangible, tactile like Death's finger. This is how Dickinson visualizes a bird beyond the sea (5), the bumblebees beyond the sun (32), the lonesome beyond the amber line (262), the stimulus beyond the grave (1001), and a wind beyond the realm of bird (1259). In this aesthetic vision, a quality of inwardness comes to the fore. It is the inward presence which paints the landscape of absence:

> The Inner – paints the Outer –
> The Brush without the Hand –
> It's Picture publishes – precise –
> As is the inner Brand –

On fine – Arterial Canvas –
A Cheek – perchance a Brow –
The Star's whole Secret – in the Lake –
Eyes were not meant to know.   [451]

The arterial canvas and the process of inner painting remain essentially inscrutable as the campaign of the interior (1188). But the poetic mind operates upon this inscrutability and renders it legible through the metaphor. The whole external world is internalized, and in the process the external world loses it externality without losing itself. This conception is fully explained in Rilke's famous letter to Witold Von Hulewicz, which deserves quotation here:

> We must introduce what is *here* seen and touched into the wider, into the widest orbit. Not into a beyond whose shadow darkens the earth, but into a whole, into *the whole.* . . . It is our task to imprint this provisional, perishable earth so deeply, so patiently and passionately in ourselves that its reality shall arise in us again "invisibly." *We are the bees of the invisible.* . . . The earth has no way out other than to become invisible: *in* us who with a part of our natures partake of the invisible, have (at least) stock in it, and can increase our holdings in the invisible during our sojourn here,—*in* us alone can be consummated this intimate and lasting conversion of the visible into an invisible no longer dependent upon being visible and tangible, as our own destiny continually *grows at the same time* MORE PRESENT AND INVIS-IBLE in us. . . . We are, let it be emphasized once more, *in the sense of the* Elegies; *we are these transformers of the earth; our entire existence,* the *flights and plunges of our love, everything qualifies us for this task* (beside which there exists, essentially, no other).[7]

The air of ambivalence and mystery is widely pervasive in the landscape of Dickinson's poetry. The whole earth becomes transformed in her poetic vision, though it remains always present in the highest sense. Dickinson embodies the tension of absence-presence in the imagery and symbolism of mists, veils, riddles, seals, "Arrestless as invisible," "Best Things dwell out of Sight," "With something hid in Her," "The Gem were best unknown," "out of sight," "Lands with Locks," "To disappear enhances," "Upon a Wheel of Cloud," "The Suburbs of a Secret," "In feats inscrutable," "Enchantment's Syndicate," "reportless places," " 'Tis threaded in the Air," "A Route of Evanescence," "Above the Haunts of men," "To pastures of Oblivion," "That somewhere," "And guile is where it goes," "ablative to show," and "Unnoticed dwell." [8] However, the tangibility of the all-inclusive landscape is a constant reality in the human consciousness which cannot be shown in terms of an external topography:

> Conscious am I in my Chamber,
> Of a shapeless friend –
> He doth not attest by Posture –
> Nor Confirm – by Word –
>
> Neither Place – need I present Him –
> Fitter Courtesy
> Hospitable intuition
> Of His Company –
>
> Presence – is His furthest license –
> Neither He to Me
> Nor Myself to Him – by Accent –
> Forfeit Probity –   [679]

Also, the awareness of the landscape can occur suddenly like a flash, and reveal what has so far been in and of the dark:

> The Lightning is a yellow Fork
> From Tables in the sky
> By inadvertent fingers dropt
> The awful Cutlery
>
> Of mansions never quite disclosed
> And never quite concealed
> The Apparatus of the Dark
> To ignorance revealed.   [1173]

The domestic images of fork, tables, and cutlery make the awful impact of the lightning bearable. The spatial metaphor

of the sky refers to the outer expanse of the inner depth. The
"inadvertent fingers" enhance our sense of mystery and point
out the sudden nature of the awakening. In this awareness,
which is dialectical ignorance or childlike wisdom as opposed
to egocentric knowledge, the mansions of mirage or wonder
fully reveal themselves. "Of our greatest acts we are ignorant,"
says Dickinson (L330). It is in this posture that the mythic,
half-disclosed, half-concealed apparatus of the dark comes to
light. Emily Dickinson refers to this revelation also as the light
of the spring, a season of rebirth and regeneration, a season
that follows a period of long and dark winter:

> A Light exists in Spring
> Not present on the Year
> At any other period –
> When March is scarcely here
>
> A Color stands abroad
> On Solitary Fields
> That Science cannot overtake
> But Human Nature feels.
>
> It waits upon the Lawn,
> It shows the furthest Tree
> Upon the furthest Slope you know
> It almost speaks to you.
>
> Then as Horizons step
> Or Noons report away
> Without he Formula of sound
> It passes and we stay –
>
> A quality of loss
> Affecting our Content
> As Trade had suddenly encroached
> Upon a Sacrament.   [812]

The poem dramatizes the uniqueness of the light in spring,
which cannot be explained by science, but which can be felt
and grasped by human nature. This light illuminates the furthest tree upon the furthest slope of the external as well as

the internal landscape. It seems to communicate with us. But it passes as the "Noons report away." The tension involved in "It passes and we stay" and encroachment upon a sacrament is integral to the creative act. It is in this creative tension that the poet learns the secret of the light, and learns to look at it as a sacrament, a permanent inner truth. In the creative act, however, the passing away of the light and its waiting upon the lawn are simultaneous realities. Nature seems to move in a sequential pattern of seasons, but in the human imagination or creativity all seasons are simultaneous: "On our *developed* eyes / Noons blaze" eternally (63). The poet masters the art of perpetuating what normally seems to escape. It is by the feeling of loss or absence of light that Dickinson proposes the presence of light.

In discussing absence as *distance* or *beyond,* I have implied throughout that Emily Dickinson does not evince any posture of escape from the world. On the contrary, like a true existentialist-romanticist, she gazes upon the world so intensely, and encounters its mystery and paradoxes so passionately, that the whole external world becomes a concrete metaphor of her life and art. Like Hopkins, she dramatizes the notions of *inscape* and *instress:* inscape means an empathic confrontation with, and a diving into, the abyss of reality as a source of true identity; instress implies a transmuting power, a grace, or the creative energy of a god that unveils the interior of things, animate and inanimate, and an intuitive mode of perception.[9]

Absence as *withdrawal* embodies a special type of retreat from the world, a retreat in which the artist cultivates his or her own mode of encountering the world. This withdrawal is not a running away from reality, but a process by which the artist ripens to a deeper perception of reality. Dickinson's own "deliberate and conscious" [10] seclusion and aesthetic privacy should be interpreted as creative devices to meet the world on her own terms. In the solitude of her Amherst room, she inscapes the vast horizons of human experience, some eighteen thousand years of human woe and bliss (1168). The world becomes more present to her in her withdrawal from it. She guards her spiritual solitude and the absence of the world with jealous care because she apprehends:

> The Soul's Superior instants
> Occur to Her – alone –
> When friend – and Earth's occasion
> Have infinite withdrawn –
>
> Or She – Herself – ascended
> To too remote a Hight
> For lower Recognition
> Than Her Omnipotent –
>
> This Mortal Abolition
> Is seldom – but as fair
> As Apparition – subject
> To Autocratic Air –
>
> Eternity's disclosure
> To favorites – a few –
> Of the Colossal substance
> Of Immortality   [306]

The revelation of immortality or eternity takes place beyond the realm of the ordinary human and earthly intercourse though not beyond the world itself. It occurs when the soul is alone. Its autocracy and favoritism are merely masks to suggest that the experience is not common. It can happen to those who choose to be spiritually alone. Thoreau tells us that the experience of solitude does not necessarily exclude us from others:

> I find it wholesome to be alone the greater part of the time. . . . I love to be alone. I never found the companion that was so companionable as solitude. We are for the most part more lonely when we go abroad among men than when we stay in our chambers. A man thinking or working is always alone, let him be where he will. Solitude is not measured by the miles of space that intervene between a man and his fellows.[11]

Spiritual solitude is indeed conducive to creativity. It is far
from being a condition of merely physical isolation, which in
most cases proves unhealthy. Dickinson extends the scope of
creative solitude by adding to it a dimension of human relationship, as she sees it in her existential-aesthetic perspective
and vision:

> I would paint a portrait which would bring the tears, had I
> canvass for it, and the scene should be – *solitude,* and the
> figures – solitude – and the lights and shades, each a solitude. I
> could fill a chamber with landscapes so lone, men should pause
> and weep there; then haste grateful home, for a loved one left.
> (L176)

Like Rilke, Dickinson belongs to solitude, and she derives all
her strength from this detachment. But, in this aesthetic detachment the identity of the whole created world presses upon
her mind with such a force that she finds no privacy in nature:

> To my quick ear the Leaves – conferred –
> The Bushes – they were Bells –
> I could not find a Privacy
> From Nature's sentinels –
>
> In Cave if I persumed to hide
> The Walls – begun to tell –
> Creation seemed a mighty Crack –
> To make me visible –   [891]

What seems to be only a centripetal movement of the leaves,
the bushes, and the walls, impinging upon the privacy of the
poet from without, is also a centrifugal force of the "quick
ear" which makes nature resonant from within. The whole
creation attempts to make the poet "visible," because creation
is a reflection of the poet's mind as she sees her in her own
image. This brings out the paradox of privacy: in the state of
withdrawal, the poet becomes more indrawn; the poet retreats
from the world, but the world remains a constant concern of
the poet, and in this tension between the outer and the inner
worlds a new world is born from within, a world full of the

depth of the seas and the expanse of the open skies. It is in
this aesthetic context alone that the drama of withdrawal in
Dickinson's biography should be understood. Allen Tate is
more than justified in saying: "All pity for Miss Dickinson's
'starved life' is misdirected. Her life was one of the richest and
deepest ever lived on this continent. . . . When she went up-
stairs and closed the door she mastered life by rejecting it." [12]
The words "closed" and "rejecting" are not meant to be taken
literally. I have said before that her withdrawal constitutes a
mode of encounter with the world. This mode explains the
paradox of art—the artist withdraws from his fellow men into
the world of art, only to enter more deeply into dialogue with
humanity. It should be emphasized that it is from the spiritual
force of her position of withdrawal that Dickinson writes:

> This is my letter to the World
> That never wrote to Me –
> The simple News that Nature told –
> With tender Majesty
>
> Her Message is committed
> To Hands I cannot see –
> For love of Her – Sweet – countrymen –
> Judge tenderly – of Me   [441]

But the spiritual grandeur, or perhaps compassion, is not
without a certain pathos. Dickinson is quite aware of the indifference of the world that never wrote to her. And yet she
implores her countrymen to judge her tenderly. This implor-
ing is, in a sense, ironical because she knows that the conflict
between the poetic world and the mundane world is not easy
to resolve; and that the poet in choosing her destiny chooses
the tragic position of being neglected by the world she aims to
transform. Dickinson finds an analogy of this tragic situation
in the life of Jesus (John 15:16) and gladly shares the fate of
Christ whom she regards as a type of the poet:

> "They have not chosen me," he said,
> "But I have chosen them!"

> Brave – Broken hearted statement –
> Uttered in Bethleem!
>
> *I* could not have told it,
> But since *Jesus dared* –
> Sovreign! Know a Daisy
> Thy dishonor shared!   [85]

However, the "dishonor" of Jesus and the poet is paradoxical. The tragedy consists in the failure of the world to comprehend the poet. The poet does not fail, because she, as she must, ever creates a new world out of her creativity. By remaining firm and brave, though broken-hearted in the face of enormous human apathy, the poet never really loses faith and hope in the world:

> They might not need me – yet they might –
> I'll let my Heart be just in sight –
> A smile so small as mine might be
> Precisely their necessity –   [1391]

Absence as *deception* highlights the authenticity of the dream or the spontaneous. Poetry proposes the world of imagined reality as opposed to the world of actuality. This aesthetic proposing has been described variously: as semblance by Schiller, as illusion by Nietzsche, as otherness by Langer, and as dream by Jung.[13] Like semblance or illusion, deception is highly paradoxical insofar as it destroys and creates *reality* at once. However strange and incompatible a work of art might seem to our ordinary human sensibility, its chief aim is to penetrate life and alter our angle of perception according to its central vision. Ortega y Gasset observes that "far from going more or less clumsily toward reality, the artist is seen going against it. He is brazenly set on deforming reality, shattering its human aspect, dehumanizing it." [14] But the paradox or deception consists precisely in this: art humanizes by dehumanizing; it creates its own self or antiself as opposed to the egotistical self which functions within the narrow alleys of our matter-of-fact existence. It is indeed true that "the poet ag-

grandizes the world by adding to reality, which is there by itself, the continents of his imagination." [15] But these "continents of imagination," paradoxically, grow out of the tension
between creativity and reality. The artist creates the illusion or
semblance in order to reconcile man to the terrors and sor-
didness of life, while preparing him to perceive life through
its transparency, its mythopoeic reality. Susanne Langer has
rightly noted: "To produce and sustain the essential illusion,
set it off clearly from the surrounding world of actuality, and
articulate its form to the point where it coincides unmistakably
with forms of feeling and living, is the artist's task." [16] Emily
Dickinson's poetry achieves the task of creating the illusion in
which reality becomes dream and dream becomes reality:

> Within that little Hive
> Such Hints of Honey lay
> As made Reality a Dream
> And Dreams, Reality –   [1607]

In this imaginative metamorphosis, the structure of lived reality gains freedom from its repressive, restrictive, intellectual
actions, its objective-abstract generalizations, and its rational,
temporal standards of morality. Reality, like the dream, becomes metaphoric and, hence, spontaneous, irrational, subjective, psychic, nondefinitive.[17] The affirmation of dream as reality is within the power of the imagination which enkindles
the realm of the possible:

> The gleam of an heroic Act
> Such strange illumination
> The Possible's slow fuse is lit
> By the Imagination   [1687]

Imagination is the fire which burns down the artificial constructs of our day-to-day empirical reality, and creates in their
stead symbolic forms through which we can perceive the dark,
deep dimensions of our individual souls, and, by analogy, of
all of human existence. Imagination helps us to grasp the mys-

tery of life, because it is the preceptor of the whole (1556). It creates several forms of *deception*—a metaphor for poetic clarity—in which one realizes the possibilities of one's primal reality or truth, above moral judgment and speculative thought:

> One Blessing had I than the rest
> So larger to my Eyes
> That I stopped gauging – satisfied –
> For this enchanted size –
>
> It was the limit of my Dream –
> The focus of my Prayer –
> A perfect – paralyzing Bliss –
> Contented as Despair –
>
> I knew no more of Want – or Cold –
> Phantasms both become
> For this new Value in the Soul –
> Supremest Earthly Sum –
>
> The Heaven below the Heaven above –
> Obscured with ruddier Blue –
> Life's Latitudes leant over – full –
> The Judgment perished – too –
>
> Why Bliss so scantily disburse –
> Why Paradise defer –
> Why Floods be served to Us – in Bowls –
> I speculate no more –   [756]

In this structure of poetic experience, the poet-dreamer records the features of the dream-poem from within the dream. The dream reveals the measureless, enchanted size of the realm of the poet's perception. The paradoxes of paralyzing bliss and contented despair are harmonized in the dream-prayer of the poet for whom the experiences of want and cold—images of poverty and lack of warmth or affection—are merely phantasms. The dream which creates this new value in the soul is the supremest earthly sum. This means to say that the dream is realizable here and now—in the heaven below—

in the very fullness of existence. The dream-poet relationship suggested by this poem, brings me to the problem of absence as *perception*.

I mentioned before that *perception* reveals instant relationship between the perceiver and the perceived in the act of creation. By this I am not suggesting a transcendence of subject-object dichotomy in normal human perception. Nor am I implying a reconciliation of the two within the empirical realm. In the creative process, the perceived emanates from the perceiver; the objectivity of the perceived remains infinitely bound to the subjectivity of the perceiver. In poetics, since the perceived is rendered as a metaphor or a symbol, it is, strictly speaking, neither subject nor object, though it is understood as both simultaneously.[18] This conjugation is always present at the root of poetic perception:

> Whether my bark went down at sea –
> Whether she met with gales –
> Whether to isles enchanted
> She bent her docile sails –
>
> By what mystic mooring
> She is held today –
> This is the errand of the eye
> Out upon the Bay. [52]

The bark in the poem is not a simple object; it is a persona of the poet. Although it has been presented as an objective symbol, it derives its meaning from the subjectivity of the poet. The sea, the gales, the enchanted isles, and the mystic mooring which form the experience of the bark, in its journey within existence, are both outside and inside the "eye" of the poet. Poetic perception clarifies the relationship between the poet and the world of objects (metaphors or symbols) which she creates in order to see her own being—"This is the errand of the eye / Out upon the Bay" of life. The images of isles enchanted and mystic mooring heighten the ambivalence of the experience and the absent-present character of the boat-

sea relationship. Poetic perception explores a vast variety of
complex relationships, imagined and autonomous, and
thereby proposes endless possibilities of existence in the existential-aesthetic mold:

> They called me to the Window, for
> " 'Twas Sunset" – Some one said –
> I only saw a Sapphire Farm –
> And just a Single Herd –
>
> Of Opal Cattle – feeding far
> Upon so vain a Hill –
> As even while I looked – dissolved –
> Nor Cattle were – nor Soil –
>
> But in their Room – a Sea – displayed –
> And Ships – of such a size
> As Crew of Mountains – could afford –
> And Decks – to seat the skies –
>
> This – too – the Showman rubbed away –
> And when I looked again –
> Nor Farm – nor Opal Herd – was there –
> Nor Mediterranean –   [628]

This is one of Dickinson's many poems describing the succes-
sive pictures which sunset offers. However, the three stages in
which the poem opens up are not mutually exclusive; they are
simultaneous in the human imagination. The poet is invited to
witness, as "some one said," the scene of sunset, symbolizing
the landscape of death. But through the window of perception, the creative "I" sees a sapphire farm, and a single herd of
opal cattle, feeding upon a distant hill—all symbols of the
landscape of life and motion. Soon, however, perception dissolves the appearance of cattle and the soil, and projects upon
consciousness a sea, a symbol of both life and death, or life-
and-death continuum. The ships having a crew of mountains,
and decks large enough "to seat the skies" suggest the limits of
human desire and the magnitude of the sea, concrete and possible only in the imagination. This is not all. The next stage or
level of perception is complicated by the fact that now there is

nothing to see. The "showman" has rubbed away the farm, the opal herd, and the Mediterranean. Perception seems to have transcended perception: there is no life, no death, no life-death flux. The whole vision appears to be Oriental insofar as it suggests a cyclic pattern of life and death, and also the ultimate freedom from the cycle. Apart from that, the role of perception as both creator and destroyer comes to light. The metaphors of sunset, sapphire farm, soil, sea, ships, skies, and showman are also the several relations of the "I" of the poem. The metaphors are human forms and they communicate as such.[19] The fundamental feature of these forms is their presence in the creative imagination of the poet, and not so much in the sphere of ordinary observation:

> I went to Heaven –
> 'Twas a small Town –
> Lit – with a Ruby –
> Lathed – with Down –
>
> Stiller – than the fields
> At the full Dew –
> Beautiful – as Pictures –
> No Man drew.
> People – like the Moth –
> Of Mechlin – frames –
> Duties – of Gossamer –
> And Eider – names –
> Almost – contented –
> I – could be –
> 'Mong such unique
> Society – [374]

Dickinson achieves the effect of an immediate relationship with the invisible in a large variety of metaphoric structures:

> The Mountains stood in Haze –
> The Valleys stopped below
> And went or waited as they liked
> The River and the Sky.

> At leisure was the Sun –
> His interests of Fire
> A little from remark withdrawn –
> The Twilight spoke the Spire,
>
> So soft upon the Scene
> The Act of evening fell
> We felt how neighborly a Thing
> Was the Invisible.   [1278]

The hazy mountains, motionless valleys, and the sun at leisure
indicate a temporary suspension of life. The twilight of evening provides a soft hue for the tapering pyramid of existence, which is ever renewed by the bright light of the sun.
The "act" of evening falls softly upon the scene of life and
shrouds it in the dark. But life is revived by the sun, which is
withdrawn from notice only for a little while. In the perception of the twilight scene, we discover a close bond between
life and death, between the visible and the invisible. Once the
relationship is perceived, the act of evening becomes soft—
death ceases to be a harsh reality, it becomes a neighborly
thing.

Absence as *love* increases our capacity for self-annihilation
and the ability to remain in uncertainties. This ability has been
described by Keats as *"Negative Capability,* that is, when a man
is capable of being in uncertainties, mysteries, doubts, without
any irritable reaching after fact and reason." [20] In love, we go
out of ourselves to *find* ourselves. Our identity unveils itself in
the form of a process—a continual unfolding of the mystery
of human existence. In this sense, the negative capability becomes the most *positive* capability imaginable, to use Lionel
Trilling's expression. [21] The presence of love is beyond the
realm of discursive interpretation. It imposes its own pattern
of paradoxical ignorance upon the one who goes through the
experience of love:

> We learned the Whole of Love –
> The Alphabet – the Words –

> A Chapter – then the mighty Book –
> Then – Revelation closed –
>
> But in Each Other's eyes
> An Ignorance beheld –
> Diviner than the Childhood's –
> And each to each, a Child –
>
> Attempted to expound
> What Neither – understood –
> Alas, that Wisdom is so large
> And Truth – so manifold!   [568]

Apocalyptic love is the subject of this poem. Its perception cannot be rendered through the analytical forms of knowledge. The wisdom or truth of love is so vast and multidimensional that the human lovers find themselves at a loss to understand its size and mystery. Its perception is possible only when the lovers are "each to each, a Child," and when they behold in each other's eyes an ignorance more divine than childhood's. The divine ignorance is the source of all perception, though divinity dwells under seal (662). The sealed character of the divinity of lovers makes love a human-divine secret which like "the Arc of a Lover's conjecture / Eludes the finding out" (1484). The revelation occurs in the human heart, which among other things, is the secret seat of love, and which cannot vocalize its eloquent silence: "Eloquence is when the Heart / Has not a Voice to spare," writes Dickinson (1268). The speechless, secret nature of love makes it impossible for it to be rendered in prose statement. Poetic language alone can provide a structure of images which matches the evanescent and ambivalent experience of love. Emily Dickinson creates several poetic structures in order to express her feelings on the subject of love, which also involves her experience of poetry. One of them may be noted here:

> The Love a Life can show Below
> Is but a filament, I know,
> Of that diviner thing

That faints upon the face of Noon –
And smites the Tinder in the Sun –
And hinders Gabriel's Wing –

'Tis this – in Music – hints and sways –
And far abroad on Summer days –
Distils uncertain pain –
'Tis this enamors in the East –
And tints the Transit in the West
With harrowing Iodine –

'Tis this – invites – appalls – endows –
Flits – glimmers – proves – dissolves –
Returns – suggests – convicts – enchants –
Then – flings in Paradise –   [673]

In the opening lines, the contrast does not seem to be so much between human and divine love, as Anderson states,[22] as between the love that a human life "embodies" and the love that a human life can "show." Dickinson does not sound apologetic for "below," because that is the sphere of her poetic creation. The problem seems to me to be that of communication. Love is essentially a divine thing, and therefore inexpressible. When love receives expression in an all-too-human context, it is reduced to the state of being a "filament" as compared to its subtle divine substance. This does not mean to say that *true* human love is less divine in any sense. Dickinson is fully aware of the divinity of love and its paradoxical nature. Love eludes all definitions. It strikes the fiery spark in the sun, and yet grows indistinct before the face of noon. It can be more efficient than the wings of the archangel Gabriel in reaching for the vision of latitudes unknown (78). It can be likened to music in its "inmost essence of sensuousness," to use Kierkegaard's phrase,[23] because it moves in an oscillating pattern of psychic "hints." It distils uncertain pain from the beauty of summer days. The east-west symbolism refers to dawn and dusk, rise and fall, life and death. Love enamors us with life, but it also impels us toward death, though the latter movement is not without pain. In the last four lines, Dickinson ex-

tends the limits of her tentative " 'Tis this," and advances a
long list of contradictory actions performed by love, actions
that aim to define love, which is indefinable. Love finally flings
her into paradise, the paradise of her mind (PF99) and art
(657), in which she deals with the whole of existence in the
same ambivalent terms she uses for love itself. Underlying this
highly intricate structure of words and meanings, there is a
certain clarity. We should try to apprehend the poem's meaning in the spirit in which it was created. Jung is right in assert-
ing that "we perceive when we are able to let the work of art
act upon us as it acted upon the artist. To grasp its meaning,
we must allow it to shape us as it once shaped him. Then we
understand the nature of his experience." [24] In other words,
we should, like the poet, first become nothing in order to
become everything.[25] Emily Dickinson achieves impersonality
which, paradoxically, implies the creation of a personality, in a
variety of ways:

> I'm Nobody! Who are you?
> Are you – Nobody – too?
> Then there's a pair of us!
> Don't tell! they'd banish us – you know!
>
> How dreary – to be – Somebody!
> How public – like a Frog –
> To tell your name – the livelong June –
> To an admiring Bog!   [288]

The final direction of Dickinson's poetry is toward the realization of identity or self—self which is not "somebody." The
poem dramatizes the loss of a public identity and the discovery
of a personal one simultaneously. It is a difficult ideal to
achieve but

> Each – it's difficult Ideal
> Must achieve – Itself –
> Through the solitary prowess
> Of a Silent Life –   [750]

The theme of self-annihilation and self-discovery is presented
with symbolic subtlety in the following poem:

> Which is the best – the Moon or the Crescent?
> Neither – said the Moon –
> That is best which is not – Achieve it –
> You efface the Sheen.
>
> Not of detention is Fruition –
> Shudder to attain.
> Transport's decomposition follows –
> He is Prism born.   [1315]

The symbolism of the crescent and the moon refers to a peri-
odic creation and recreation: the birth of the crescent from
the new moon, its process of becoming the full moon, its vanishing into the dark, and its re-emergence from the dark. On
the human level, the symbolism embodies the fundamental
problems of existence: birth and rebirth. Rebirth involves a
constant process of regeneration, a process of becoming full.
The truly regenerated person transcends the cycle of birth-
rebirth; he no more belongs to the world of vegetation. But
man attains this level only through the imagination: man becomes "that which is not" through the creative act. In this
sense, the poem also embodies romantic concepts of life as a
process and as a quest for the dialectical "that which is not." It
is only by achieving this paradoxical "nothing" that one can
transcend the condition of mere external growth and efface
the seeming splendor of outward reality. In this lies our true
freedom. Fulfillment does not consist in being confined to the
world; therefore, one should shudder to achieve the fruition
which lies in "detention." Ironically, one also shudders to attain true freedom. Worldly transport or ecstasy decays because it is ego-centered and, hence, shows signs of arrest.
True happiness is, in a sense, "Prism born"; one finds it
through the prismatic dome of life. By annihilating or tran-
scending the outward forms of identity or personality, by going
through the prism, the poet attains the real self or the condi-

tion of love. But the act of going *through* the prism of life is a necessary step toward the discovery of one's identity.

Absence as *death* performs the dual function of nullifying and intensifying life. Death is generally considered as a mere negation of existence, though, paradoxically, it enhances the meaning of existence. Life derives its meaning from death, and death cannot exist without life, because only that which lives can die. The moment of death is an integral part of the whole act of living. Our perception of life is dependent upon our perception of death:

> By a departing light
> We see acuter, quite,
> Than by a wick that stays.
> There's something in the flight
> That clarifies the sight
> And decks the rays   [1714]

Emily Dickinson views death from various angles and calls it by several names. But an aura of heavy ambivalence hangs over her wanderings in the landscape of nothingness. Even when the sight is clarified "by a departing light," we are left with the nameless "something" which is our only source of illumination. Nevertheless, the perception of this "something" in the moment of death is vital to our sense of being:

> I've seen a Dying Eye
> Run round and round a Room –
> In search of Something – as it seemed –
> Then Cloudier become –
> And then – obscure with Fog –
> And then – be soldered down
> Without disclosing what it be
> 'Twere blessed to have seen –   [547]

The images of cloud and fog enhance the elusiveness of this "something" and the inevitable obscurity of death, but they do not conceal the blessedness of the dying eye in having seen what it searched for so eagerly. Dickinson likes to watch the

play of death from a close angle, because death triggers her
imaginative power:

> So fleet thou wert, when present –
> So infinite – when gone –
> An Orient's Apparition –
> Remanded of the Morn –   [788]

Since she defines death by such varied phrases as "the supple
Suitor" (1445), "the recallless sea" (1633), "Costumeless Consciousness" (1454), and "Languor of the Life" (396), it is obvious that her tone is far from being decisive. She knows that
"Behind the hill is sorcery / And everything unknown" (1603).
Therefore, it is on this side of the grave, on the margin of life
and death, that Dickinson often explores the possibilities of
perceiving the distance between ourselves and the dead (949).
Distance is her polar image which means both remoteness and
nearness. In terms of time, the distance implies the past, but
she asserts that "It is the Past's supreme italic / Makes the
Present mean" (1498). Curiously enough, Dickinson creates
presence out of the absence of the dead:

> I see thee clearer for the Grave
> That took thy face between
> No Mirror could illumine thee
> Like that impassive stone –
>
> I know thee better for the Act
> That made thee first unknown
> The stature of the empty nest
> Attests the Bird that's gone.   [1666]

On the death of Higginson's daughter, Louisa, Dickinson
writes: "The Face in evanescence lain / Is more distinct than
our's" (L630 and 1490). She also believes that all we secure of
beauty is its evanescences (L781). In another poem of more
subtle meaning she affirms the life-giving quality of death:

> A Death blow is a Life blow to Some
> Who till they died, did not alive become –

> Who had they lived, had died but when
> They died, Vitality begun. [816]

To some people, death makes the dead more alive: it is after
the incident of death that the ones who died start living in the
minds of the friends who survive, in a vital manner. This is
also the meaning of "The stature of the empty nest / Attests
the Bird that's gone" (1666). On a metaphorical level, the
poem also means that those who experience death's blow deep
in their souls start living in a far more meaningful way than
they did before. Vitality begins only after we have known the
significance of death within our own selves. This experience
indicates heightened consciousness which points toward one's
identity:

> This Consciousness that is aware
> Of Neighbors and the Sun
> Will be the one aware of Death
> And that itself alone
>
> Is traversing the interval
> Experience between
> And most profound experiment
> Appointed unto Men –
>
> How adequate unto itself
> It's properties shall be
> Itself unto itself and none
> Shall make discovery.
>
> Adventure most unto itself
> The Soul condemned to be –
> Attended by a single Hound
> It's own identity. [822]

This poem affirms that man's consciousness or psyche, which
is aware of objects as near as the neighbors and as distant as
the sun, will eventually become aware of death. The awareness
of death is a process, a continual drama or the "most profound experiment" in which men are involved, so that they

may find a core of their reality which no one can discover for
others. This awareness is an inward movement, an "Adventure most unto itself," which indicates the struggle of the soul
chased by its own identity. The human soul is condemned to
be *itself* through its journey into the realm of death. This implies the symbolic death of man's false selfhood, and a complete surrender of self-seeking, egotistical existence. This also
constitutes a condition in which man realizes his being
through nonbeing. But, all this happens in and through the
despair of becoming one's self.[26] Dickinson makes concrete
the experience of *despair* and death in "There's a certain Slant
of light," one of her finest poems, which also captures the
spirit of absence-presence in a perfect form:

> There's a certain Slant of light,
> Winter Afternoons –
> That oppresses, like the Heft
> Of Cathedral Tunes –
>
> Heavenly Hurt, it gives us –
> We can find no scar,
> But internal difference,
> Where the Meanings, are –
>
> None may teach it – Any –
> 'Tis the Seal Despair
> An imperial affliction
> Sent us of the Air –
>
> When it comes, the Landscape listens –
> Shadows – hold their breath –
> When it goes, 'tis like the Distance
> On the look of Death –   [258]

The mood created by the opening stanza is that of oppres-
siveness and pain. The consciousness of life's mutability is
heightened by the solemn hymnal and funereal music of the
church choir. But by giving us a "Heavenly Hurt," the slant of
light in the winter afternoons assumes a spiritual significance.
The providential wound does not cause any visible scar; it
operates on the psyche of the individual, which is the reservoir

of life's meanings. The sense of hurt is absolute and thus it cannot be shown or explained empirically. It can be defined only as "the Seal Despair" or as an "imperial affliction" which comes to us from the realm of the celestial, and which creates the internal difference or the psychological metamorphosis. In this context, the coming and going of the slant of light seem somewhat ambiguous and paradoxical. On the surface, the light certainly comes and goes. But its inherent despair, being a divine condition of life, abides. It is only by living in despair that one can experience freedom from despair. When despair becomes presence, "the Landscape listens," the human consciousness becomes attuned to its soul-burdening music. The shadows or images of the creative mind "hold their breath." When despair reaches its own culmination, or when the light goes, " 'tis like the Distance / On the look of Death," a dark vision in which one realizes the presence of death. The distance on the look of death could suggest several things at once. It could simply mean the unseeing gaze of the dead. It could also mean that death is its own perceiving organ, and distance is its measure of fulfillment insofar as it beckons man toward itself. Distance may be taken as the pause between life and death. In this sense, death becomes a phenomenon of life: man lives but, in the consciousness of death and by living in this awareness, lives more intensely and freely. This clarifies the relationship between light and darkness. The winter under cultivation is as arable as spring, says Dickinson (1707). Therefore, to read the poem for negative despair, depression, and desolation is to read it incorrectly.[27] Without wishing to stress the point any further, I should add here that death as pure negation is not the finale of Dickinson's poetic world, and that she never proclaims life as purely absurd and futile. She does not aim to sound unnecessarily conclusive in a world which in itself is not conclusion (501). Her poetry embodies the never-ending odyssey of her mind:

> Such are the inlets of the mind –
> His outlets – would you see

> Ascend with me the eminence
> Of immortality –   [1421]

Absence as *time* and *deity* embodies man's ascension, which, according to Dickinson, has a "muffled" route (L945)—a route of eternity through time, of deity through human life—which is present as an everlasting possibility. In the ontological sense, past, present, and future are irrelevant categories of time. Time is eternally present: forever is composed of nows (624). Past and future are subsumed in this eternal present. Time is deity in that it creates, preserves, destroys, and ever creates anew. The riddle of time and deity can be solved only in the eternal presence, in the typology of the Christ-man relation.[28] Aesthetically, by being eternally present in the temporal moment, we reverse temporality into eternity. It is only through time that the artist transcends its finiteness. The creative imagination plunges into the reality of the lived moment and transforms it into its eternal significance by perceiving the temporal and the eternal at once. The simultaneity of vision should not be called nondramatic.[29] Dickinson's perception of time is highly dramatic, because it constitutes her whole poetic action in which time and eternity are the dramatis personae:

> I heard, as if I had no Ear
> Until a Vital Word
> Came all the way from Life to me
> And then I knew I heard.
>
> I saw, as if my Eye were on
> Another, till a Thing
> And now I know 'twas Light, because
> It fitted them, came in.
>
> I dwelt, as if Myself were out,
> My Body but within
> Until a Might detected me
> And set my kernel in.
>
> And Spirit turned unto the Dust
> "Old Friend, thou knowest me,"

> And Time went out to tell the News
> And met Eternity. [1039]

The relationships between the vital word and existence, eye and light, body and kernel, self and might, dust and spirit lead up to the final relationship between time and eternity. The ear, eye, and body are related to dust in time, and to spirit in eternity. Time and eternity are the two aspects of life or the realm of the sensuous. In life, time goes out to meet eternity. Eternity absorbs time; it does not annihilate the temporality of time. Time is a process: time does go on (1121); its tomorrow is "of alibi" and a mere "hallucination" (1367). It is infinite, but remains ever present in the finite:

> The Infinite a sudden Guest
> Has been assumed to be –
> But how can that stupendous come
> Which never went away? [1309]

It dissolves itself (1774) only in its ever creative activity. Since eternity can be obtained in time (800), it defines the God-man relationship. It also defines the limitless boundaries of love and death. To her lover, a Christ figure, Dickinson says:

> You constituted Time –
> I deemed Eternity
> A Revelation of Yourself –
> 'Twas therefore Deity
>
> The Absolute – removed
> The Relative away –
> That I unto Himself adjust
> My slow idolatry – [765]

The transformation of time into eternity changes the nature of the lover-beloved relationship. In eternity, the lover is truly and wholly revealed, and to apprehend him is to apprehend deity. The absolute nature of relationship or perception keeps the relative out of sight, though the relative is an integral part of the absolute to which the beloved offers her devotion. In deeming time as eternity or deity, the poet expresses her attitude toward time itself, which is "The Finite—furnished / With the Infinite" (906). Dickinson contemplates the vast circumference of time in many ways, and achieves "the Stupendous Vision / Of His Diameters" (802). She believes that by expanding the range of one's perception, one can realize eternity in the now and here of this existence.[30]

The foregoing discussion of the landscape of absence, through its several forms and metaphoric relationships, does not exhaust the full scope of interpenetrating themes in Dickinson's poetry. Its chief aim has been to illuminate the themes and to provide a guideline for the all-inclusive subject of perception in her poetry.

3

Perception

THE BILLOWS OF CIRCUMFERENCE

> There grew
> A power within me of enormous ken,
> To see as a god sees, and take the depth
> Of things as nimbly as the outward eye
> Can size and shape pervade.
>
> —Keats, *The Fall of Hyperion*

Poetic perception is the nucleus of creativity.[1] Embodying the way of seeing, creativity clarifies the relationship between the seer and the seen in the act of creation.[2] Thus a poem, which is a symbolic construct, carries within itself, explicitly or implicitly, a fourfold structure, defining the nature of correspondence between the poet and the realm of existential reality, the poet and the poetic experience, the poet and the creative process, and the poet and the poem. The romantic-existentialist theory of poetic perception or aesthetics should not be considered adequate unless it deals with this fourfold structure of imagination in which the poet is the central figure or the hero. It is from this point of view that I intend to explore Emily Dickinson's theory of perception, and show its uniqueness insofar as it emerges from and is integral to the entire range of her poetic creation. However, the above-noted structure of relationships poses a difficulty: whereas the relationships have to be assumed as being discussed simultaneously, it will be trite and repetitious if they are restated with the rendition of individual poems or cluster of poems. In order to cope with this problem, I propose to discuss each angle of the fourfold structure separately but not exclusively, because the discussion of any one of the four will necessarily involve the other three. The whole discussion, then, is being offered in four parts, which are integral.

THE POET AND THE REALM OF
EXISTENTIAL REALITY

Concerning the relationship between the poet and the realm of existential reality it has been pointed out elsewhere in this study that the poet's eye or the poetic perception is essentially metamorphic. The poetic seeing is apocalyptic in that it transmutes ordinary, vegetative existence into a vision. It is in this sense that to see is to create. This means "an intimate seeing, a grasping and being grasped." [3] This seeing may also be described as an involvement with and a penetration into reality which is invariably the starting point of creativity. Poetic reality assembles and gives form to all the free possibilities of life which the human existence in its chaotic state lacks. The aesthetic consciousness repulses what ordinarily seems or appears to be "real" in existence; it consists in lending "wakeful reality to the dream, and dream-like liberating spontaneity to wakeful life." [4] Emily Dickinson achieves the union of reality and dream in her poetic vision, and affirms that the days can bring

> No numb alarm – lest Difference come –
> No Goblin – on the Bloom –
> No start in Apprehension's Ear,
> No Bankruptcy – no Doom –
>
> But Certainties of Sun –
> Midsummer – in the Mind –
> A steadfast South – upon the Soul –
> Her Polar Time – behind –

The Vision – pondered long –
So plausible becomes
That I esteem the fiction – real –
The Real – fictitious seems –

How bountiful the Dream –
What Plenty – it would be –
Had all my Life but been Mistake
Just rectified – in Thee   [646]

Dickinson's perception dramatizes the experience of perception: the poem about perception tells us what there is to perceive. Perception, like the day, becomes the source of light, and we see into the essence of things. We are no longer worried by the torpid fears and anxieties of mundane existence. The image of the bloom hounded by the goblin captures fully the feeling that, under normal circumstances, life is being chased by a demon into some form of absurdity. But it is not so in the aesthetic perception: there is no sudden, shocking movement of dissonant sounds in "Apprehension's Ear" which perceives harmony out of the din of voices. There is no emptiness, there is no doom—the death that condemns and destroys forever. In aesthetic existence, there are only "Certainties of Sun," the forms of awareness. The human mind becomes conscious of life's fullness, symbolized here by midsummer:

It's like the Morning –
Best – when it's done –
And the Everlasting Clocks –
Chime – Noon!   [297]

Spiritual awakening assumes the form of a never-altering reality, and time's polarity ceases to intrude upon the ontological present. This vision becomes plausible as a result of long and steady pondering. The vision which is, in a sense, created or fictive becomes "real," and the outward flux of experiential reality assumes the form of "the Dream," which is another name for the fictitious or the visionary. The creative man finds this dream or vision bountiful, and thus he rectifies the mistake of looking at life and the plenty of its creation through vegetable eyes. Emily Dickinson emphasizes the importance of "furnished" eyes in poetic perception. In a letter to Higginson, she writes:

> I was thinking, today – as I noticed, that the "Supernatural," was only the Natural, disclosed –
>
> Not "Revelation" – 'tis – that waits,
> But our unfurnished eyes –   [L280]

With her furnished or "developed" eyes (63), Dickinson confidently sees "Some Rainbow – coming from the Fair! / Some Vision of the World Cashmere" (64)—the far-off landscape of India. The poet takes "no less than skies," and her "Basket holds – just – Firmaments" (352). The light of poetic perception, however, does not provide an easy escape from the darknesses of existence; it simply lends man the courage or vision to put up with existence as such:

> And so of larger – Darknesses –
> Those Evenings of the Brain –
> When not a Moon disclose a sign –
> Or Star – come out – within –
>
> The B[r]avest – grope a little –
> And sometimes hit a Tree
> Directly in the Forehead –
> But as they learn to see –
>
> Either the Darkness alters –
> Or something in the sight
> Adjusts itself to Midnight –
> And Life steps almost straight.   [419]

When eyes grow accustomed to the dark, they can pierce through existential wastes, blank and steady wilderness, and infinites of nought (458). The perceiver can measure every grief he meets, with narrow, probing eyes (561). Dickinson's favorite images of perception are star, sun, noon, light, lightning, and thunder.[5] It is in and through these images that she

realizes her "Compound Vision" which encompasses man's
finitude and his sense of eternity:

> 'Tis Compound Vision –
> Light – enabling Light –
> The Finite – furnished
> With the Infinite –
> Convex – and Concave Witness –
> Back – toward Time –
> And forward –
> Toward the God of Him –   [906]

The perception of light or lightning reveals to Dickinson that
fountain of spiritual existence which consummates man's experience of life: it reflects that "Mortality's Ground Floor / Is
Immortality" (1234), and it lends meaning to man's encounter
with the concrete realities of love and death. This perception
also ignites the spark of her own creativity to which she dedicates herself so daringly. The light which is "waylaying," and
which strikes as powerfully as the lightning and as furiously as
thunder, lays the basis of her poetics:

> The farthest Thunder that I heard
> Was nearer than the Sky
> And rumbles still, though torrid Noons
> Have lain their missiles by –
> The Lightning that preceded it
> Struck no one but myself –
> But I would not exchange the Bolt
> For all the rest of Life – . . .
> It founds the Homes and decks the Days
> And every clamor bright
> Is but the gleam concomitant
> Of that waylaying Light –
> The Thought is quiet as a Flake –
> A Crash without a Sound –
> How Life's reverberation
> It's Explanation found –   [1581]

The poem renders a psychic experience in terms of the images borrowed from time and nature. The inner thunder continues to rumble even when the torrid noons have ceased their operation—the excessive heat and energy of the torrid noons cause rain, lightning, storm, and thunder in outer space. The poet internalizes the lightning, and does not wish to exchange the bolt for all the rest of life, because the luminosity of the bolt or the flash of lightning makes her comprehend more than all the things of life put together. This bolt helps her in creating the innumerable bolts of melody (505) which constitute her poetic life. Thunder, then, is the poetic reality which illuminates human life. Every other illumination of existence springs from the waylaying light with which thunder is coexistent. The waylaying light or thunder of poetry, paradoxically, robs man of his ordinary eyesight. It turns man inward, into the realm of intuition where the experience of thunder is analogous to the sensation of thought, which moves as quietly as a flake of snow. The crash occurs, but without a sound: thunder enters the silent regions of the human psyche in which are stored the answers to life's reflections, though they can never be stated in nonmetaphoric language. This poem seems to clarify and resolve the problem of subject-object polarity: the external world of thunder and lightning is made subjective in terms of the thought which in "its deepest recesses is a sensuous, formative process: spontaneous, not controlled by any extrinsic will or consciousness," [6] and the internal world of poetic vision is objectivized in terms of the images and metaphors which belong to nature in its widest context. It highlights, through tone and implication, the importance of intuition which stresses man's ability to apprehend reality by direct spiritual insight. Dickinson describes the power of intuition in these verses:

> You'll know it – as you know 'tis Noon –
> By Glory –
> As you do the Sun –
> By Glory –

As you will in Heaven –
Know God the Father – and the Son.

By intuition, Mightiest Things
Assert themselves – and not by terms –
"I'm Midnight" – need the Midnight say –
"I'm Sunrise" – Need the Majesty?

Omnipotence – had not a Tongue –
His lisp – is Lightning – and the Sun –
His Conversation – with the Sea –
"How shall you know"?
Consult your Eye! [420]

The poem is crowded with the images of perception. Intuition being the central organ of perception, it works as the eye of distant vision to which the mightiest things reveal themselves. The God-Son or the God-man relationship is authentic for a man who can intuit, but not for a person whose skeptical eye is caught up in proximate seeing. To a man of intuition, the Creator, who is silence par excellence, speaks through the lightning. Through the sun, God converses with the sea of life and death. The poet, in using the images of lightning and sun to define the nature of the poetic experience, appropriates the role of a god. But the poet does not compete with God; he creates his own essentially tongueless experience in the symbolic forms which are as primordial as lightning or the sun.

The role of intuition in creativity brings us to the complex and paradoxical problem of poetic subjectivity versus poetic impersonality. The stress on the faculty of intuition or creative imagination in perception is stress on the subjectivity of the poet.[7] Objective reality seems to play a secondary role in the poetic creation, because external nature derives its meaning from the inwardness of the poet:

The Outer – from the Inner
Derives it's Magnitude –
'Tis Duke, or Dwarf, according
As is the Central Mood –

> The fine – unvarying Axis
> That regulates the Wheel
> Though Spokes – spin – more conspicuous
> And fling a dust – the while.   [451]

The wheel of perception is regulated and moved by the un-
varying axis of the human psyche where the central mood is
located in its ambivalent form, though the "spokes"—the external points of contact with reality—seem more conspicuous
because of their spinning dance. The movement of the spokes
flings a dust into the eyes of a beholder, but the creative perceiver plunges across the screen of dust, moves freely back
and forth, in and out of the objective realm, and creates the
world anew from the depths of his or her own spiritual life.
This implies a process of individuation in which the subjectivity of the creator seems to be emphasized at the cost of the
objective reality of the perceived phenomena. Dickinson's
theory of perception endorses the romantic view of the creative mind as projecting its own inner truth upon the forms of
life; this contrasts sharply with the view of the perceiving
mind as a mere reflector of the external world.[8] While projecting the inner truth upon the outer world, the creative mind
establishes a constant relationship between the knower and the
known. Objective reality attains its fullest meaning in the vision of the artist in being subjectivized. Subjectivity, in this
context, does not refer to a state of the ego; it refers, paradoxically, to the loss of ego, and an abundance of spirituality in
which the artist has no personal axe to grind. It is in this
dimension of awareness that a continuous conversion of the
external into the internal, and of the internal into the external, takes place. The emphasis on the inwardness or withinness of the poet, however, is an integral part of the process
of poetic perception.[9] Dickinson uses the word "interior" as a
metaphor for internalized space which expands into infinity in
the imagination. The interior is the locus where the self and
the other, being and nonbeing meet. In other words, the sub-

ject-object relationship is fundamental to Dickinson's way of perception. The subject-object interpenetration results in true perception in which the whole objective realm is appropriated by the subject, and is transformed "into a unity of subjective feeling," to use Whitehead's phrase.[10] Dickinson achieves this perspective in the following poem:

> Perception of an object costs
> Precise the Object's loss –
> Perception in itself a Gain
> Replying to it's Price –
> The Object Absolute – is nought –
> Perception sets it fair
> And then upbraids a Perfectness
> That situates so far – *
>
> * *variant reading:*
> that 'tis so Heavenly far –   [1071]

Perception describes the confrontation between the perceiver and the perceived: the perceiver moves toward the object and enters it, so as to transform it according to his or her spiritual reality. In this process the object loses its objectivity, externality, and opacity, and the subject loses its self-conscious subjectivity or ego. The object's loss does not refer to the negation of the material existence; it simply posits the relative position of the objective reality insofar as it derives its full meaning from the spirituality of the perceiver, and insofar as it is re-created within the perceiver. The object's loss as mere object, then, represents, metaphorically, perception's gain, which is the creativity of the poet. Since creativity or creation is a process and not the end product, the poet considers the "Object Absolute" as nothing. The question is not so much that absolute reality is beyond the limits of human perception as it is an observation that poetry or the poet's perception does not concern itself with the metaphysical absolute. Poetic perception only sets the absolute object in its true perspective: the absoluteness of creativity is the creative process itself. Poetic

perception upbraids the "Perfectness" which is situated
beyond the creative realm. In this context, Albert Gelpi has
rightly noted that Dickinson "is concerned not with the 'Perfectness' of the ultimate reality 'that 'tis so Heavenly far,' nor
with the object which is 'nought' in itself, but with the poet's
perception, which more than compensates for the sacrifice of
the negligible phenomenal existence." [11]

In creative perception, the emphasis falls on how the perceiver creates from within himself and how he transforms external reality into a typology of his own inner experience. Perception provides a ground for the union of the inner with the
outer, though the inner always remains as its focus. It should
be obvious here that in a theory of perception which brings
into prominence the role of the creative perceiver, there is
little room for the Lockean view of mind as a mere passive recipient of sense data, a tabula rasa acted upon by external
stimuli. Emily Dickinson affirms the primacy of the creative
mind which apprehends simultaneously the reality of sensuous experience and its transparency, and which creates the experience anew by viewing it through the spirit:

> To hear an Oriole sing
> May be a common thing –
> Or only a divine.
>
> It is not of the Bird
> Who sings the same, unheard,
> As unto Crowd –
>
> The Fashion of the Ear
> Attireth that it hear
> In Dun, or fair –
>
> So whether it be Rune,
> Or whether it be none
> Is of within.
>
> The "Tune is in the Tree – "
> The Skeptic – showeth me –
> "No Sir! In Thee!"   [526]

The experience of hearing the oriole's song can be commonplace. But the same experience can become truly divine if the listener's ear is attuned accordingly. The nature of perception in this case is determined by the fashion of the ear, which derives its quality from within. It is the poet's perception of the song that gives it meaning. The poem seems to perform a double function: as the emphasis in the case of the bird's song falls on the inner perception of the listener, the poem which is the poet's song demands of the reader to have that within which will enable him to apprehend its meaning. The reader should be able to apprehend creatively the bird-bard's song in his or her own being. This means that our response to poetry is dependent upon and reflective of the quality of our inner life. Hearing in this poem includes seeing: the auditory images "sing," "ear," and "tune" are merged with the visual images "dun," "fair," and "tree." Although it seems that it is the interiority of the poet which shapes poetic perception, ontologically, interiority does not exclude exteriority.[12] The bird's song is integral to the process of inner hearing: "The Spirit is the Conscious Ear" (733). It is in this sense that the tune which to the skeptic is in the tree is the tune which to the poet is "In Thee!"

Emily Dickinson's theory of perception, which is at once a theory of knowledge and a theory of poetic creation, shows marked resemblances to the ideas of several creative writers and thinkers of the past as well as to those of poets and phenomenologists of today.[13] It is not within the scope of the present study to offer a full-length treatment of the romantic theory of perception as enunciated in the writings of the romantic tradition in poetry or in philosophical thought. But a few examples which bring out the view of the perceiving mind as an imaginative act and as a creative power radiating objective reality may be cited here, in order to reinforce Dickinson's own view of perception. In his "Dejection: An Ode," Coleridge, like Plotinus and Schlegel, asserts the role of the poet's own spirit in creating a world of perceptions:

> Though I should gaze for ever
> On that green light that lingers in the west:
> *I may not hope from outward forms to win*
> *The passion and the life, whose fountains are within.*
>
> *O Lady! we receive but what we give,*
>   *And in our life alone does Nature live:*
> Ours is her wedding garment, ours her shroud!
> And would we aught behold, of higher worth,
> Than that inanimate cold world allowed
> To the poor loveless ever-anxious crowd,
>   Ah! *from the soul itself must issue forth*
> *A light, a glory, a fair luminous cloud*
>   *Enveloping the Earth –*
> And from the soul itself must there be sent
> A sweet and potent voice, of its own birth,
> Of all sweet sounds the life and element!
>
>   [lines 43–58; italics mine]

The fountains of the passion and the life are within. The soul or the creative mind is what Coleridge calls the "shaping spirit of Imagination." Blake feels that "This World Is a World of Imagination & Vision," though "Every body does not see alike." He further observes: "to the Eyes of the Man of Imagination, Nature is Imagination itself. As a man is, so he sees. As the Eye is formed, such are its Powers." [14] In a note to the "Immortality Ode," Wordsworth records: "I was often unable to think of external things as having external existence, and I communed with all that I saw as something not apart from, but inherent in, my own immaterial nature." [15] Thoreau declares in *Walden:* "Wherever I sat, . . . the landscape radiated from me accordingly." [16] The contours of outward reality are determined by the poet's vision, for they are the external lineaments of his inner perception:

> Packed in my mind lie all the clothes
> Which outward nature wears,
> And in its fashion's hourly change
> In all things else repairs.[17]

Emerson observes likewise in his essay on nature: "Every natural fact is a symbol of some spiritual fact. Every appearance in nature corresponds to some state of the mind, and that state of mind can only be described by presenting that natural appearance as its picture." [18]

Rilke, in a letter to Clara Rilke (March 8, 1907), delineates the process which testifies that external phenomena are the "means to the end of expressing indirectly something in his own inner life that he could hardly express in any other way." [19] The process is stated in these words:

> Gazing is such a wonderful thing, about which we know little; in gazing we are turned completely outward, but just when we are so most, things seem to go on within us, which have been waiting longingly for the moment when they should be unobserved, and while they are happening in us, intactly and strangely anonymously, independently of our consciousness, their significance gradually grows in the object without, a convincing, powerful name, their only possible name, in which we joyfully and reverently recognize the happening within our soul, without being able to reach it, only quite gently, quite remotely comprehending it under the symbol of a thing that immediately before was quite strange to us and in the next moment is again estranged from us.[20]

Wallace Stevens's poetry or poetics demonstrates fully the connection between external and internal reality; it seeks to relate the creative mind and the objects of perception in a network of poetic metaphors. Like Penelope in "The World as Meditation," the poet awakens the world in which he dwells. In "Credences of Summer," Stevens writes:

> Let's see the very thing and nothing else.
> Let's see it with the hottest fire of sight.
> Burn everything not part of it to ash.
>
> Trace the gold sun about the whitened sky
> Without evasion by a single metaphor.

> Look at it in its essential barrenness
> And say this, this is the centre that I seek.

The "hottest fire of sight," a metaphor for the poetic imagination, indicates the mind's ultimate dominance over the visual
landscape. This is how the poet can "sing in face / Of the Object." The ambivalence of the subject-object relationship is a
part of the complex relation between the self and the outside
world, as shown in "The Man with the Blue Guitar." Stevens
believes that the poet must first experience existential reality
within his own mind or heart in order to be able to tell about
it. "The Snow Man" fully embodies this view:

> One must have a mind of winter
> To regard the frost and the boughs
> Of the pine-trees crusted with snow;
>
> And have been cold a long time
> To behold the junipers shagged with ice,
> The spruces rough in the distant glitter
>
> Of the January sun; and not to think
> Of any misery in the sound of the wind,
> In the sound of a few leaves,
>
> Which is the sound of the land
> Full of the same wind
> That is blowing in the same bare place
>
> For the listener, who listens in the snow,
> And, nothing himself, beholds
> Nothing that is not there and the nothing that is.

It should be clear from the above poem that it is the "subjectivity" of the poet, which is neither purely subjective nor
strictly objective, that makes the rendering of all the metaphoric relations between the inside and the outside world possible. In the process of actualizing these relations, as is shown
in Stevens's poem, one becomes the frost in order "to behold
the junipers shagged with ice." The listener merges with the
wind and the sound, in order not to think of any misery in the

sound of the wind, and the self is metamorphosed into "noth-ing himself" before it can see "Nothing that is not there and the nothing that is." In the structure of Stevens's perception, "a mind of winter" is one with "the hottest fire of sight"; the opposites meet here as freely as they do in Dickinson's po-etry.[21]

Examples concerning the primacy of the perceiving mind in its creative experience of the world can be multiplied by quot-ing from several other poets, as well as from modern phenom-enologists such as Husserl, Heidegger, and Merleau-Ponty.[22] But, for the sake of continuity, I must resume my discussion of Emily Dickinson. The emphasis on the creative powers of the poetic mind in Dickinson's poetry should not be confused with some sort of narcissism, for creativity is expansion, a search for fullness, and not self-centeredness. The poet's per-sonal sense of solitude or loneliness does not betray any sign of neurosis. On the contrary, it shows spiritual awareness (1092). Loneliness is the "Maker of the soul" (777), and it "Is richer than could be revealed / By mortal numeral" (1116). It is the "sumptuous solitude" (1495) which is the source of Dick-inson's inner strength, her creative imagination, her poetic perceptions. The sense of being alone does not generate in her any feeling of self-sufficient egocentrism; nor is it a mode representing one-way traffic from the external to the internal, from the known to the unknown. Rather, paradoxically, it is a creative condition of being in which personal destiny or the in-terior world constantly interpenetrates the outside world, showing the "I-thou" relationship in a metamorphic process. It is through her solitude or "polar privacy" (1695) that Emily Dickinson strives to achieve the *whole* of her poetic vision; she does not permit any external impingements to thwart or dis-turb this syncretic effort. She seeks the whole and writes:

> Without this – there is nought –
> All other Riches be
> As is the Twitter of a Bird –
> Heard opposite the Sea –

> I could not care – to gain
> A lesser than the Whole –
> For did not this include themself –
> As Seams – include the Ball?   [655]

The creative voice of Dickinson's poetry is full-throated, not
the low-toned chirp of a distant bird. The sea is the battlefield
of her perception and creativity. Daring as she is, she does not
intend "to gain / A lesser than the Whole." This also speaks
for her total commitment to her art. Her unique sense of creative fidelity makes her perceive in these demiurgic terms:

> My Faith is larger than the Hills –
> So when the Hills decay –
> My Faith must take the Purple Wheel
> To show the Sun the way –   [766]

Dickinson does not "stint a faith / On which so vast depends."
For her, it is the "Experiment of Our Lord" (300). It is in-
herited with life, and, therefore, losing it means to lose one's
being (377). It relieves one from trepidation and fear of death
(392), because it adores the dark (7). It is the organ of perception: "What I see not, I better see – / Through Faith" (939),
writes Dickinson. It creates the presence in the landscape of
absence:

> Faith – is the Pierless Bridge
> Supporting what We see
> Unto the Scene that We do not –
> Too slender for the eye
>
> It bears the Soul as bold
> As it were rocked in Steel
> With Arms of Steel at either side –
> It joins – behind the Vail   [915]

Faith involves resignation and "negative capability." But it
also involves fulfillment and assertion. As an aesthetic category
faith means consecration to the terror of creation.[23] It is this
poetic fidelity which prompts her to sing: "I'm Nobody! Who

are you?", "The Service without Hope," and "How happy is
the little Stone." [24] It also implies the endless search for identity, the "Haunted House" of art, that Dickinson fixes in her
verses.[25] She grapples with the process and mystery of human
existence, and affirms the sovereignty of the poet's mind in
these words:

> The Brain – is wider than the Sky –
> For – put them side by side –
> The one the other will contain
> With ease – and You – beside –
>
> The Brain is deeper than the sea –
> For – hold them – Blue to Blue –
> The one the other will absorb –
> As Sponges – Buckets – do –
>
> The Brain is just the weight of God –
> For – Heft them – Pound for Pound –
> And They will differ – if they do –
> As Syllable from Sound –   [632]

Dickinson uses the words brain, mind, heart, intuition, imagination, and consciousness synonymously. She believes that the
poet's mind or the brain comprehends all the worlds from
here to eternity. It is wider than the sky—a domed structure
which contains the limits of externality. Its depth matches the
depth of the sea. It is "an inland soul" which dips into eternity
(76). In its creative exuberance the poet's mind assumes the
role of a god and surpasses nature:

> The One who could repeat the Summer day –
> Were greater than itself – though He
> Minutest of Mankind should be –
>
> And He – could reproduce the Sun –
> At period of going down –
> The Lingering – and the Stain – I mean –
>
> When Orient have been outgrown –
> And Occident – become Unknown –
> His Name – remain –   [307]

   The poet's perceptions are the only permanent realities in a
transient world. His poems are "Roses of a steadfast summer"
(163). They are the "continents of summer," and the "firmaments of sun" (180). Dickinson calls her art a summer day
(397) which lasts a solid year (569). In nature, summer slips
into autumn as life fades into death (1346 and 1506), but in
the poetic imagination the summer would not cease (1014).
Therefore, the poet can repeat the summer day, and stop the
sun from going down by making a picture of the sun (188).
The poetic consciousness is a zone "whose Sun constructs perpetual Noon / Whose perfect Seasons wait" (1056). Hence,
Dickinson's assertion:

> I reckon – when I count at all –
> First – Poets – Then the Sun –
> Then Summer – Then the Heaven of God –
> And then – the List is done –
>
> But, looking back – the First so seems
> To Comprehend the Whole –
> The Others look a needless Show –
> So I write – Poets – All –   [569]

However, Emily Dickinson is quite familiar with the poet's
human predicament. The poet's sense of pain and anguish
caused by his alienation from the source of primal existence
has been captured most successfully in these verses:

> To learn the Transport by the Pain –
> As Blind Men learn the sun!
> To die of thirst – suspecting
> That Brooks in Meadows run!
>
> To stay the homesick – homesick feet
> Upon a foreign shore –
> Haunted by native lands, the while –
> And blue – beloved air!
>
> This is the Sovreign Anguish!
> This – the signal wo!

> These are the patient "Laureates"
> Whose voices – trained – below –
>
> Ascend in ceaseless Carol –
> Inaudible, indeed,
> To us – the duller scholars
> Of the Mysterious Bard!   [167]

The poet has to master the art of going through anguish and woe, in order to reach the state of internal bliss. He must experience want (731) so that he may be fulfilled. The poet remains haunted by the memory of the native lands of primordial existence, and feels homesick. The land of our daily habitation looks like a foreign shore to him. To recover the primal reality of being is the mythic errand of the patient bard on this earth. The "ceaseless Carol" of the poet is dedicated to this end. Emily Dickinson reproaches "the duller scholars" to whom the poet's song of suffering remains inaudible or who find it difficult to accept the value of suffering in arriving at the source of existence.

In order to be able to participate in the creative vision of the poet, and share some of his insights, we must have an almost identical degree of imaginative experience. Dickinson demands that her readers show a high level of imaginative awareness, because

> Reportless Subjects, to the Quick
> Continual addressed –
> But foreign as the Dialect
> Of Danes, unto the rest.
>
> Reportless Measures, to the Ear
> Susceptive – stimulus –
> But like an Oriental Tale
> To others, fabulous –   [1048]

Without the imagination and the sensitivity, the reader will not be able to comprehend the uncommon themes and rhythms of the poet's world. Dickinson defines the imagination in terms of the metaphors of air and wind, and calls the

"Happy Air" an "Essential Host in Life's faint, wailing Inn"
(1060). She believes that wind ushers liberty (1137). To her,
the speech of wind is "like the Push / Of numerous Humming
Birds at once / From a superior Bush," and

> His Countenance – a Billow –
> His Fingers, as He passed
> Let go a music – as of tunes
> Blown tremulous in Glass –   [436]

Dickinson suggests that the imagination has its roots in the
sea—the symbol which encompasses the whole of existence:

> I think that the Root of the Wind is Water –
> It would not sound so deep
> Were it a Firmamental Product –
> Airs no Oceans keep –
> Mediterranean intonations –
> To a Current's Ear –
> There is a maritime conviction
> In the Atmosphere –   [1302]

It is through the imagination that the poet achieves a priestly
status:

> How mighty the Wind must feel Morns
> Encamping on a thousand dawns
> Espousing each and spurning all
> Then soaring to his Temple Tall –   [1418]

And, again, it is through the imagination that the poet succeeds in wearing the garb of paradoxical humility, the barefoot rank (L265), which is essential to her barefoot vision
(523), the spiritual center of Dickinson's poetic perception.[26]

THE POET AND THE POETIC EXPERIENCE

Dealing with the perplexing problem of the genesis of Dickinson's creative experience, which is linked with the larger
problem of perception, it should be admitted at the outset that

there is no clear-cut, scientific method by which one can determine the causes and track down the intrinsic mystery of the poetic experience which occurs in the imagination. Herbert Read illuminates the problem in these words:

> Some kind of immateriality is, of course, intrinsic to the poetic process. Poetry is consistent only in its shadowiness, its indeterminacy, its intangibility. In writing poetry we have a sense of the inexhaustible depth of our subjectivity; and out of that depth, flowing as spontaneously as water from a spring, comes this sensuous utterance in rhythmic verse. Of course, it is spiritual or psychic, as water is earthy. Spirituality is generated by it, as "a sudden flash of transcendental feeling," but not added to it.[27]

Poets have always found it difficult to describe the precise sources of their creative experience, because behind every creation there is chaos, which is never precise; it has myriad roots and branches. Psychology and psychoanalysis have done very little to help with the task of exploring the true nature of poetic experience from the point of view of literary criticism. Though creativity is a mental and psychic activity, it is against the canon of literary taste to try to trace it mainly from the instinctual, unconscious biography of the artist. I am not being indifferent to the several dynamic uses of psychology insofar as it can inform us about the functions of the human mind, particularly the mind of the creative artist. I only wish to warn against excessive psychologism and clinical analysis of literary works, because psychology perhaps will never be fully equipped to translate for us the ambiguous sources of artistic creations, especially literature. Rollo May frankly admits that "most of our approaches to creativity in psychology have been strikingly inadequate." [28] Describing the ambivalent nature of the poetic experience, Brewster Ghiselin mentions that "the poem seems to issue from the dark of the mind without much awareness of how it comes." [29] Since the sources of the poetic experience are generally obscure, and since the "dark" mind of the poet is beyond any rational analysis, we cannot com-

pletely rely on genetic theories. The best way, then, to talk
about the origins of poems is to focus our attention on the
poems themselves. Allen Tate offers a sound observation in
this matter:

> Poets, in their way, are practical men; they are interested in
> results. What is the poem, after it is written? That is the ques-
> tion. Not where it came from, or why. The Why and Where can
> never get beyond the guessing stage because, in the language of
> those who think it can, poetry cannot be brought to "laboratory
> conditions." The only real evidence that any critic can bring
> before his gaze is the finished poem.[30]

The genesis of the poem is contained within the poem itself.
The poem also brings into being something new of which we
are at first only vaguely aware. The poem invites the reader to
encounter its imagery and share with it the fullness of the
knowledge that it embodies. The poem is a live creature; to
read it is to participate in its concern, its movement, its drama,
its inner metamorphosis. In this sharing process, the poet and
the reader become one. In order to achieve the poetic experience, we should go to the poet and his creation, and become
involved in his particular scheme of things. We should not
merely ask the poet, as Coleridge reminds us in his "Dejection:
An Ode,"

> What this strong music in the soul may be!
> What, and wherein it doth exist,
> This light, this glory, this fair luminous mist,
> This beautiful and beauty-making power.   [lines 60–63]

Emily Dickinson's poetry is an embodiment of her creative
experience which can be described as mythopoeic, ontological,
tragic, and existential, to repeat the observation made earlier
in this study. The highly connotative images and symbols such
as fire, volcano, lightning, thunder, bolt, crash, water, well,
sea, flood, ecstasy, agony, love, sacrament, beauty, truth, pang,
thorn, affliction, suffering, despair, life, death, immortality,
self, soul, being, god, awe, terror, palsy, abyss, cave, cocoon,

grass, earth, sky, heat, cold, noon, and frost are some of the innumerable archetypes of her poetic experience. In poem after poem, she plays with the terror and awe of creation. She tells Higginson, "My Business is Circumference" (L268), and writes:

> Circumference thou Bride of Awe
> Possessing thou shalt be
> Possessed by every hallowed Knight
> That dares to covet thee   [1620]

In terms of the creative experience, here is the grand merger of "the themes of sexual, religious and aesthetic fulfillment in the union of the bride and the knight, Circumference and Awe," to use Gelpi's insight.[31] Terror is the womb that crystalizes the experience of poetry; thunder and lightning are the accompaniments of its birth. Awe provides the mood and atmosphere. Describing the process of birth of the poetic character and its abiding nature, Dickinson writes:

> It struck me – every Day –
> The Lightning was as new
> As if the Cloud that instant slit
> And let the Fire through –
>
> It burned Me – in the Night –
> It Blistered to My Dream –
> It sickened fresh upon my sight –
> With every Morn that came –
>
> I thought that Storm – was brief –
> The Maddest – quickest by –
> But Nature lost the Date of This –
> And left it in the Sky –   [362]

The storm of lightning. and fire, blistering "Me" and "My Dream," seems to provide a clue to Dickinson's "terror – since September" (L261). The realization of this symbolic storm within her, each day and night, constitutes, to my mind, the genesis of her poetry. No wonder she refers to the experience of poetry in terms of thunder (1247 and 1581). To her, even "the Minutest Bee / That rides – emits a Thunder" (591), and "A Thunder storm combines the charms / Of Winter and of Hell" (1649). Joseph Campbell informs us that "the thunderbolt (*Vajra*) is one of the major symbols in Buddhist iconography, signifying the spiritual power of Buddhahood (indestructible enlightenment) which shatters the illusory realities of the world." [32] In Dickinson's expanded perception, "thunderbolt" plays the same part. In her poetic world as well as in Hindu mythology, thunder is a spiritual metaphor having a cathartic significance. Dickinson experiences thunder as a "stop-sensation" on her soul (293), and tells Higginson, in equally paradoxical vein, the way she experiences poetry: "If I read a book [and] it makes my whole body so cold no fire ever can warm me I know *that* is poetry. If I feel physically as if the top of my head were taken off, I know *that* is poetry. These are the only way[s] I know it. Is there any other way" (L342a: Higginson's words in a letter to his wife).

The feeling of numbness, or the loss of body-consciousness, is symptomatic of the sense of wonder at the haunting aspects of creation. For Dickinson, the terror and mystery of existence is identical with the terror of poetry which enacts that mystery. Nature or existence haunts Dickinson, and she feels palsied at the mere contemplation of life's "Haunted House" (L459a). The only way to relieve herself of the burden of mystery is to re-create it in her own words, making the enactment of "Haunted House" possible in terms of poetry, the art to which she is consecrated. This is what she conveys to Higginson: "My dying Tutor told me that he would like to live till I had been a poet, but Death was [as] much of Mob as I could master – then – And when far afterward – a sudden light on Orchards, or a new fashion in the wind troubled my attention – I felt a palsy, here – the Verses just relieve – " (L265).

For Emily Dickinson, poetic experience is the "wondrous sea" whose shore is eternity (4), and it stays like grief and hills (89).[33] It is called "Being's Road" or "a Sealed Route" (615).

Once obtained, there is no retreat possible. It is the "escapeless sea" (1264 and L390). It is the "Magic passive but extant" (1231). Its awe is pervasive and integral to the creative process: "I work to drive the awe away, yet awe impels the work," says Dickinson (L891).[34] Emily Dickinson literally feeds on awe (1486). The creative urge in her is that fire which cannot be put out, and it is that flood which cannot be folded (530). It is "a new Content – / That feels to her – like Sacrament" (535). It is a threadless way on which it is lighter to be blind (761), for the poet in this blindness can look within herself, the circumference of a poetic vision. The inward direction of Dickinson's creative experience is the source of her poetic power. Poetry takes its birth in the silence of the poet's mind:

> The reticent volcano keeps
> His never slumbering plan;
> Confided are his projects pink
> To no precarious man.   [1748]

But the silence of the poet's mind is volcanic; from it unceasingly erupts the fluid body of his poetry. Dickinson poetizes the paradoxical and complex nature of the poet's mind in which the initial experience of poetry takes place:

> On my volcano grows the Grass
> A meditative spot –
> An acre for a Bird to choose
> Would be the General thought –
>
> How red the Fire rocks below –
> How insecure the sod
> Did I disclose
> Would populate with awe my solitude   [1677]

The grass represents the outward tranquillity of the poet's mind threatened by volcanic forces beneath. It also represents poetry: before the grass grows or poetry comes into being, the bird-bard meditates on the volcanic spots of existence and goes through the experience of red fire, symbolic of love and suffering. The poet also experiences, in her solitude, the sense of uncertainty and insecurity between the meditative conception and the creation of poetry, without ever disclosing its awful nature to anyone. It is this deliberate choice to meditate on the volcano of existence which qualifies Dickinson as a religious poet, and her poetry as "the poetry of meditation," to use Louis Martz's phrase. The Hindu term for meditation is *Dhyâna*, the instrument of self-knowledge and liberation, vision and revelation. The poetry of meditation (*Dhyâna-Kavayah*) is what Sri Aurobindo calls *Mantra*, the culmination of poetic utterance, discovery, and insight.[35] Emily Dickinson transcribes her meditative experience into poetry, and names it "the Scarlet way," calling for the "straight renunciation" of the world, which "Requires Energy – possibly Agony" (527). The scarlet experiment (861) of her poetry enables Dickinson to achieve the spiritual height by diving deep into the sea of the human heart and exploring the darkness of its abyss with peril as a possession (1678). She plunges into and rises from the deepest layers of human existence simultaneously. The way down becomes the way up, "*down* into the concrete, *up* into the unlimited," as William Lynch puts it.[36] Emily Dickinson evinces a rare capacity to stay with life's mystery and ambiguity, to find herself by losing herself, and to create a poetic world of light out of the darknesses of existence. She writes to Susan Gilbert Dickinson: "Moving on in the Dark like Loaded Boats at Night, though there is no Course, there is Boundlessness" (L871), and "The first section of Darkness is the densest, Dear – After that, Light trembles in" (L874). Boundlessness defines the range of her poetic perception, and *dark* is the realm of her creative experience. Her poems are like the loaded boats at night, fully equipped to withstand the fury of the stormy seas. It is through the dark that we can experience light. It is ironic. But, then, irony is the mode of existence. Dickinson finds the road to her ultimate identity, her destiny, her vocation, in the dark of her inner self. It is the dark which impels "shapes to eyes at a distance, which for them have the whole area of life or of death" (L656): "Vastness – is but the Shadow of the Brain which casts it" (L735). The dark invades the whole being of the poet, and the forms of the poetic experience manifest themselves to her. She cannot describe them in prose. She gropes at shapes, and clutches at sounds (430), and eventually, in the process, the poetic utterance is born. Since the experience is original, the utterance must also be original. What this original utterance involves can, perhaps, be best described in the words of Jung:

> It is . . . to be expected of the poet that he will resort to mythology in order to give his experience its most fitting expression. It would be a serious mistake to suppose that he works with materials received at second-hand. The primordial experience is the source of his creativeness; it cannot be fathomed, and therefore requires mythological imagery to give it form. In itself it offers no words or images, for it is a vision seen "as in a glass, darkly." It is merely a deep presentiment that strives to find expression. It is like a whirlwind that seizes everything within reach and, by carrying it aloft, assumes a visible shape. Since the particular expression can never exhaust the possibilities of the vision, but falls far short of it in richness of content, the poet must have at his disposal a huge store of materials if he is to communicate even a few of his intimations. What is more, he must resort to an imagery that is difficult to handle and full of contradictions in order to express the weird paradoxicality of his vision.[37]

My discussion of Emily Dickinson's creative experience in terms of the archetypes of her poetic vision also shows the validity of my treatment of Dickinson as a mythopoeic poet. She seems to me to be successful in clothing her poetic experience in images "full of contradictions," and thereby giving her primordial experience its most appropriate expression. She can perhaps boast with the great Chinese poet, Lu Chi:

> So acute is the mind in such instants of divine comprehension,
> What chaos is there that it cannot marshal in miraculous order?
> While winged thoughts, like quick breezes, soar from depths of
>   heart,

Eloquent words, like a gushing spring, flow between lips and
    teeth.
No flower, no plant, or animal is too prodigal of splendour
To be recreated under the writer's pen.[38]

THE POET AND THE CREATIVE PROCESS

It is understood that the problem of creative process is in-
dissolubly linked with the creative experience or the genesis of
poetry. However, an independent discussion of the relation
between the poet and the creative process is necessary here, so
that we may have an insight into the character of the poet in
the act of creation, in the actual coming of poetry into being.
This discussion will also demonstrate, explicitly or implicitly,
how the making of a poem involves a sacred use of language
and how the images and metaphors are used as the means of
intuitive or spiritual awareness. Dickinson has

> Inconceivably solemn!
> Things so gay
> Pierce – by the very Press
> Of Imagery –   [582]

Since Dickinson's poetry is often about the making of poetry, I intend to show this in her own words:

> So from the mould
> Scarlet and Gold
> Many a Bulb will rise –
> Hidden away, cunningly,
> From sagacious eyes.
>
> So from Cocoon
> Many a Worm
> Leap so Highland gay,
> *Peasants* like me,
> Peasants like Thee
> Gaze perplexedly!   [66]

The poem is *made*. The act of creation has taken place. The poet has given birth to a poetic form from the scarlet mold of her being. Many a bulb or many a poem is just waiting to be born of the creative womb of the poet, though they are as yet hidden even from her own sagacious view. The poem is to the poet as the worm is to the cocoon. As poem after poem emerges from its chrysalis, the "peasants," the pastoral spectators of Dickinson's world of perception, only gaze perplexedly—a most fitting posture for the audience of Creation. Poetry, like creation itself, cannot be rationalized; no definite meaning can be deduced from it. Its symbolic structure is ambiguous, indeterminate, and multiple. The real gazer, therefore, cannot help feeling perplexed at its amorphous shape. The voice of the poet in the poem is that of both the creator and the creation. In terms of the poem's symbolism, the poet is both the mold and the bulb, the cocoon and the worm. She is also the peasant, a person of uncorrupted sensibility. The poem's symbolism is, thus, "the symbolic process dramatizing itself." The poem also shows that "a creative man *is* creativity itself; a man who acts is act." [39] The cocoon is one of Dickinson's favorite metaphors, which she uses here very effectively to convey the process of birth. The cocoon's secret, which is creation itself, perches in ecstasy and defies imprisonment (129). But cocoon symbolism also refers to the process of death and destruction. The cocoon is at both the beginning and the end of creation. It is at once the womb and the tomb. "From Cocoon forth a Butterfly" (354) describes the purposeless wanderings of a butterfly after the initial experience of birth from the cocoon. The journey takes place in a land where life struggles with death, where the contenders move like phantoms without direction, as if in a "purposeless Circumference," and where finally everything—sun, men, butterfly—is extinguished in the sea. In "He parts Himself – like Leaves" (517), the eternal strife between life and death is captured through the images of rose and buttercup, day and night, world and frost. The journey of the persona ends on a point of uncertainty which is terminated by a sepulchre, a coffin or a mansion, a tomb or a cocoon. These poems (354 and 517) show Dickinson's bafflement at the mystery of creation. The circumference which is the "Bride of Awe" (1620), or the circumference which is her business (L268) becomes here the purposeless circumference or a "Tropic Show" (354). In this way, however, the poems offer us a faithful description of the mood of ambivalence which prevails over the nature of poetic reality, the mood which is the core of perception and the creative process. If going back to the sea or the cocoon means to go back to the embryonic form in order to be reborn, the womb-tomb symbolism has a functional value. It can be treated as Dickinson's aesthetic strategy to experience a birth-death continuum, a sort of immortality which subsumes an everlasting possibility of rebirth. Such a theme would necessarily involve doubt and perplexity, though the poet's job is to actualize the experience entailing these and much else besides:

> My Cocoon tightens – Colors teaze –
> I'm feeling for the Air –
> A dim capacity for Wings
> Demeans the Dress I wear –
>
> A power of Butterfly must be –
> The Aptitude to fly
> Meadows of Majesty concedes
> And easy Sweeps of Sky –
>
> So I must baffle at the Hint
> And cipher at the Sign
> And make much blunder, if at last
> I take the clue divine –   [1099]

The poem is about perception. The poet makes concrete the whole experience of perception by feeling simultaneously the inside wall of the womb and "A dim capacity for Wings," the urge to be born. The tightening cocoon symbolizes captivity as well as freedom. Although the act of birth seems to imply the demeaning of the chrysalis, it is necessary to alienate oneself from the embryo so that the experience of the butterfly state will be possible. Butterfly symbolizes the will to be free. The butterfly state itself does not mean ultimate freedom; it is a stage in the process of freedom, which is, paradoxically, contained in the captivity of the cocoon. In the butterfly state, man is in the larger womb, which is this world. In order to be free from the chrysalis called world, and in order to "take the clue divine," one has to free oneself from the encircling walls of this great womb. Bafflement, guessing, blundering are natural to the process of discovery, which is our true freedom, our rebirth. The symbolic process of "My Cocoon tightens – Colors teaze," seems to me to be analogous to the experience contained in the words of Hermann Hesse: "The bird fights its way out of the egg. The egg is the world. Who would be born must first destroy a world. The bird flies to God. That God's name is Abraxas." [40] Embodying this analogy, the poetic experience or the genesis of poetry becomes the poem, and the poem breaks the limits of its linear language and assumes a symbolic form, the body of perfect freedom.

Emily Dickinson describes the creative process through several other symbolisms. When she writes: "Mountains drip with Sunset," "the Fire ebbs like Billows," "Dusk crawls on the Village," and "Dome of Abyss is Bowing / Into Solitude," she is arresting the "Visions" in the language of poetry. In such moments, she feels as if paralyzed with gold.[41] The creative process brings back the creative experience with a sense of real vitality conveyed through the paradoxical paralysis of gold. In "Dare you see a Soul *at the White Heat?*" (365), Dickinson seems to describe the poet as a blacksmith, the poetic experience as the "vivid" ore, and the creative process as the passing of the ores through the forge. The ore becomes the "Designated Light," which is poetry. It is self-evident that the creative process involves great effort; the poet-blacksmith gives shape to his ores with hammer and the anvil. The power of poetry can be gained by strategy (359), by clutching at and diving into the roots of experience (427). The poet weaves the

fabric of poetry as the spider who "plies from Nought to
Nought – / In unsubstantial Trade," and "Supplants our Tapestries with His – / In half the period" (605). The spider sews
"at Night / Without a Light / Upon an Arc of White" (1138).
Dickinson regards the spider as the neglected son of genius
(1275), an artist who weaves his net from within. Considering
the spider as a metaphor for inwardness, she presents it as a
figure that assiduously creeps into the silence of one's mind
(1167). This spider is the builder of the "fairest Home" of her
poetry (1423).

It should be clear from the above-noted symbolisms that the
relation between the poet and the poetic creation cannot be
stated directly; it requires a vast range of images and metaphors to clothe its naked mystery. Emily Dickinson describes it
in these verses:

> This is a Blossom of the Brain –
> A small – italic Seed
> Lodged by Design or Happening
> The Spirit fructified –
>
> Shy as the Wind of his Chambers
> Swift as a Freshet's Tongue
> So of the Flower of the Soul
> It's process is unknown.
>
> When it is found, a few rejoice
> The Wise convey it Home
> Carefully cherishing the spot
> If other Flower become.   [945]

The mystery of the poetic creation cannot be known through
intellect alone. It is the flower of the human soul or a blossom
of the brain which is wider than the sky, and deeper than the
sea (632). In its nascent stage, it is the "italic Seed," which is
fructified by the spirit into a blooming flower. The poet does
not concern herself so much with the problem of how the seed
got there as she does with the fact of its discovery. Emily
Dickinson clutches at the discovery in a mood of religious fer-
vor because she is aware that if and

> When it is lost, that Day shall be
> The Funeral of God,
> Upon his Breast, a closing Soul
> The Flower of our Lord. [945]

The poetic creation is, then, the flower of our Lord, and the poet is its creator-custodian, as well as its instrument on earth.

Poetry comes into being when the poet exerts his sinews. Dickinson describes this striving in terms of the flower-perfume metaphor:

> Essential Oils – are wrung –
> The Attar from the Rose
> Be not expressed by Suns – alone –
> It is the gift of Screws –
>
> The General Rose – decay –
> But this – in Lady's Drawer
> Make Summer – When the Lady lie
> In Ceaseless Rosemary – [675]

Wringing is an existential act; it implies self-discipline through pain and suffering. It is only through suffering that man can realize the "Essential Oils" of existence. Suffering being the existential imperative, essence and existence are integral to the creative process, as the perfume and flower are in nature. The attar is the expression of the rose, as the poetic creation is the expression of the poet. But this expression occurs when the flower-poet goes through the experience of psychic as well as physical pressures. The "gift of Screws" is the secret of artistic fulfillment. It refers to the artist's capacity to undergo pain in order to create. It also refers to craftmanship and discipline, which are necessary ingredients in the making of an artist. The rose-petals must be seasoned in the process of becoming the attar. The last four lines reveal Dickinson's strategy of making the attar or the poetic creation appear to be of permanent character, in contrast to the transiency of existence which is not particularized in the mold of aesthetic experience. The job of the poet is to save the things of this world from decaying. The only way to do so is by preserving their essence in the

edifice of poetry. Emily Dickinson achieves this goal and
enacts the experience in this form:

> This was a Poet – It is That
> Distills amazing sense
> From ordinary Meanings –
> And Attar so immense
>
> From the familiar species
> That perished by the Door –
> We wonder it was not Ourselves
> Arrested it – before –
>
> Of Pictures, the Discloser –
> The Poet – it is He –
> Entitles Us – By Contrast –
> To ceaseless Poverty –
>
> Of Portion – so unconscious –
> The Robbing – could not harm –
> Himself – to Him – a Fortune –
> Exterior – to Time –   [448]

In the creative process, the poet arrests the flux of our perish-
able existence. He creates pictures of immortality, and when
these rich visions are disclosed to us in the form of images and
metaphors, our daily world fades by contrast into ceaseless
poverty. It is in these images of permanence that we experience the amazing sense, or the "Attar so immense" of his art.
The world of familiar objects or ordinary meanings stands
transformed before our very sight. In this transformation or
distillation of our experiential reality, the poet achieves the
ontological status of being exterior to time like the "artist in
the city of Kouroo." [42] The word "attar," derived from the
Persian *atar-gal,* essence of roses, which has been used here as
a metaphor for poetry, carries an aura of meaning for Dickinson. Charles Anderson explores the deep meanings of attar
and its association with India, which makes it "Attar so immense" for Dickinson. He writes that the attar is

one of the most costly ingredients of perfume, described in her Webster in terms of its exotic origin: "A highly fragrant concrete obtained in India from the petals of roses." India was a loaded word for her, typifying opulence in awesome degree, and this is certainly included in her meaning here. To a young friend getting married she sent her congratulations "that the shortest route to India has been supremely found," and in a poem on her own moment of love she defines it in the concluding line as "My drop of India." These refer to the ecstasy of love, but since she frequently equates love with poetry, it becomes clear that for her India, brought into this poem by "Attar from the Rose," is symbolic of the heaven-on-earth that includes them both.[43]

That the poetic creation or the creative process impels the poet to use language in a sacred way, in order to dramatize the mystery of existence as actualized in the imagination, should be clear from the foregoing discussion. Dickinson's particular use of words and images such as attar, cocoon, butterfly, spider, blacksmith, ore, light, grief, flood, volcano, grass, gaze, circumference, air, rose, and screws, to mention only a few of them from the vast fund of her poetic vocabulary, demonstrates a highly metamorphic character of poetic language which alone can express the primordial experience of the poet. This does not mean to say that the poet is completely free from the intrinsic tension involved in the making of a poetic medium.[44] The poet is perfectly aware that "A Word made Flesh is seldom" (1651), or the "Morning's finest syllable" looks "Presumptuous" by the evening (1266). Moved by the force of her emotional experience, Dickinson writes: "If I could tell how glad I was / I should not be so glad" (1668); for the expressed words "Are paltry melody / But those the silent feel / Are beautiful" (1750). The "silent" words are the hardest to come by:

> Your thoughts don't have words every day
> They come a single time
> Like signal esoteric sips

> Of the communion Wine
> Which while you taste so native seems
> So easy so to be
> You cannot comprehend its price
> Nor it's infrequency   [1452]

The manuscript of "Your thoughts don't have words every day," like the manuscripts of hundreds of Dickinson's poems, fully supports the point of view contained in the poem. There are words and words everywhere, but it is a strenuous job, dictated alike by intuition and skill, to select the precise word for the poetic transcription of the experience. The variant words for some particular word, image, or metaphor, as contained in Dickinson manuscripts, should clarify the point involved here. But Emily Dickinson shows a rare sensitivity for the inner meanings of the words, their divine power, their energizing role. "A Word is inundation, when it comes from the Sea," says Dickinson (L965). She writes of the interior structure of words or poetic language in these verses:

> A Man may make a Remark –
> In itself – a quiet thing
> That may furnish the Fuse unto a Spark
> In dormant nature – lain –
>
> Let us divide – with skill –
> Let us discourse – with care –
> Powder exists in Charcoal –
> Before it exists in Fire.   [952]

In terms of the language, then, the poem becomes the epiphany of the poetic creation. "In itself – a quiet thing," the silent-speaking symbol, poetry carries within it the necessary fuse to cause the spark of intuitive enlightenment. The charcoal-fire symbolism reinforces the fuse-spark energy which is at the core of poetic perception.

Using the language as she does, Emily Dickinson evolves her aesthetics of ambiguity from the still-flowing brook of the human heart (136), and the amber hands of the moon (429), from the pathos of the butterflies and the ecstasy of the flowers (137), from the secret of the crocus (22) and the power of the cloud (293). The poetic creation, thus, means to her the world of endless possibilities. What she cannot create is unknown to possibility (361). Dickinson emphasizes the dimensions of possibility (1208), and tells us:

> I dwell in Possibility –
> A fairer House than Prose –
> More numerous of Windows –
> Superior – for Doors –
>
> Of Chambers as the Cedars –
> Impregnable of Eye –
> And for an Everlasting Roof
> The Gambrels of the Sky –
>
> Of Visiters – the fairest –
> For Occupation – This –
> The spreading wide my narrow Hands
> To gather Paradise –   [657]

The windows in this fairer house of possibility are in themselves the wide open doors of poetic perception. The "Chambers as the Cedars" enhance the supernatural quality of the house of poetry. The ordinary human eye cannot pierce through its haunting structure whose outer limits extend up to the sky, the symbol of man's ultimate sense of freedom. But the poet can "gather Paradise" here because she knows the art of spreading wide her "narrow Hands." By this art the poet learns to dwell in her haunted house of poetry. Hands symbolize man's mental life. The narrow hands indicate an unregenerated state. Man is in the everlasting necessity of widening his narrow hands. Only then can he "gather Paradise" in the *now* and *here* of existence.[45]

THE POET AND THE POEM

To poetic creation everything is possible, though it reflects itself through paradox, irony, tension, and ambiguity. In poetry, what matters is intensity and not cold logic. Intensity of utterance can be experienced through and in the relationship between the poet and the poem. It is significant to understand what the poet becomes though the poem, how he shapes and is shaped by his art, how he assumes various symbolic forms to dramatize his experience of reality, and finally how he performs his social obligation toward mankind.

Emily Dickinson declares that poetry is "that Keyless Rhyme," that perfect music of a Mozart, which no one could play the second time (503). Poetry comes to the poet with a sense of finality in an otherwise impermanent world. Poetry abides and in a sense fixes the poet, though the poet must constantly strive to keep it. By way of metaphor, it salvages mankind from the curse of mortality: a page of "prancing Poetry" can "take us Lands away," because it is "the Chariot / That bears the Human soul" (1263 and L400). By consecrating himself to poetry, the poet consecrates himself to himself because it is the call of his destiny. It is through poetry that the poet *becomes himself*. Poetry is the poet's power which makes him sing: "I taste a liquor never brewed . . . Inebriate of Air – am I – / And Debauchee of Dew" (214). To the poet, "Much Madness is divinest Sense" (435). He continues to create, "Although Annihilation pile / Whole Chaoses on Him" (806). He outstrips "Time with but a Bout," and outstrips stars and sun (865). In his creativity, the poet is like the Lord in "the Zones of Paradise" (871). "His Labor is a Chant – / His Idleness a Tune" (916). His mind is a "too minute Area" (936). His voice "stands for Floods," and his face "makes the Morning mean" (1189). He is one of the "imperial few" to whom is due the "Auroral light" (1577). His courage *to be* is unique: the arrows and venoms of existence do not "rankle" in his heart (1629). Poetry is "His remedy for care" (1723). He learns "to like the Fire / By playing Glaciers" (689). He builds "the infinite Relations" in the realm where affliction is "but a Speculation – And Wo / A Fallacy, a Figment" (1040). He knows that

> The hallowing of Pain
> Like hallowing of Heaven,

> Obtains at a corporeal cost –
> The Summit is not given
>
> To Him who strives severe
> At middle of the Hill –
> But He who has achieved the Top –
> All – is the price of All –   [772]

This is what the poet becomes through the poem. In the very heart of the creative process, the poet arrives at the vision of divine pain. Corporeality of existence has to be sacrificed in order that one should be born to the realm of holy pain. This is the summit of human experience. But this cannot be possible unless one is prepared to lose all. The last verse conveys the paradoxical wisdom of the poet. That we should lose all in order to find all is the message of the poem, conveyed creatively and not didactically. The word "all" also defines the limits of our existential commitment to transmute the daily experience of pain and suffering into a holy one which is rare, though possible. The poet gives *all* to his poetic creation, and thereby becomes immortal like the creation itself. Poetry confers upon him the status of permanence. The poet enters the arena of "a steadfast land, / Where no Autumn lifts her pencil – / And no Reapers stand!" (163). His "swamps are pink with June," a metaphor for constant heat and life (22). In the poetic sense, he becomes permanent like the "Hosts" of feelings and emotions, a "Recordless Company," which comes to the mind but is never gone (298). The poet stays in an "immortal Place / Though Pyramids decay" (946). Emily Dickinson claims that her art, like her love, will survive the hills and the heavens (400). She is conscious of being a great poet, because she evinces confidence in the continuity of her voice:

> I shall keep singing!
> Birds will pass me
> On their way to Yellower Climes –
> Each – with a Robin's expectation –
> I – with my Redbreast –
> And my Rhymes –

> Late – when I take my place in summer –
> But – I shall bring a fuller tune –
> Vespers – are sweeter than Matins – Signor –
> Morning – only the seed of Noon –   [250]

Even when the poet is dead and gone, her creation, which embodies an infinite process, continues to disseminate her circumference of light (883) in the heart of humanity:

> My Splendors, are Menagerie –
> But their Competeless Show
> Will entertain the Centuries
> When I, am long ago,
> An Island in dishonored Grass –
> Whom none but Daisies, know.   [290]

Poetry is earth-bound, as conveyed here in the image "menagerie," but it is no less splendid for that, because both poetry and the earth represent a "Competeless Show," signifying the grandeur of the creative process and the infinite play of existence. For Dickinson, poetry is "Her deathless Syllable" (1183). The poems are, then, her "Splendors," fit enough to survive the transitoriness of man.[46] In Dickinson's poetry, earth expands from here to eternity; it is the place where she gathers her paradise (657). Earth is also the center of her circumference, which is her business (L268). In her imagination, the earth reverses her hemispheres and takes her "out upon Circumference" (378). Circumference is Dickinson's metaphor for resurrection (515). Circumference, which is the earth's outer limit, offers her a simultaneous experience of life and death or life in death:

> She staked her Feathers – Gained an Arc –
> Debated – Rose again –
> This time – beyond the estimate
> Of Envy, or of Men –
>
> And now, among Circumference –
> Her steady Boat be seen –

> At home – among the Billows – As
> The Bough where she was born – [798]

The image of feathers stands for the human imagination, "Arc" stands for the curve of circumference which seems beyond the reach of an unimaginative person in this poem. However, the persona of the poem is at home among the billows of circumference. The circumference becomes the sea of life and death on which the poet alone can keep his boat steady. Thus, the earth provides Dickinson with the imaginative powers of the expansive consciousness: a coffin can contain a citizen of paradise (943), writes Dickinson. In the mold of her imagination, the restricted size of the grave expands into a "Circumference without Relief – / Or Estimate – or End" (943). For Dickinson, "Ages coil within / The minute Circumference / Of a single Brain" (967). The poet "carries a circumference" within her mind, which is her secret, her mystery (1663), and which enables her to become like the saint:

> No matter where the Saints abide,
> They make their Circuit fair
> Behold how great a Firmament
> Accompanies a Star. [1541]

The word "saint" may be understood as describing the type of a poet. It is full of varied and paradoxical meanings. The saint is the one who experiences holiness on earth. He is the yogin-artist who fully experiences the pathos, irony, comedy, and tragedy of existence. He is humorous, he is serious; he laughs, he weeps. He is poor, he is rich. He is body, he is soul. He is silence, he is sound. Love and death are his pastime, because he comprehends the play of life. He can perform any role at will; he can exercise empathy with all the forms of creation. He suffers, he is above suffering. He is process, he is completion. Emily Dickinson the poet, who becomes what she becomes through her art, is a paradigm of such a type. Her art is a process of this possibility. The poet Emily Dickinson passes through and lives with all the contradictions of life. In

her various poetic postures, she becomes the bee, the butterfly, the rose, the spider, the lark, the bird, the magician, the
caterpillar, the moon, the beloved, the lover, to mention only a
few. The poet becomes the bee "that brew – / A Honey's
Weight / The Summer multiply" (676), and a bird who knows
the secret of the skies (191). The poet identifies herself with
the robin "That speechless from her Nest / Submit that
Home – and Certainty / And Sanctity, are best" (828). She is
the black berry who "wears a Thorn in his side" (554). She is
the butterfly who obtains but little sympathy for his sense of
freedom (1685).[47] She is the bluebird whose "conscientious
Voice will soar unmoved / Above ostensible Vicissitude"
(1395).[48] The poet is the caterpillar who is intent upon its own
career (1448). She is the moon whose "Bonnet is the Firmament – / The Universe – Her Shoe – / The Stars – the Trin-
kets at Her Belt – / Her Dimities – of Blue" (737). She is the
carpenter who builds temples (488). The poetic forms that the
poet assumes can be multiplied infinitely, because whatever she
touches she becomes. Since the forms are hermaphroditic, the
interplay or the shifting use of the masculine and feminine
pronouns he and she, him and her should not be considered
as a grammatical flaw in Dickinson's poetry. The aesthetic purpose of these forms is to show that the poet is above personality in the narrow sense of the word, but is engaged in realizing
the all-inclusive personality or being through art. By moving
in and out of the various forms, the poet experiences true
freedom. She challenges existential anxiety and fear by assuming the forms of the bee and the flower, because bees and
flowers are "unafraid" (869).[49] Dickinson launches her drama
of freedom and calls it her revolution against the systems,
generated by the "Winds of Will" (1082). The poet creates
these forms and is in turn created by them. By being in possession of these forms, the poet becomes "the mere incarnation, or mouth-piece, or medium" of their power.[50] The poet
realizes himself through his art, and the art realizes itself
through the poet. The paradoxical conception of art realizing

its own destiny through the artist is explained by Jung in these words:

> Art is a kind of innate drive that seizes a human being and makes him its instrument. The artist is not a person endowed with free will who seeks his own ends, but one who allows art to realize its purposes through him. As a human being he may have moods and a will and personal aims, but as an artist he is "man" in a higher sense—he is "collective man"—one who carries and shapes the unconscious, psychic life of mankind. To perform this difficult office it is sometimes necessary for him to sacrifice happiness and everything that makes life worth living for the ordinary human being.[51]

Emily Dickinson dedicates herself to her art and becomes its instrument, without hankering after any fame as a writer of poetry:

> I was a Phebe – nothing more –
> A Phebe – nothing less –
> The little note that others dropt
> I fitted into place –
>
> I dwelt too low that any seek –
> Too shy, that any blame –
> A Phebe makes a little print
> Upon the Floors of Fame –   [1009]

Dickinson regards fame as "a fickle food / Upon a shifting plate" (1659). She thinks that "Glory is that bright tragic thing" which ends in oblivion (1660). To her way of looking,

> Fame is a bee.
> It has a song –
> It has a sting –
> Ah, too, it has a wing.   [1763]

Fame has no arms to lift anyone above "Oblivion's Tide" (1531), and "Fame is the tint that Scholars leave / Upon their Setting Names" (866). She considers that

Fame is the one that does not stay –
It's occupant must die
Or out of sight of estimate
Ascend incessantly –
Or be that most insolvent thing
A Lightning in the Germ –
Electrical the embryo
But we demand the Flame   [1475]

But all this does not mean that Dickinson is averse to genuine
fame. The point is that she does not wish to be considered as
writing simply for the sake of some cheap glory. She has a
kind of fame in mind, which comes from within oneself, and
which comes only when one has fulfilled one's self, one's destiny, one's vocation. She calls it the "Fame of Myself":

Fame of Myself, to justify,
All other Plaudit be
Superfluous – An Incense
Beyond Necessity –

Fame of Myself to lack – Although
My Name be else Supreme –
This were an Honor honorless –
A futile Diadem –   [713]

The real fame does not come by seeking; it comes in proportion to our realization of ourselves. Dickinson states her methodology of arriving at the condition of fame in these verses:

To earn it by disdaining it
Is Fame's consummate Fee –
He loves what spurns him –
Look behind – He is pursuing thee.

So let us gather – every Day –
The Aggregate of
Life's Bouquet
Be Honor and not shame –   [1427]

Emily Dickinson's poetic career is full of rigors. She imposes
severe discipline on herself in order to serve the Muses. She

writes and writes intensely, but she does not care to publish. She thinks "Publication – is the Auction / Of the Mind of Man" (709). She writes to Higginson:

> I smile when you suggest that I delay "to publish" – that being foreign to my thought as Firmament to Fin –
> If fame belonged to me, I could not escape her – if she did not, the longest day would pass me on the chase – and the approbation of my Dog, would forsake me – then – My Barefoot-Rank is better. [L265]

Dickinson's commitment to her art verges on religious passion; she does not like to profane it with publicity. She goes through life as one passes through a sacred place, and tries to assimilate in her own being the mystery of the human existence. Northrop Frye observes that there is "something Oriental in her manner of existence." [52] But, without trying to make her look like an Indian or a Chinese poet, her Oriental manner should mean a certain way of life in which one apprehends the paradoxical or seemingly duplicate nature of reality, not by way of passive acceptance of creation but by active participation in its process in which there are contradictions, ironies, and tensions. Her poetry embodies a gigantic effort to comprehend reality or truth through the creative process. Dickinson realizes that in order to find truth, as seen through the creative eye of the imagination, one has to live until death in the presence of beauty (1654). Beauty and truth meet in the womb-tomb of existence (449). For Dickinson, as for Keats, truth and beauty are one in the aesthetic vision. The realm of beauty is the realm of imagination and spontaneity, and "Estranged from Beauty – none can be – / For Beauty is Infinity" (1474). Dickinson insists that man should discover the fountain of his primordial spontaneity from within himself, for truth is internal. Imagination, beauty, truth, spontaneity—all are abstract words and are made concrete within the human being. In the imagination every form of feeling or life is concrete and thus actualized, although this cannot be demonstrated empirically. When Dickinson refers to truth, she uses such expressions as "The Truth never flaunted a Sign" (1207), "A Wisdom, without Face, or Name" (1104), "But Truth, outlasts the Sun" (1455), "The Truth – is stirless" (780), "And Truth – so manifold" (568), "Truth is good Health – and Safety, and the Sky" (1453), and

> Truth – is as old as God –
> His Twin identity
> And will endure as long as He
> A Co-Eternity –
>
> And perish on the Day
> Himself is borne away
> From Mansion of the Universe
> A lifeless Deity.   [836]

The universe is the creation of God. Truth being the twin identity of God, it is integral to creation itself: a co-eternity. As long as there is creation, there is truth. Similarly, for the poet, his creation is his truth. In terms of the poetic process, the truth cannot be stated directly. Poetry is creativity and not speculative philosophy. The only way it can speak is the way of indirection. Art can tell the truth, but obliquely. Hence Dickinson's advice:

> Tell all the Truth but tell it slant –
> Success in Circuit lies
> Too bright for our infirm Delight
> The Truth's superb surprise
> As Lightning to the Children eased
> With explanation kind
> The Truth must dazzle gradually
> Or every man be blind –   [1129]

The truth's splendid surprise is dazzling. Since we are not able to behold its vision, we should not be impatient with it. We should learn it gradually and through the metamorphic process of some "explanation kind." The success of poetic communication depends upon the circuitous or symbolic manner of utterance. "Circuit" is Dickinson's synonym for circumference, which means circle, the symbol of perfection, the round container of all opposites, the maternal womb where the masculine and the feminine meet. The poetic utterance which contains truth in it is the *Mandala* of human consciousness, the dawn of all knowledge.

The culmination of poetic perception is symbolized by the dawn which shows the beginning of creation after the night of chaos. Poetic perception is rebirth in which all deaths and births are syncretized. The function of the poet is to show us that dawn which means the light of awareness. Emily Dickinson awakens us through her favorite metaphors of sunrise, day, dawn, morn, morning, noon, aurora, and apocalypse. In the creative sense, the break of day (13) means the blossoming of consciousness. It is the different dawn when one finds what one waked for (87). The day comes after mist in which some lose their way (113). Morning stands for "Just revelation – to the beloved" (300). "Two Dawns upon a single Morn, / Make Life a sudden price" (1610), says Dickinson.[53]

In order to perform his social obligation toward humanity, the poet sacrifices his personal interests and challenges all hazards. Dickinson states her position in these verses:

> If I could bribe them by a Rose
> I'd bring them every flower that grows
> From Amherst to Cashmere!
> I would not stop for night, or storm –
> Or frost, or death, or anyone –
> My business were so dear!
>
> If they w'd linger for a Bird
> My Tamborin were soonest heard
> Among the April Woods!
> Unwearied, all the summer long,
> Only to break in wilder song
> When Winter shook the boughs!   [179]

The poet stops the human heart from breaking (919), but, paradoxically, instils such pain as cannot be healed by "Herb of all the plain" (177). He teaches us the art of suffering, so that we may be able to transcend suffering. Without poetic insights, we will remain strangers, in a foreign world (1096). With his "pang," the poet creates the art of peace (544). He chooses maturity by blossom's "gradual process," and when ripe, he gives away his life to us (567). He lends "an Ample Sinew / Unto a Nameless Man / Whose Homely Benediction / No other – stopped to earn" (767). His service is without hope of any reward (779). He plans to "Advocate the Azure / To the lower Eyes" to meet the obligation of Paradise (1348). His only price is that one should comprehend the worth of his mind, which is like the fabrics of the east (1446). In one of the finest leaps of her imagination, Dickinson conveys how the poet operates on the mind of one who willingly submits to the poet's spell:

> He fumbles at your Soul
> As Players at the Keys
> Before they drop full Music on –
> He stuns you by degrees –
> Prepares your brittle Nature
> For the Etherial Blow
> By fainter Hammers – further heard –
> Then nearer – Then so slow
> Your Breath has time to straighten –
> Your Brain – to bubble Cool –
> Deals – One – imperial – Thunderbolt –
> That scalps your naked Soul –
>
> When Winds take Forests in their Paws –
> The Universe – is still –   [315]

The whole movement has been described very sensuously. To start with, the poet gropes at the human soul, as if taking the initial steps of his journey to the heart of man. He shapes our fragile nature by hammering it slowly, almost inaudibly, so that in the process we may become ready to bear the weight of his full music as delicately as one does "the Etherial Blow." He stuns, but by degrees. Our breath remains smooth and un-hampered, and our brain remains calm and cool. And then, once the poet has achieved this harmonious relationship with us, he deals one imperial thunderbolt, Dickinson's symbolic instrument of light, the source of enlightenment and vision. In this moment, the poet scalps our naked soul. The whole process seems sexual: the poet is the masculine power trying to enter the feminine soul. The soul remains passive only in the paradoxical sense. The last two lines of the poem convey the ultimate truth of poetic perception: when the human imagination, symbolized here by the winds, comes to grips with the forests or the bewildering nature of reality, the whole universe becomes calm and quiet. The faculty of imagination enables the poet to perceive stasis in process, motionlessness in motion, silence in sound, and vice versa.

In the process of creative perception, the poet shows empathy with the whole creation, and enacts his vision of the world in the form of his poetry. In order to comprehend fully the nature of this enactment, the reader must be able to perceive the poetic perceptions and re-create them in his own mind. It is the job of a critic to enact these perceptions in terms of literary criticism. To perform this task, the literary critic should look for the poetic "sincerity" (1671) of the work, which is central to perception and creation. Emily Dickinson demands of her readers and critics to step lightly on the breast which "These Emerald Seams enclose" (1183). She asks her countrymen to judge her as tenderly (441) as one should judge life:

> Surgeons must be very careful
> When they take the knife!
> Underneath their fine incisions
> Stirs the Culprit – *Life!* [108]

Even the most perceptive reader of Emily Dickinson's poetry cannot help remaining in awe and wonder at the bewildering variety of moods and postures in which she enacts the perplexing drama of her perceptions. She is indeed a difficult poet to bring into focus. But a concentrated search into the heart of her poetic perplexity can be both challenging and rewarding. It is with this awareness and hope that I intend to explore further her themes of love, death, and self—"the Roses / In life's diverse boquet" (93)—in the chapters that follow.

4

Love

THE GARMENT OF FIRE

With wide-embracing love
Thy spirit animates eternal years,
Pervades and broods above,
Changes, sustains, dissolves, creates and rears.

Though Earth and moon were gone
And suns and universes ceased to be
And thou wert left alone
Every Existence would exist in thee

There is not room for Death
Nor atom that his might could render void:
Since thou art Being and Breath,
And what thou art may never be destroyed

—Emily Brontë, "No Coward Soul Is Mine"

I should begin by saying that the poetry of perception is the poetry of love, not only in the sense in which the poet creates his work as a service of love, but also in the sense that both perception and love mean creativity: to love is to create. Love is that action which Dickinson calls redemption (L726). It is a deed which cannot be theorized, for it springs from the inwardness of the lover. It is the experience in which the finite and the infinite, the temporal and the eternal meet. It is a constant striving, a process of becoming what is being. It is not a system, but a way of life that continually unfolds the myriad dimensions of human existence. Like poetry, it is ambivalent

135

and hence without result, without finality. It is a secret, silent, lifelong pursuit of truth. Its mode of communication is not direct, because it resides in the spirit and aspires to the divine state of relationship. The essential content of love, its spiritual center, cannot be the subject of objective dialogue.[1] These attributes do not exhaust the inexhaustible character of love, though they seem to describe its most crucial dimension—the God-man relationship—through which the finite man apprehends his ultimate destiny and apprehends it by persistent striving.

Emily Dickinson's aesthetics of love, which is central to the whole of her creative experience, is a poetic directive for man to realize his own destiny, and realize it in and through the prism (1602) of existence: the prism symbolizes a constant movement, an endless play of hues which represent forms of human emotions, feelings, and complex experiences. As several colors are integrated in the prism, many moods and postures are syncretized in the structure of love. In this sense, love is energy; it is imagination to which alone all forms are possible. It is inclusive of the contradictory postures of self-surrender and self-assertion, search for self and search for the other, living in death and dying into life. It generates the opposing moods of happiness and woe, pleasure and pain, remembering and forgetting, freedom and bondage. It is sensuous, it is spiritual. It is fleeting, it is abiding. It is speech, it is silence. It is ignorance, it is wisdom. It is water, it is fire. It is dark, it is light. It is absence, it is presence. In its human form divine it is male, it is female.

The above-noted framework of reference is fundamental to our understanding of the involute theme of love in Dickinson's poetry, as it is necessary to our appreciation of the tradition in which eroticism merges with asceticism; where *Eros* is reconciled with *Agape*. The following pages will demonstrate this point of view.

Dickinson believes in the might of human love (1648), and she writes to Higginson: "Love is it's own rescue, for we – at

our supremest, are but it's trembling Emblems" (L522). Ontologically speaking, love demands total commitment, total energy, which few of us can offer:

> Sometimes with the Heart
> Seldom with the Soul
> Scarcer once with the Might
> Few – love at all   [1680]

In this posture, Dickinson considers might as the chief instrument of love: might is inclusive of the heart and the soul.
Love is, then, the power of a god, his compassion, which can
"warm / The bosoms where the frost has lain / Ages beneath
the mould" (132). She argues that love is life, and life has immortality (549). She realizes that the long road of love passes
through pain and "many a turn – and thorn" (344), but feels
that "To wait Eternity – is short – / If Love reward the end"
(781). Love imposes its own dangers and perils on existence,
but "In insecurity to lie / Is Joy's insuring quality" (1434). Love
is the inward bliss; each individual is uniquely aware of its
value. Its loss can make a person utterly alone; it cannot be
bought because it is not sold (840). Its presence cannot be
proved; it is tenderness which "decreases as we prove" (860).
"That Love is all there is, / Is all we know of Love" (1765), says
Dickinson. To her, "Love – is that later Thing than Death –
/ More previous – than Life" (924). She writes:

> Love – is anterior to Life –
> Posterior – to Death –
> Initial of Creation, and
> The Exponent of Earth –   [917]

One can resolve within oneself the contradictions of life and
death, the foot upon the earth and the foot upon the grave, if
one is even faintly assisted by love (960). While keeping man
tied to earth, love takes him "Beyond earth's trafficking frontier" (1435). It is highly paradoxical: it is "The Boon of all
alive," but "To lack of it is Woe – / To own of it is Wound"

(1438). It is a "solemn nameless need," and "The only Food that grows" (1555). Dickinson considers "A face devoid of love or grace" as "A hateful, hard, successful face" (1711)—the word *successful* seems to have been used here sarcastically, implying the end of growth.

The foregoing, widely scattered observations are enough to show Dickinson's deep understanding of the emotion of human love. She shapes her vision of love with great passion. Love epitomizes her whole existence; for it is in love that she experiences death and realizes her true self. Love enables her to give abundantly, and it is by giving that she receives. She writes to Susan Gilbert Dickinson:

> I think of love, and you, and my heart grows full and warm, and my breath stands still. The sun does'nt shine at all, but I can feel a sunshine stealing into my soul and making it all summer, and every thorn, a *rose*. And I pray that such summer's sun shine on my Absent One, and cause her bird to sing! [L88] [2]

In a mood of perfect consecration, she writes to Otis P. Lord:

> My lovely Salem smiles at me. I seek his Face so often – . . . .
>   I confess that I love him – I rejoice that I love him – I thank the maker of Heaven and Earth – that gave him me to love – the ex-ultation floods me. I cannot find my channel – the Creek turns Sea – at thought of thee – . . . .
>   Incarcerate me in yourself – rosy penalty – threading with you this lovely maze, which is not Life or Death – though it has the intangibleness of one, and the flush of the other – waking for your sake on Day made magical with you before I went. [L559]

However, Dickinson's aesthetics of love should not be in-terpreted entirely in terms of her personal relationship with any particular individual. She is known for the intensity of her feelings and expression. She writes equally intensely to her brother Austin, her cousins Louise and Frances Norcross, her friends Dr. and Mrs. J. G. Holland, and several others. She projects upon the recipients of her letters and poems her inner drama of love, and regards love, poetry, and God as coeval (1247). She writes to Dr. and Mrs. J. G. Holland: "My business is to love" (L269), and realizes her true identity through the art of poetry. In other words, the act of true love implies going back to the source of creation and creativity: "Till it has loved – no man or woman can become itself – Of our first Creation we are unconscious," says Dickinson (L575). It is in this spiritual and primordial sense that Dickinson explores within herself the endless possibilities of love, and makes concrete her explorations in the form of her poems and letters. She addresses particularly those who are instrumental in the realization of her own being. In this connection, Millicent Todd Bingham has aptly observed:

> The Greeks imagined that the miracle of vision resided not in the eye alone, but in the eye plus the object looked at; in other words, that certain rays emanate from the eye and, when they strike an object, it is seen. So it was with Emily Dickinson's genius. When she encountered a person who could precipitate an expession of her thought, could cause her feeling to crystallize in words, the release was for her a gift so royal that she could but adore the giver.
>
> Those who cherish the legend of a lifelong renunciation because of a broken heart in youth may prefer not to entertain the thought that her fidelity was not confined to one person. Faithful indeed she was; but faithful above all to her own integrity, to that power within her which, no matter how slight the stimulus, and it might be no more than an exchange of glances, could create a poem. To those persons who cling to the legend it can be said only that against a cherished belief, mere truth is a feeble antagonist. Be that as it may, and when all is said, explanations do not explain. Mystery remains, but it is the mystery of genius.[3]

Literary critics should resist the temptation of tracing love affairs in Dickinson's poetry which is primarily about love and creativity. The poetic theme of love has, strictly speaking, nothing to do with love affairs which are "more or less accidental episodes that happen between men and women," to use Ortega y Gasset's expression.[4] Loving as contrasted with love affairs "is perennial vivification, creation and *intentional* preservation of what is loved." [5] The poet Emily Dickinson is mainly concerned with such a process only, and she dramatizes her search for an endless love in a variety of poetic poses. That she is not interested in merely physical love can be shown through interpretation of her love poems. She strives to achieve that love "Of which this (our) living world is but the shade" (PF41).

Since the character of that which Dickinson calls love is ultimately psychic, the sexual symbolism in her poetry does not pertain exclusively to the amatory urges of man. She does not glorify sexual activity, like D. H. Lawrence, for instance. She has no sex vision like Whitman's in his "Children of Adam" and "Calamus" poems. In short, she has her own way of exploring the mythology of love, and she explores it in the plumbless abyss of the human heart. In the process of this inward journey, she experiences all sorts of contradictory emotions and, by passing through several levels or phases of suffering and moral pathos, comprehends the true nature of love. The levels of suffering and moral pathos are integral to the levels or dimensions of love, which are not mutually exclusive.

In the temporal dimension of love, Emily Dickinson craves others to be sure and certain in their love of her (156), although she herself experiences oscillation between remembering and forgetting the warmth and light of love (47). She thinks of the reluctant partings with the objects of love (1614), and goes through the moral pathos and pain of having been forgotten (1683). In this state, she remains "Love's stricken" (1368), and her inner strength does not alleviate the despair caused by the loss of the loved (882). She fully realizes that "Each that we lose takes part of us" (1605). On being grievously hurt by the scars of temporal love, she longs for a different type of love or grace, and still in sheer agony she pleads: " 'Just Once' Sweet Deity" (1076). She shows signs of restlessness when the summer troubles her or when the rose is ripe because her lover is so far from her (956). The whole experience of love at this level summarizes man's craving for the intense but temporal moments of life and consequently his sense of immediacy, transient enjoyment, and moral pathos. But, however transitory this level of love or longing for relationships may be, it has its own function to perform. By being in this state over a long period, man's sense of suffering and pain takes roots in him and finally fructifies into what Unamuno calls the tragic sense of life.[6] It is through this tragic sense that man transcends the transiency of human conditions and becomes greater and even more sorrowful. He realizes the fleeting and "indiscreet" nature of love at the temporal level (1771 and L695). The pain of this dimension of love persists and ultimately compels man to be himself, because man alone is burdened with the ontological responsibility *to become himself,* to become free.[7] Freedom is the essence of love; freedom is spontaneity and creativity. However, paradoxically speaking, the way of love is the way of bondage, or to put it this way, the way of freedom lies through the way of bondage and commitment. Emily Dickinson shows perfect awareness of this bondage and a deep sense of pain, which are coexistent with the spiritual dimension of love:

> You left me – Sire – two Legacies –
> A Legacy of Love
> A Heavenly Father would suffice
> Had He the offer of –
>
> You left me Boundaries of Pain –
> Capacious as the Sea –
> Between Eternity and Time –
> Your Consciousness – and Me –   [644]

In this poem the lover-beloved relationship is of infinite quality. The beloved cherishes the gifts of love and boundaries of pain which her sovereign lover has bestowed upon her. Such a love in which the beloved evinces the willingness and the capacity to suffer infinitely for the sake of her lover would please even God. Infinite love and infinite suffering are the requirements in man's relationship to God. In this state, the beloved's consciousness of herself and her princely lover, symbolic of the God-man relationship, expands from the limits of time to eternity. But the truly spiritual dimension of love is a continual process. The necessary step toward the realization of this sacred level is through the consummation of love between man and woman or between man and man. Dickinson views the spiritual or the integrative love between man and woman or between two human beings as a typology of the God-man relationship, as our road to God lies through his creation, to use Buber's insight.[8] While assuming several symbolic postures and moods, she poetizes this experience with rare candor and sincerity.

In the nontransient, perpetual, conjugal dimension of love, Dickinson's poetry is permeated with sexual symbols. But, there is nothing of sex for sex's sake in her vision of love. Sexual love is shown as representing man's sense of longing as well as union. If it is spiritually conceived and effected, sexuality can become the source of human fulfillment. Its mystery and force can never be uttered:

> So bashful when I spied her!
> So pretty – so ashamed!
> So hidden in her leaflets
> Lest anybody find –
>
> So breathless till I passed her –
> So helpless when I turned
> And bore her struggling, blushing,
> Her simple haunts beyond!
>
> For whom I robbed the Dingle –
> For whom betrayed the Dell –
> Many, will doubtless ask me,
> But I shall never tell!   [91]

The beautiful, shy beloved whom the lover must possess is the external manifestation of the lover's inner reality. The breathless, and seemingly helpless, beloved surrenders to the active power of the lover, though she struggles and blushes in the process of being possessed. Once possessed by the lover, the beloved's thoughts travel beyond the limits of normal perception. At this level, the sexual experience does not destroy the temporal dimension of love; rather, it transforms it. Its spiritual center cannot be vocalized; it can only be felt: "The incidents of love / Are more than it's Events" (1248), writes Dickinson. In the final stanza the beloved becomes the dingle or the dell, a deep valley shaded with trees, symbolizing a state of fertility and regeneration which man must gain in order to redeem himself from his vegetative existence. This act constitutes Dickinson's "whole Experiment of Green" (1333). The words "robbed" and "betrayed" are used here as images of violence and power, dialectically but effectively employed to indicate that man must show spiritual strength in order to possess his regenerated self, which is his true identity, the source of the God-man relationship in time.

For Dickinson, love is "The peace – the flight – the Amethyst" of life (106): as flowers derive their colors from the sun, man derives his quality from the fountain of love. In love, there is no repose; it is like "Tugging at the Forge" (109). It is the lightning and the sunrise which compel man to see (480). In this sense, love is perception. It is that water which if "denied to drink" would mean "condemned lip" (490). It is that page in a letter which the lover-beloved cannot write, and which is ever silent and sealed in the human heart (494). It has "but the power to kill, / Without – the power to die" (754). It comes from "Eminence remote" (1128). It grows like a hurricane within the human heart, which is its congenial ground (1745). All these varied expressions show the depth and immensity of Dickinson's experience of love.

By playing the persona of the beloved who is prepared to

sacrifice all in order to behold the face of her lover, Dickinson
shows great insight into the mystery of the human heart:

> What would I give to see his face?
> I'd give – I'd give my life – of course –
> But *that* is not enough!
> Stop just a minute – let me think!
> I'd give my biggest Bobolink!
> That makes *two* – *Him* – and *Life!*
> You know who *"June"* is –
> I'd give *her* –
> Roses a day from Zenzibar –
> And Lily tubes – like Wells –
> Bees – by the furlong –
> Straits of Blue
> Navies of Butterflies – sailed thro' –
> And dappled Cowslip Dells –   [247]

The ecstasy and bliss of beholding the face of the lover is so
complete in the beloved's heart that all her sense of life and its
prized possessions is obliterated in a moment. In another
poem, the beloved is portrayed as willing to pay all her diamonds, rubies, and topaz for just a single smile of the lover
(223). The lover's face or his presence can efface the burden
of time from the beloved's heart, which she has borne in waiting for him (1507). In this dimension of love, looking at each
other's faces creates in the lovers a psychic awareness or consciousness of the human form divine, and this activity is precisely what is called the lover-beloved's spiritual luxury:

> The Luxury to apprehend
> The Luxury 'twould be
> To look at Thee a single time
> An Epicure of Me
>
> In whatsoever Presence makes
> Till for a further Food
> I scarcely recollect to starve
> So first am I supplied –

> The Luxury to meditate
> The Luxury it was
> To banquet on thy Countenance
> A Sumptuousness bestows   [815]

"Not in this World to see his face – / Sounds long" (418), says
Dickinson. In her imagery or poetic iconography, the lover-
beloved's face acquires a deep and meditative significance.[9]
She associates the face of the lover with the enormous wealth
of the East:

> I'm sure 'tis India – all Day –
> To those who look on You –
> Without a stint – without a blame,
> Might I – but be the Jew –
>
> I'm sure it is Golconda –
> Beyond my power to deem –
> To have a smile for Mine – each Day,
> How better, than a Gem!
>
> At least, it solaces to know
> That there exists – a Gold –
> Altho' I prove it, just in time
> It's distance – to behold –   [299]

In "Again – his voice is at the door," Dickinson writes: "I
look on all this world *contains* – / *Just his face* – nothing more!"
(663). She wishes to spend her whole life in the presence of
the lover's face, and when her time on earth is up she hopes
to carry this face, metaphorically, with her to the heavenly
abode:

> The face I carry with me – last –
> When I go out of Time –
> To take my Rank – by – in the West –
> That face – will just be thine –
>
> I'll hand it to the Angel –
> That – Sir – was my Degree –
> In Kingdoms – you have heard the Raised –
> Refer to – possibly.

He'll take it – scan it – step aside –
Return – with such a crown
As Gabriel – never capered at –
And beg me put it on –

And then – he'll turn me round and round –
To an admiring sky –
As one that bore her Master's name –
Sufficient Royalty!   [336]

Contemplating the "future" life, the poet Dickinson declares
that it would be dull and uninteresting for her if she fails to
find in her redeemer's face the face of her lover:

The "Life that is to be," to me,
A Residence too plain
Unless in my Redeemer's Face
I recognize your own –   [1260]

In a sense, she identifies the lover with the savior, the rescuer
of human freedom. She describes the face of the human-
divine lover with subtle emotive nuances.

Showing the process of the nontransient, conjugal dimension of love, the poet Dickinson emphasizes the emotional experience in which one finds the physical distance between the
lover and the beloved undesirable, and imagines the possibility
of merging their souls and not merely their bodies. She also
believes that when two human beings love with spiritual love,
distance abates (1155) and becomes meaningless. It is the
merely physical love or the conjugal love without spiritual involvement which generates separation and not fusion. In "The
Rose did caper on her cheek" (208), Dickinson visualizes the
fusion of lovers and describes it as a dance to "the immortal
tune": the lovers in this pulsating dance eventually tick "into
one." It is in the spiritual sense, in which the lovers unite and
harmonize into each other, that she beckons her lover and
sings:

Spring comes on the World –
I sight the Aprils –

> Hueless to me until thou come
> As, till the Bee
> Blossoms stand negative,
> Touched to Conditions
> By a Hum. [1042]

Without the lover, the world seems hueless to the beloved, and
the blossoms hold no charm for her even in the heart of the
spring. As the flowers appear to hear the vitalizing song of the
bee in order to come to their true form and expression, the
beloved needs the presence of the lover to feel life in and
around her. The lovers are to each other a true source of regeneration and awakening. They are each other's emanation:
when "I" and "thou" meet and form a unity of spiritual sharing, the experience of love leads one to the primordial
wholeness of being.[10] The posture of realization of this type
of love through the instrumentality of relationship with the
"other" which, paradoxically speaking, is not nonself but more
than self, is characteristic of several of Dickinson's poems to be
studied in this chapter. It is the "I-thou" relationship, the core
of human-divine merger, which characterizes the mood of the
following poem:

> Wild Nights – Wild Nights!
> Were I with thee
> Wild Nights should be
> Our luxury!
>
> Futile – the Winds –
> To a Heart in port –
> Done with the Compass –
> Done with the Chart!
>
> Rowing in Eden –
> Ah, the Sea!
> Might I but moor – Tonight –
> In Thee! [249]

The images of wild nights and luxury do not indicate a mere
sexual urge. In symbology, night stands for the feminine principle, the source of all creation. Night also stands for the dark-

ness which precedes light; it is the matrix of fertility. In this symbolic sense, the meeting of "I" with "thee" marks the ritual of creativity. In the process of consummation of this relationship, the dangers of existence do not enter. Not that the perils of life cease to be, but that they cease to worry the lovers. The winds cannot strike "a Heart in port." The ship of love moves on toward its destination without the aid of the compass or the chart. The act of love constitutes for Dickinson the "Rowing in Eden," the landscape of our primordial existence, the sea of all loves. Therefore the wish: "Might I but moor – Tonight – / In Thee!" Mooring in the "other" expresses an aspect of love in its nontransient, conjugal dimension. In this mood the lovers sing to each other:

> Our's be the tossing – wild though the sea –
> Rather than a Mooring – unshared by thee.
> Our's be the Cargo – *unladen – here –*
> Rather than the *"spicy isles – "*
> And thou – not there –   [368]

Emily Dickinson's Eden is in the here and now of existence, and she wishes it to come to her slowly (211). In love of "thee," she transcends all time by experiencing it in the dynamism of the present moment:

> Forever might be short, I thought to show –
> And so I pieced it, with a flower, now.   [434]

"If you were coming in the Fall" (511) dramatizes Dickinson's power to while away the years, even centuries, if there exists a possibility of her ultimate union with the lover. She is willing to throw her life away, as one does the peel of a fruit, or as a tree surrenders its bark, or as a snake leaves its skin, if she is assured of her final union with the lover:

> If certain, when this life was out –
> That your's and mine, should be
> I'd toss it yonder, like a Rind,
> And take Eternity –   [511]

The throwing away of life is paradoxical, because by losing the peel, the bark, and the skin, the fruit, the tree, and the snake do not lose their identity; rather they achieve it. By losing life in love, one finds eternity. The process of love is both self-destroying and self-fulfilling. Keats's lines in *Endymion* can sum up this experience for us:

> there are
> Richer entanglements, enthralments far
> More self-destroying, leading, by degrees,
> To the chief intensity: the crown of these
> Is made of love.   [lines 797–801]

Emily Dickinson's voice of longing, which resounds through such expressions as "Bee! I'm expecting you" (1035), "Not to see what we love, is very terrible" (L262), "I tend my flowers for thee – / Bright Absentee" (339), to quote a few, can be construed as the voice of earthly yearning for a human lover only. But Dickinson's voice is deeper and more subtle than that. Its music vibrates the endless variations on the theme of human-divine love. Dickinson sings the "Love terrene," "Love Marine," and "Love celestial" (1637) simultaneously. Each love imposes its own inherent will upon the person who experiences it. Although suffering and self-surrender are common to all forms of love, they differ in their degree and intensity in the varying levels of love. In the temporal dimension of love, the suffering and self-surrender of the lovers are transient and do not lead to any serious commitment and spiritual involvement; in the nontransient, conjugal dimension of love, suffering and self-surrender become moral and spiritual necessities for the lovers, and in the purely spiritual or religious level of love, suffering and self-surrender become psychic forces which shape the lives of the lovers, according to their own inscrutable purpose. The suffering and the negation of self in the last two dimensions of love are highly paradoxical: the woe becomes the source of exultation (1642), and self-annihilation means self-assertion. In this posture of paradoxical exultation, Dickinson is willing to give to her lover the whole of herself, and the "last Delight" that she owns, and to dwell timidly with him, though he may "Sift her, from Brow to Barefoot," and finally drop her before "the Fire's Eyes" (275). She promises to remain "Obedient to the least command" that the lover's eye may impose on her (429). She kneels before her lover whom she calls "Teneriffe," the volcanic mountain, in a state of perfect resignation and stillness (666): she is constant and firm in her love, although the mountain retreats to a little rest after the eruption. She is "a Dedicated sort": she does not seem to mind the withdrawal of her imperial lover who once puts "the Belt" around her life, because to her it constitutes the "folding up" of her lifetime (273). While the river of her love continually flows toward the lover, she pleads with him for his acceptance of her:

> My River runs to thee –
> Blue Sea! Wilt welcome me?
> My River waits reply –
> Oh Sea – look graciously –
> I'll fetch thee Brooks
> From spotted nooks –
> *Say* – Sea – Take *Me!*   [162]

Water symbolism indicates constant movement and inner restlessness. Love, like water, is the prime source of existence; rather it *is* existence. Existence moves regardless of any cause outside itself. Therefore, "My River waits reply" is paradoxical. It can be a pose, or perhaps the beloved's sense of discipline, who does not wish to appear as intruding upon the freedom of the lover. But, then, there is no essential difference between the freedom of the river and the freedom of the sea: sea, river, brook are all different names of the same being:

> The Sea said "Come" to the Brook –
> The Brook said "Let me grow" –
> The Sea said "Then you will be a Sea –
> I want a Brook – Come now"!   [1210]

Since the river and sea are parts of the same process, the pleading of the river: "Oh Sea – look graciously" shows paradoxical humility, and *"Say* – Sea – Take *Me!"* (162) reveals the beloved's sense of surrender not to anything outside herself but to her own larger identity. This paradox is also embodied in the following poem:

> In lands I never saw – they say
> Immortal Alps look down –
> Whose Bonnets touch the firmament –
> Whose Sandals touch the town –
>
> Meek at whose everlasting feet
> A Myriad Daisy play –
> Which, Sir, are you and which am I
> Upon an August day?   [124]

In the landscape of imagination, the lover assumes the form of the immortal Alps, at whose everlasting feet a myriad daisy, the persona of the beloved, meekly plays. The lover looks downward with infinite love for his beloved. And, in the process of this love-play, the lovers lose their separate identities. The August day symbolizes the moment of sacred experience in which the lovers unite. After this experience, it is hard to make any distinction between the lovers, to know whose bonnet touches the firmament and who plays at whose everlasting feet. In this paradoxical state of self-negation, Dickinson also experiences the loss of the power of speech, which, metaphorically, proves that the relationship between the lovers is governed by inner silence, and that it is beyond worldly dialogue:

> I taught my Heart a hundred times
> Precisely what to say –
> Provoking Lover, when you came
> It's Treatise flew away   [1449]

However, the silence of the lovers is louder than the nearest noise; it speaks with great effect and clarity, it is "the Teller's eye" (619). It is the symptom of man's affection (1681). It is infinity (1251), and it is love's only mode of communication:

We talked with each other about each other
Though neither of us spoke –
We were listening to the seconds Races
And the Hoofs of the Clock –
Pausing in Front of our Palsied Faces
Time compassion took –
Arks of Reprieve he offered to us –
Ararats – we took –   [1473]

The meeting in which the lovers communicate with each other through silence is hallowed by the pausing of ever-moving time, the God of creation and destruction. Time takes pity on the palsied faces of the lovers and offers them arks of reprieve. In this respite from the continuous movement of time, the lovers arrive at a level of awareness by which ever-creating, ever-destroying time is properly perceived. The paradox of respite from time implies that the lovers, by listening to the seconds' races in the depth of their own silence, apprehend the mystery of ever-flowing creation. The lovers accept the offer of time, as Noah (Genesis 8:4) accepts Ararat after the deluge in which the world was swept away, in order to be recreated. In "The Winters are so short" (403) Dickinson remarks that "Ararat's a Legend – now – / And no one credits Noah." But, Noah's presence on Ararat, after the deluge, symbolizes a continuing process, a continual end and beginning of creation.[11] The point involved here is that when time shows compassion for the silent lovers, the lovers perceive the mystery of creation and the nature of the endless process, and by apprehending these they earn respite: they are no longer baffled by the phantasm of reality, they perceive reality itself and their love becomes timeless. Love, in this sense, is the whole of perception, and the act of loving takes man back to the roots of his mythology. It is this love which Paul Tillich designates as "a seeing love, a knowing love, a love that looks through into the depth of the Heart of God, and into the depth of our hearts."[12]

Emily Dickinson dramatizes the centrifugal movement of

the human psyche through her art, and makes it possible for the perceptive reader to share with her the mythology of love. Dickinson's search for the "other"—"he," "his," "him," "you," "thee," "thou"—constitutes her spiritual initiation into *Eros* (human-divine love), which can also be described as *Agape* (divine love).[13] She delineates her feeling toward her lover in terms of her most opulent image, East India (202). She regards herself as the "Brain of His Brain – / Blood of His Blood / Two lives – One Being – now" (246). The consciousness of her lover dawns upon her like sunrise following the night of chaos (347): "I saw the sunrise on the Alps since I saw you" (L321), writes Dickinson. She mentions to her lover: "My Heart ran so to thee / It would not wait for me" (1237). She reacts to the loss of the lover in these words: "More Life – went out – when He went" (422). And the presence of her lover gives her the feeling of being doubly alive:

> How good – to be alive!
> How infinite – to be
> Alive – two-fold – The Birth I had –
> And this – besides, in – Thee!   [470]

Her love is like a song to which she offers a perennial commitment: "For thee to bloom, I'll skip the tomb / And row my blossoms o'er!" (31). The constancy of her love is comparable to the permanence of the hills and the sun, and her passion is like the insatiable craving of the flowers for the dew:

> Alter! When the Hills do –
> Falter! When the Sun
> Question if His Glory
> Be the Perfect One –
>
> Surfeit! When the Daffodil
> Doth of the Dew –
> Even as Herself – Sir –
> I will – of You –   [729]

She becomes completely egoless in her love, and negates herself to the point where all polarities of existence seem to her to

have been resolved, and where the opposites appear to be
equally true. She speaks to her lover in this manner:

> You said that I "was Great" – one Day –
> Then "Great" it be – if that please Thee –
> Or Small – or any size at all –
> Nay – I'm the size suit Thee – . . .
>
> So say – if Queen it be –
> Or Page – please Thee –
> I'm that – or nought –
> Or other thing – if other thing there be –
> With just this Stipulus –
> I suit Thee –   [738]

The lover's presence can transform the beloved into the
"fairest of the Earth." Therefore, to the beloved, this experience is worth all the waiting:

> Time to anticipate His Gaze –
> It's first – Delight – and then – Surprise –
> The turning o'er and o'er of my face
> For Evidence it be the Grace –   [968]

But, in this relationship, physical distance does not enter: the
real distance is of the will and "not of Mile or Main" (863).
The lovers constitute one identity which distance cannot mar:

> Nor separate, Herself and Me
> By Distances become –
> A single Bloom we constitute
> Departed, or at Home –   [1037]

Since the realm of the lover symbolizes for Dickinson the
whole of existence, she does not visualize any life or death
beyond its vast space. There are no "Earths to come – / Nor
Action new" excepting those which can be realized within the
orbit of the lover's realm (1398). This means to say that the
lover comprehends all. Dickinson declares:

> The "Life that is" will then have been
> A thing I never knew –

> As Paradise fictitious
> Until the Realm of You –   [1260]

To be alive in the lover's realm is to experience "A warmth as near as if the Sun / Were shining in your Hand" (1568). To be in the lover's company is to become immortal:

> Perceiving thee is evidence
> That we are of the sky
> Partaking thee a guaranty
> Of immortality   [1643]

Emily Dickinson cannot afford to lose the "other" or the lover, because without him "Emptiness / Is the prevailing Freight" (834). The lover embodies her "Mansion of Identity" (1689), and by being with him she surveys infinity, which implies her being "face to face with Nature" and "face to face with God" (643). In one of her moments of longing for the human-divine lover, when she imagines herself to have been denied the privilege of being with him, Dickinson undergoes the experience of helplessness, inner pathos, and the fear of remaining "in Everlasting Night." She envies those who have access to her lover:

> I envy Seas, whereon He rides –
> I envy Spokes of Wheels
> Of Chariots, that Him convey –
> I envy Crooked Hills
>
> That gaze upon His journey –
> How easy All can see
> What is forbidden utterly
> As Heaven – unto me!
>
> I envy Nests of Sparrows –
> That dot His distant Eaves –
> The wealthy Fly, upon His Pane –
> The happy – happy Leaves –   . . .
>
> I envy Light – that wakes Him –
> And Bells – that boldly ring
> To tell Him it is Noon, abroad –
> Myself – be Noon to Him –   [498]

But she realizes very soon, as she almost invariably does, that the reality of her human-divine lover does not exist outside herself. The "other" is a part of one's self which exists outside one's self only in the paradoxical sense. The fusion which takes place in objective reality is always preceded by the harmonious act within the self. However, the "other" or the objective self helps in establishing the perspective through which one can realize the God-man relationship on earth. Without the "other," the self would have no meaning for humanity, though the pure subjectivity of the created being can be understood in terms of its own dynamism—an examination of the phenomenon of pure subjectivity will be offered in chapter six of this study. Dickinson dramatizes the syncretistic structure of her heart in which the "other" or "thee" is inevitably bound with the self, in these verses:

> Empty my Heart, of Thee –
> It's single Artery –
> Begin, and leave Thee out –
> Simply Extinction's Date –
>
> Much Billow hath the Sea –
> One Baltic – They –
> Subtract Thyself, in play,
> And not enough of me
> Is left – to put away –
> "Myself" meant Thee –
>
> Erase the Root – no Tree –
> Thee – then – no me –
> The Heavens stripped –
> Eternity's vast pocket, picked –   [587]

The human-divine lover is so inextricably fused in the very being of the poet Dickinson that she describes him as the single artery of her heart, which, if removed, would result in her extinction. The integrity of the lover-beloved relationship is analogous to the completeness of the wave-sea relationship. Since "myself" means "thee" to Dickinson, the subtraction of one from the other is impossible. As a tree cannot exist without its root, the self cannot manifest itself without the "other," which is the source of its identity: "Neither would be a Queen / Without the Other" (458). "Where You were not – / That self – were Hell to Me" (640), says Dickinson. In another poem, she describes the utter mutuality of the lover-beloved relationship in these authentic words:

> But since We hold a Mutual Disc –
> And front a Mutual Day –
> Which is the Despot, neither knows –
> Nor Whose – the Tyranny – [909]

The images of disc and day refer to death and life in Dickinson's poetry. "Despot" and "Tyranny" are images of power. In indicating the forceful and eternal nature of the lover-beloved relationship, these images are consistent with the idea of self-assertion. For the opposite notion of self-negation, Dickinson compares herself to a timid pebble, and her lover to a bolder sea (966). As death is integral to life, self-assertion is one with self-negation. In a similar way, "thee" is a part of "me," which cannot be separated from the self without destroying the whole:

> If Blame be my side – forfeit Me –
> But doom me not to forfeit Thee –
> To forfeit Thee? The very name
> Is sentence from Belief – and Home – [775]

The "I-thou" drama of the nontransient, conjugal dimension of love does not conclude here. Dickinson solemnizes the relationship by wearing the symbolic garb of a bride, by becoming the mythic wife, and by taking upon herself the crucifix of God. This level, however, can be realized only in the human imagination. Mundane existence does not permit the fructification of such a love. What life in its temporal state cannot offer, the imagination bestows, and the artist enjoys the advantage of making the experience concrete in the form of his or her art. This does not mean to say that the imagination completely bypasses life in its temporality and mundaneness; rather, it helps us to experience the transiency, the moral pathos, and the fear and trembling of our everyday existence. The imagination does not leave out anything; it contains all. In this sense, great works of art are always deeply and truly existential. Biographically speaking, Dickinson is quite aware of the existential impingements which normally come in the way of the human desire to achieve spiritual relationships at various levels. She is conscious that with her kind of dedication to poetry, and with her kind of sensibility, she cannot allow herself to marry like an ordinary woman. But she faces the predicament of her temporal existence boldly, and finally resolves her inner contradictions through her art. The marriage which cannot take place in her outward life is actualized in her poems. Dickinson the person shows hesitancy and suspicion toward the accomplishment of an "I-thou" relationship in our day-to-day existence, but Dickinson the poet feels confident of its fulfillment in the human imagination. The poetic understanding of the "I-thou" relationship does not lack the human perspective; rather, it arises from a full awareness of the human context. As a very young person, almost ten years before Dickinson began to discuss herself as a poet, she wrote to Susan Gilbert:

> You and I have been strangely silent upon this subject, Susie, we have often touched upon it, and as quickly fled away, as children shut their eyes when the sun is too bright for them. I have always hoped to know if you had no dear fancy, illuminating all your life, no one of whom you murmured in the faithful ear of night – and at whose side in fancy, you walked the livelong day; and when you come home, Susie, we must speak of these things. How dull our lives must seem to the bride, and the plighted maiden, whose days are fed with gold, and who gathers pearls every evening; but to the *wife,* Susie, sometimes the *wife forgotten,* our lives perhaps seem dearer than all others in the world; you have seen flowers at morning, *satisfied* with the dew, and those same sweet flowers at noon with their heads bowed in

anguish before the mighty sun; think you these thirsty blossoms will *now* need naught but – *dew*? No, they will cry for sunlight, and pine for the burning noon, tho' it scorches them, scathes them; they have got through with peace – they know that the man of noon, is *mightier* than the morning and their life is henceforth to him. Oh, Susie, it is dangerous, and it is all too dear, these simple trusting spirits, and the spirits mightier, which we cannot resist! It does so rend me, Susie, the thought of it when it comes, that I tremble lest at sometime, I, too, am yielded up. [L93]

The letter is revealingly frank in tone and matter. It portrays Dickinson's conflicting attitudes toward the states of virginity and wedlock: it betrays the longing to be scathed and ravished by the mighty "man of noon," and the trembling at the thought of being "yielded up." In the experiential realm, there is no easy way to resolve these contradictory emotions. In other words, the temporal state of being does not permit one to choose to be married and yet remain virgin or keep what Gelpi calls "the separate identity of the ego." [14] Emily Dickinson considers her spiritual needs, and finally chooses not to be the plighted maiden in the temporal sense. Her choice is difficult and soul-scathing: she chooses to experience the heat of the sunlight and the peace of the dew through the imagination. She achieves the status of the virgin-bride through her aesthetics of marriage in which she can both possess and be possessed simultaneously.

In her aesthetic vision, Dickinson perceives the true bridal ceremony as a mark of baptism, an initiation into purity which confers meekness as well as pride on the recipient (473). She visualizes this ceremony also as a type of resurrection which takes place before the judgment seat of God where the "Fleshless Lovers" meet, and are "Born infiniter – now" (625). However, this rebirth becomes real in the now of the imagination only as a continual process:

> Dominion lasts until obtained –
> Possession just as long –

> But these – endowing as they flit
> Eternally belong.
>
> How everlasting are the Lips
> Known only to the Dew –
> These are the Brides of permanence
> Supplanting me and you.   [1257]

Worldly marriage does not hold any charm for the "Brides of permanence." Though they never fully obtain the dominion of their lovers, their prize belongs to them eternally. For them, love is a continual radiation and not an end-product. As the lips of the sun-god never tire of the dew, the lovers never grow weary of their brides; their love is renewed with each morn.

In "I'm 'wife' – I've finished that" (199), Dickinson passes through the experience of pain and oddity of the girl's life, and becomes woman or wife. She calls this change a "soft Eclipse," a state in which she can be oblivious of the ways of the earth. She expresses her new status with a sense of authenticity: "I'm 'Wife'! Stop there!" She becomes "two" in order to cross the deep sea of love which is "Nicknamed by God – / Eternity" (453). In another poem she describes the experience of becoming a wife in terms of the images of daybreak, sunrise, east, and victory, and addresses her lover in this manner: "Eternity, I'm coming – Sir, / Savior – I've seen the face – before!" (461). The religious overtones are integral to this aesthetic and spiritual experience. When called upon to be the wife of the human-divine lover, she renounces every other pleasure of her life:

> She rose to His Requirement – dropt
> The Playthings of Her Life
> To take the honorable Work
> Of Woman, and of Wife –
>
> If ought She missed in Her new Day,
> Of Amplitude, or Awe –

> Or first Prospective – Or the Gold
> In using, wear away,
>
> It lay unmentioned – as the Sea
> Develope Pearl, and Weed,
> But only to Himself – be known
> The Fathoms they abide –   [732]

Dickinson, or the persona of the poem, undertakes the honorable work of wifehood with a sense of utter dedication. She readily sacrifices the playthings of her life, and in her new day, she does not miss anything of abiding nature. She loses only her finiteness which is transformed into the amplitude of her primordial vision, symbolized here by the first prospective. This new day, the dawn of Dickinson's perception, is the source of awe and spiritual terror. The gold symbolizes emanation or ascension through fire. Dickinson does not mention this new day to anyone, and becomes more inward like the sea where pearl and weed grow side by side. The mystery and the depths of the sea abide and are known only to the lover. Sea is the symbol of creation and destruction; it represents both water and fire. The "Fire ebbs like Billows" (291) in Dickinson's imagination. The pearl-weed symbolism is parallel to the symbolism of the sea in so far as pearl means the wanted and weed means the unwanted, and in so far as both mean life and death. In terms of the poem's symbolisms, then, the work of the wife touches the ultimate spiritual dimension, the dimension of living and dying simultaneously. Dickinson describes the metamorphosis involved in this love, in these verses:

> The World – stands – solemner – to me –
> Since I was wed – to Him –
> A modesty befits the soul
> That bears another's – name –
> A doubt – if it be fair – indeed –
> To wear that perfect – pearl –
> The Man – upon the Woman – binds –
> To clasp her soul – for all –

A prayer, that it more angel – prove –
A whiter Gift – within –
To that munificence, that chose –
So unadorned – a Queen –
A Gratitude – that such be true –
It had esteemed the Dream –
Too beautiful – for Shape to prove –
Or posture – to redeem!   [493]

Dickinson's marriage transforms her world-view. In the presence of her lover, everything in the world seems sacred to her. She feels that in carrying the name of the lover as a sign of her identity, the beloved expresses the humility of her soul. It is through this humility and self-effacement that the beloved can "wear that perfect pearl" the symbol of creation, which "The Man – upon the Woman – binds." The whole picture of binding seems erotic, but it is that *Eros* (human passion) in which the lover clasps the beloved's soul, and the love act becomes a kind of prayer, an angelic act of creativity. This is what Dickinson calls a "whiter Gift within," the gift of revelation and self-illumination. She regards this gift as a splendidly generous act of the lover in whose presence she perpetually humbles herself by calling herself "unadorned." There is no limit to her gratitude for the lover who has fulfilled her dream which is "Too beautiful – for Shape to prove – / Or posture – to redeem!" However, her sense of humility and gratitude is paradoxical. She is quite proud but fully aware of the spiritual implications of her role as a divine beloved:

Title divine – is mine!
The Wife – without the Sign!
Acute Degree – conferred on me –
Empress of Calvary!
Royal – all but the Crown!
Betrothed – without the swoon
God sends us Women –
When you – hold – Garnet to Garnet –
Gold – to Gold –

> Born – Bridalled – Shrouded –
> In a Day –
> Tri Victory – *
> "My Husband" – women say –
> Stroking the Melody –
> Is *this* – the way?   [1072]

The "whiter Gift within" (493) entitles Dickinson to be a human-divine beloved. She becomes the wife without any outward ceremony. The whole experience of being the divine beloved is summed up in the words "acute degree," signifying a sense of intense involvement and suffering, legitimate enough in the nontransient, conjugal dimension as well as the spiritual or religious dimension of love. In becoming the "Empress of Calvary," she undergoes an experience of agony which is comparable to that of the Crucifixion itself. Her royalty is without the crown. She is betrothed, but without the happy swoon of a plighted maiden. Holding "Garnet to Garnet – / Gold – to Gold" symbolizes the psychic drama of going through the forge—both garnet and gold symbolize passion and fire, in this case not the consuming fire but the consummating fire. God creates women in order to perpetuate the feminine principle of creativity on earth, but it is by going through the fire of the spirit that a woman can realize the "Tri Victory" of being "Born – Bridalled – Shrouded" in a single day of illumination. It is through this fire that Dickinson perceives the mystery of birth, love, and death. Her spiritual and aesthetic marriage is far more daring and abiding than the customary marriages in which women call their lovers by the label "my husband." Dickinson asks if this is the way of fulfillment: can men and women achieve regeneration and spiritual rebirth within the confines of social institutions? The answer to her question is stated in terms of the metaphors of her art.

Dickinson's art is the art of suffering. She apprehends the mystery of human-divine love through the symbol of the

* An additional line from the variant draft of this poem.

Cross: each must bind "the Other's Crucifix," and realize the
"new Marriage" through "Calvaries of Love" (322). With "such
a Crucifixal sign," she enters her new Jerusalem, and captures
the love experience in all its primordial sensuousness:

> He touched me, so I live to know
> That such a day, permitted so,
> I groped upon his breast –
> It was a boundless place to me
> And silenced, as the awful sea
> Puts minor streams to rest.
>
> And now, I'm different from before,
> As if I breathed superior air –
> Or brushed a Royal Gown –
> My feet, too, that had wandered so –
> My Gipsy face – transfigured now –
> To tenderer Renown – . . .   [506]

In her vision of love, Dickinson views silence and death as
integral to the totality of the experience. The pattern of death
is that of the tapestries of paradise which are made so "note-
lessly" (278). "I cannot live with You" (640) captures fully the
paradox of death—the death of the lover and his ultimate resurrection which Dickinson calls new grace. "I cannot live with
You" and "I could not die – with You" stage the continually
unfolding drama of living in death and dying into life. There
is no end in sight, and Dickinson prefers it that way. On the
surface, this might indicate the impossibility of fulfillment, or
some other type of doom, in love. But, in terms of the poetic
reality, it refers to the process of love which is never complete
and which is like an endless sensibility. Dickinson tells her
lover:

> So We must meet apart –
> You there – I – here –
> With just the Door ajar
> That Oceans are – and Prayer –
> And that White Sustenance –
> Despair –   [640]

As long as the door of perception remains ajar, the physical distance between the lover and the beloved, between here and there, will not be of any consequence. As the oceans subsume the distance between life and death, the lovers' prayer, which is the true act of love, will keep them together though physically apart. In this spiritual state of love, despair becomes the "White Sustenance," a divine condition of being, and not some earthly anguish over the loss of a beloved or a lover: "We must through much tribulation enter into the Kingdom of God" (Acts 14:22), because "we are appointed to afflictions" (I Thessalonians 3:3). This despair constitutes Dickinson's spiritual or psychic dimension of love. This is the "Grace so unavoidable – / To fail – is Infidel" (387). The mere thought of its departing afflicts her with a double loss: " 'Tis lost – And lost to me" (472). The mystery of love cannot be apprehended by everyone. It is the secret which God calls eternity:

> Love – thou art Vailed –
> A few – behold thee –
> Smile – and alter – and prattle – and die –
> Bliss – were an Oddity – without thee –
> Nicknamed by God –
> Eternity – [453]

Love is Dickinson's diadem which she must continually harmonize with the dome or the circumference of her poetry:

> 'Tis little I – could care for Pearls –
> Who own the ample sea –
> Or Brooches – when the Emperor –
> With Rubies – pelteth me –
>
> Or Gold – who am the Prince of Mines –
> Or Diamonds – when have I
> A Diadem to fit a Dome –
> Continual upon me – [466]

The images and metaphors of pearls, the ample sea, diamonds, diadem, and dome adequately describe Dickinson's poetic strategy of realizing the interpenetrating relations be-

tween love and death, death and self, self and poetry, and so
on.

The spiritual eroticism or the *Eros* embodied in Dickinson's
poetry forms the basis of her awareness of the God-man relationship. Her poetry dramatizes all the possibilities of love and
suffering which are fundamental to this relationship. In order
that such a relationship should be fully realized within one's
own being, one must be willing to sacrifice his dearest earthly
possessions. Dickinson illustrates the quality of sacrifice in
"Abraham to kill him" (1317). She believes that eternal suffering is the prerequisite for the "coronation" of love, which surpasses all other crowns (356). Even God, whom Dickinson portrays as "a distant – stately Lover," loves us "as He states us –
by His Son," who is a paradigm of suffering and sacrifice (357).
The death of Jesus on the Cross is the supreme example of
God's *Agape*. As Anders Nygren writes: "Apart from the Cross
we should never have known God's love and learnt its depths
of meaning." [15] God's love for man, then, should be understood as a typology of man's own spiritual love for his fellow
men through whom alone he can reach God and love him *in
concreto*. The typology of Jesus on the Cross would serve man,
then, as a pattern of his own suffering and consecration, his
love and death. Dickinson's poetry portrays this typology in a
variety of ways. She emphasizes the role of man's suffering in
his search for the primordial land which is the true source of
the mystery of love, death, and self:

> Far from Love the Heavenly Father
> Leads the Chosen Child,
> Oftener through Realm of Briar
> Than the Meadow mild.
>
> Oftener by the Claw of Dragon
> Than the Hand of Friend
> Guides the Little One predestined
> To the Native Land.   [1021]

The opening lines of the above poem seem to present a contrast with the God of the New Testament, who according to

Pauline theology is all-embracing love. The Calvinistic tone is too obvious to be overlooked, although Dickinson does not seem to be entirely concerned with the theological concepts of God's ways to man. Ontologically speaking, the "Realm of Briar" and the "Claw of Dragon" are essential to the realization of the native land, which symbolizes man's primordial consciousness, the fountain of his being. By contrast, the love of God, the "Meadow mild," and the "Hand of Friend" can prove impediments on the journey toward the inner spring. This brings out the paradox that a life of hardships takes one closer to fulfillment than a life of comforts. The purpose, then, is not to show any want of love in the Heavenly Father. Rather, the implied idea is that God prescribes the way of thorns on which alone can one find roses. It is by passing through the "Claw of Dragon," symbolizing here fire and chastity, that one can be truly born. In Dickinson's poetry, God himself is paradoxical: he is both attached and detached, near and far, compassionate and indifferent, generous and jealous. In one of her poems of God's compassion, Dickinson writes:

> The Himmaleh was known to stoop
> Unto the Daisy low –
> Transported with Compassion
> That such a Doll should grow
> Where Tent by Tent – Her Universe
> Hung out it's Flags of Snow –   [481]

The "Himmaleh" is the Indian mountain range called Himalayas or Himalayan passes. Himalaya literally means the home of snow (Him = snow, and alaya = home). In Indian mythology it is the abode of Shiva, who embodies eternal dissolution and re-creation of all life, and from whose locks the sacred river Ganga flows.[16] Dickinson's use of the word "Himmaleh" brings out most of its mythic connotations. In this poem, Himmaleh is pure compassion, which means creativity. But the daisy's universe carries the flags of snow, which symbolize death and destruction. In showing compassion for the lowly daisy and letting it grow in the heart of death, Himmaleh is fulfilling the creative-destructive-recreative role of Shiva himself. But when God's compassion turns into indifference, you cannot see him, though his house is but a step from yours (487). It is in this sense that he is both far and near. God loves man's infinite suffering and endeavor, and he rewards those who live in death:

> Victory comes late –
> And is held low to freezing lips –
> Too rapt with frost
> To take it –
> How sweet it would have tasted –
> Just a Drop –
> Was God so economical?
> His Table's spread too high for Us –
> Unless We dine on tiptoe –
> Crumbs – fit such little mouths –
> Cherries – suit Robins
> The Eagle's Golden Breakfast strangles – Them –
> God keep His Oath to Sparrows –
> Who of little Love – know how to starve –   [690]

God's love comes, though late, to those whose lips are freezing in death, presented here in the metaphor of frost. The poet surmises the sweetness of the drop of love and seems to regret the inability of the dying to taste it. The question involved here is not so much about the revival of the dying as it is about the proximity of love and death. Death has been shown quite vividly and feelingly: the lips are freezing, they are not frozen as yet. It is an experience of death-in-life. The last seven lines constitute an attempt to answer the question, "Was God so economical?" In Dickinson's vision, God's table is spread too high for us. In order to reach the food, which symbolizes energy, creativity, and fertility, we have to dine on tiptoe, signifying that we should undergo every extremity to taste even a few crumbs. Passion begets passion: the scarlet cherries suit the redbreasted robins; the eagle's breakfast is too much for their little mouths. The entire symbolism implies that in man's relationship to God it is not the quantity or size of God's love that concerns man; rather, it is the intensity with which man should receive God's love. Man, like sparrows, should know how to starve "of little Love." If man craves God's love as he craves breath, he will get it, and get it by starving for it. In its ontological dimension the poem seems to resolve the paradox of God's love for man and man's love for God. The poem suggests a two-way traffic: God's love flows, but man must exert himself and reach for it on tiptoe. In a highly religious sense, God alone or man alone is a meaningless entity; one without the other sounds absurd.[17]

The poet not only watches God's creation but also re-enacts it in his own medium and remains perpetually haunted by it. He suffers for himself in the process, but vicariously suffers for us all. By becoming the paradigm of Christ, the God-man, he experiences love and death simultaneously. He loves abundantly, and continues loving even when there is no response:

> So well that I can live without –
> I love thee – then How well is that?
> As well as Jesus?
> Prove it me
> That He – loved Men –
> As I – love thee – [456]

This posture refers to the purely spiritual or sacred dimension of love, which is completely self-effacing, and in which the poet loves without any reciprocity, selflessly, as Jesus loved men. This love is far above the realm in which the lonely housewife, on a windy, cold night, checks to see if the blinds are fast and draws her little rocking chair closer to the fire (589); in which the wife keeps house, but waits for everlasting life with her lover beyond the grave (1743); and in which marriage means the contract of a life, and love is just the "Sweet Debt of Life – Each Night to owe" but "Insolvent – every Noon" (580). This love means man's ultimate destiny, which involves his death. It is necessary to die, to be dead to the world's worldliness, in order to be able to love like a god. In order that we should possess the sensibility of "holier love," we must first pass through the ordeal of the "wheel of fire." [18]

In Emily Dickinson's aesthetics, love is intertwined with death. The symbols of life and death are infinitely fused in her vision. She expresses this cohesive insight with a subtle sense of pathos and dignity: "All this and more, though *is* there more? More than Love and Death? Then tell me it's name!" (L873). Death haunts Dickinson in many paradoxical ways. She visualizes death as an intruding force, but one which enhances our appreciation of what is alive. She writes to Mrs. Samuel E. Mack: "A friend is a solemnity and after the great intrusion of Death, each one that remains has a spectral price-lessness besides the mortal worth" (L940). And she writes to Higginson: "Perhaps Death – gave me awe for friends – striking sharp and early, for I held them since – in a brittle love – of more alarm, than peace" (L280). Death also augments her love for the dead a hundredfold (482).

Death and sacrifice are indeed integral to love. But love creates and destroys simultaneously: the great daemon is the ever-dying, ever-reviving god. The relationship between love and death, creation and destruction, may be discerned in the symbolism of the sexual act.[19] In the context of love, then, death means a point of view, an awareness, a perspective by which the lovers transcend the limitations of mortality. While living in the finite state, they experience the infiniteness of being. Love confers upon them a sense of immortality:

> Unable are the Loved to die
> For Love is Immortality,
> Nay, it is Deity –
>
> Unable they that love – to die
> For Love reforms Vitality
> Into Divinity.   [809]

Fading in love is to fade "unto Divinity" (682). Death also becomes the vantage point from which the lovers can converse with each other:

> Think of it Lover! I and Thee
> Permitted – face to face to be –
> After a Life – a Death – We'll say –
> For Death was That –
> And This – is Thee – [577]

In the dying eye of the lover-beloved, there are only "Two Armies, Love and Certainty / And Love and the Reverse" (831). But, whatever that might entail, the lovers must "bend as low as Death," because "Christ – stooped until He touched the Grave" (833). This metaphoric dying is the prerequisite of a life of love:

> Till Death – is narrow Loving –
> The scantest Heart extant
> Will hold you till your privilege
> Of Finiteness – be spent – [907]

The experience of dying—"The dying multifold – without / The Respite to be dead" (1013)—enhances our perception of love. In another poem, Dickinson writes:

> The Tenant of the Narrow Cottage, wert Thou –
> Permit to be
> The Housewife in thy low attendance
> Contenteth Me –
>
> No Service hast Thou, I would not achieve it –
> To die – or live –
> The first – Sweet, proved I, ere I saw thee –
> For Life – be Love – [961]

In love the sense of self-abnegation should be so complete that living or dying should cease to matter. Love, then, becomes life, and life becomes love. Death dies into life. The steadfast heart of love can bear itself through the tomb (1597):

> Love is like Life – merely longer
> Love is like Death, during the Grave
> Love is the Fellow of the Resurrection
> Scooping up the Dust and chanting "Live"!   [491]

To achieve the condition of love in which death ceases to hurt as it does in our limited perception, one has to brave the storms and surges of existence. Man must fathom the heart of darkness and should be able to say to himself: "I will love," though "Oceans – and the North must be – / On every side of mine" (631). Dickinson shows rare strength of character when she writes:

> Affliction would not be appeased –
> The Darkness braced as firm
> As all my stratagem had been
> The Midnight to confirm –
>
> No Drug for Consciousness – can be –
> Alternative to die
> Is Nature's only Pharmacy
> For Being's Malady –   [786]

By bracing the darkness and confirming the midnight, one can experience the genesis of light and the dawn. Darkness contains light, and the midnight is the time between night and morning, or death and life. This experience is the source of our true consciousness, which no drug can provide. Dickinson seems to be addressing the drug-addicts of today and saying that psychedelic drugs like marijuana and LSD can never provide a cure for being's malady. There is no alternative to man's death; he must meet it in the abyss of his own being by the stairway of love. By way of meeting the dangers of existence Dickinson wears "the 'Thorns' till *Sunset*" and then puts her diadem on (1737). This is how she knows that after the midnight frosts there is always the morning's sun (205). She is not deterred by death; rather, she plays with it and loves it as one loves the wound which serves as a reminder of the withdrawn pleasure of love:

> Rehearsal to Ourselves
> Of a Withdrawn Delight –
> Affords a Bliss like Murder –
> Omnipotent – Acute –
>
> We will not drop the Dirk –
> Because We love the Wound
> The Dirk Commemorate – Itself
> Remind Us that we died.   [379]

Death in this poem does not end the delight of love. Paradoxically, it perpetuates the delight by way of the wound. The re-
hearsal or the replay within ourselves of the scene of death in
which the delight is withdrawn "Affords a Bliss like Murder."
It affords bliss because this murder or killing is not ordinary;
it is infinitely powerful and intense. It celebrates itself eternally in the human mind. "We will not drop the Dirk / Because We love the Wound" establishes a posture of authentic
living in which an awareness of death lends intensity to life
and love. Lovers prove that they possess such an awareness
and, thus, do not fear death:

> They summoned Us to die –
> With sweet alacrity
> We stood upon our stapled feet –
> Condemned – but just – to see –
>
> Permission to recant –
> Permission to forget –
> We turned our backs upon the Sun
> For perjury of that –
>
> Not Either – noticed Death –
> Of Paradise – aware –
> Each other's Face – was all the Disc
> Each other's setting – saw –   [474]

In love, death becomes the organ of perception. Even when
the lovers are condemned to die, they show cheerfulness on
their faces and do nothing but see each other. They turn their
backs upon the sun, which is symbolic of life, and do not agree

to recant for its sake, for they understand the falsehood of existence without love. They do not even notice death when it
comes. They are lost in each other's face and are aware of the
paradise of love. They see each other's setting in their hearts,
represented here by their faces. Death becomes the instrument and test of love. When life fails to convince the lover
of the beloved's love, death proves helpful. The beloved embraces death as a proof of her love, though death cannot di-
minish the power of her eyes with which she sees her lover till
the end:

> The River reaches to my feet –
> As yet – My Heart be dry –
> Oh Lover – Life could not convince –
> Might Death – enable Thee –
>
> The River reaches to My Breast –
> Still – still – My Hands above
> Proclaim with their remaining Might –
> Dost recognize the Love?
>
> The River reaches to my Mouth –
> Remember – when the Sea
> Swept by my searching eyes – the last –
> Themselves were quick – with Thee!   [537]

The river and sea of death are also the river and sea of life.
When the river overflows with death, love makes the eyes, the
doors of perception, "quick – with Thee!" The hands which
are indicators of man's spiritual life, also remain above death.
Death does not interfere with the beloved's conception of the
lover. Rather, love's magnitude requires the "Services of
Snow," symbolizing death (914): "The Test of Love – is
Death – / Our Lord – 'so loved' – it saith" (573). In this vein
Dickinson demands: "So give me back to Death – / The Death
I never feared" (1632). One who challenges death sees better
in the dark:

> I see thee better – in the Dark –
> I do not need a Light –

The Love of Thee – a Prism be –
Excelling Violet –

I see thee better for the Years
That hunch themselves between –
The Miner's Lamp –sufficient be –
To nullify the Mine –

And in the Grave – I see Thee best –
It's little Panels be
Aglow – All ruddy – with the Light
I held so high, for Thee –

What need of Day –
To Those whose Dark – hath so – surpassing Sun –
It deem it be – Continually –
At the Meridian?   [611]

In the deep, dark region of the human psyche, love performs
the function of a prism, a structure of lights with myriad colors, which excels even violet, symbolic of the unattainable passion. Love throws time into relief and the years gain in perspective. They shine like the miner's lamp which nullifies the
darkness of the cave, or which liberates man from the ignorance of his closed mind. Love's grave is all aglow. Its walls are
red with life. Love's dark is that sun which surpasses even the
light of day, and it shines "Continually – / At the Meridian,"
symbolizing the zenith of one's consciousness, which in itself is
the splendid circle of light. When death and dark become life
and light, there is nothing more to experience, excepting that
one has to continue experiencing them in the perfect silence
of the heart, which is the source of man's being and freedom.
Dickinson dives deep into this silence and writes: "The time
was scarce profaned, by speech – / The symbol of a word / Was
needless, as at Sacrament," and "Each was to each The Sealed
Church" (322). While in love, Dickinson has "no answer of the
Tongue / But answer of the Eyes" (1053). She considers that

"*Speech*" – is a prank of *Parliament* –
"*Tears*" – a trick of the nerve –

> But the Heart with the heaviest freight on –
> Does'nt – always – move –   [688]

She believes that man's real wars are fought within his heart:

> To fight aloud, is very brave,
> But *gallanter,* I know
> Who charge within the bosom
> The Cavalry of Wo –   [126]

This constitutes for Dickinson the courage to be. While building her being on the spires of love and death, she regards the "little Toil of Love" as large enough for her (478). To her "cooler than the Water" is the "Thoughtfulness of Thirst" (818). She learns from time the lower way, the way of suffering and deep feeling, "That Life like This – is stopless – / Be Judgment – what it may" (463). Love teaches her the art of freedom in which she seems to transcend every form of bondage. She tells her lover:

> Where Thou art – that – is Home –
> Cashmere – or Calvary – the same –
> Degree – or Shame –
> I scarce esteem Location's Name –
> So I may Come –
>
> What Thou dost – is Delight –
> Bondage as Play – be sweet –
> Imprisonment – Content –
> And Sentence – Sacrament –
> Just We two – meet –   [725]

Love is utter freedom: "Love reckons by itself – alone. . . . Itself is all the like it has" (826). The lovers cannot be bound by anything outside love. Dickinson sings:

> Bind me – I still can sing –
> Banish – my mandolin
> Strikes true within –
>
> Slay – and my Soul shall rise
> Chanting to Paradise –
> Still thine.   [1005]

Love transforms the poet, and she assumes several poetic forms. She becomes what she sees—the flower, the bee, the spider—and ushers in true liberty:

> I said "But just to be a Bee"
> Upon a Raft of Air
> And row in Nowhere all Day long
> And anchor "off the Bar"
>
> What Liberty! So Captives deem
> Who tight in Dungeons are.   [661]

The raft of air is symbolic of the sources of creativity and imagination, which can take the bee-poet to the sea of nowhere, signifying the poet's unbounded character. Dungeons symbolize the caverns of the human mind, which is tied down to earth's earthliness. The poet also lives in the now and here of time and space, but, paradoxically, she is beyond spatio-temporal reality. At will, she can go from now and here to nowhere and vice versa. The poet's freedom lies in the captivity of her own commitment, in the captivity of womb-tomb, the source of love, creativity, life, and death.

5

Death

THE COSMIC DANCE

Fare forward.
               O voyagers, O seamen,
You who come to port, and you whose bodies
Will suffer the trial and judgement of the sea
Or whatever event, this is your real destination.
So Krishna, as when he admonished Arjuna
On the field of battle.
                       Not fare well,
But fare forward, voyagers.
                       —T. S. Eliot, "The Dry Salvages"

It has been suggested before in this study that Emily Dickinson encounters the ontological problem of death by living most deliberately. Life itself constitutes for her the "awful stranger Consciousness" (1323) into which she penetrates and discovers her creative destiny and vocation. She realizes that death is an integral part of life; it is a continual event taking place in the being's center (553). Death is inevitably woven into the schema of creation in which alone one can experience its true significance. Paradoxically speaking, death enhances the meaning of existence. Considering death from various angles, Dickinson experiences change in her moods and postures. But death remains a constant reality in her poetic vision.

Dickinson sees through nature that the symbols of death are interfused with the symbols of life. She believes that spring

178

and winter, summer and autumn, sunrise and sunset, dawn and dusk, morn and night, light and dark, green and white are man's eyes, the doors of perception, through which he can view the continuity of existence and say, "This World is not Conclusion" (501). A creative apprehension of life is man's only way to recognize the true dimensions of his mortality and to realize eternity in the very now of his being, which is a constant becoming. In the creative vision, man is in a perpetual state of being reborn. Creativity implies freedom from the sense of temporality, and a recognition of life as a continuous process in which death ceases to be absolute and final. In creative immortality, winter is as arable as spring (1707), there is no goblin on the bloom (646), and summer lasts a solid year (569). Creativity constitutes man's challenge to the notion of death as a painful absurdity. Creatively understood, death assumes the form of love, which is another name for perception or creation: "Till Death – is narrow Loving" (907), and in love, one perceives better in the dark (611). The silence and terror of death finally merge with the awe of life, as realized in the human spirit or imagination. In this process, death affirms life, and life affirms death, and the awareness of a creative unity of life and death becomes man's ultimate goal which alone can define the limits of human possibility.[1]

But the vision of life-death continuity is highly paradoxical and ambiguous. It is beyond the limits of man's judgment and practical reason. It is irrational and spiritual, and thus governed by an intuitive logic. In the face of human mortality, it represents man's most stupendous attempt to rescue himself imaginatively from the condition of impermanence and transiency. It is symbolic of man's hunger for immortality.[2] Therefore, it should be remembered that the contradictions inherent in the ontological problem of man's immortality in time cannot be explained in terms of scientific thought; only the metaphoric language can help us to assimilate the whole vision.

In order for man to be able to transcend the anxiety of

dying, it is necessary that he should face the question of his
own death creatively. Recognition of death as an existential reality is the prerequisite that man must fulfill before entering
the dawn in which the east and west meet. I have said before
that death haunts Dickinson in many paradoxical ways. Before
she realizes death as a primordial metaphor for continuation,
before she understands tomb as womb, and before she in-
tegrates these insights into her aesthetics of continuity, Dickinson undergoes the excruciating experience of death as eternal
silence and darkness, as the unknown mystery and oblivion
from which there is no return. Through the images of "Beetle
at the Candle" and a "Fife's Fame," she contemplates life and
death as proclaimed by mere accident (706). She visualizes
death as the crowning experience of life (98) which happens
to everyone, irrespective of color or caste or denomination
(970). She regards "The overtakelessness of those / Who have
accomplished Death" as more majestic than the majesties of
Earth (1691). But, still the notion of the absolute power of
death to kill or destroy, and to put an end to the process of existence seems to appal her. The ruthlessness of death, its cold,
frosty look on life distresses her "Like Time's insidious wrin-
kle / On a beloved Face" (1236). Describing the utter darkness
of the heart of death, Dickinson writes:

> His Heart was darker than the starless night
> For that there is a morn
> But in this black Receptacle
> Can be no Bode of Dawn   [1378]

On the vicious purpose and finality of death, she broods in
this manner:

> Within thy Grave!
> Oh no, but on some other flight –
> Thou only camest to mankind
> To rend it with Good night –   [1552]

Dickinson feels the intrusion of death's darkness upon life's
day in terms of the most touching pathos and despair. She

contemplates the beginning and the end of life, and utters this cry:

> Oh Life, begun in fluent Blood
> And consummated dull!
> Achievement contemplating thee –
> Feels transitive and cool.   [1130]

The frost of death lies too heavily on the pane of Dickinson's consciousness (1136). Death, like the insect, menaces the tree of her life (1716). But this does not mean to say that she gives up the fight for survival: she resists with all her spiritual strength the nullifying attempts of the "White Exploit" (922). Paradoxically speaking, the cry which is uttered in recognition of one's mortality and temporality is the cry which takes one beyond the realm of the mortal. In other words, a constant awareness of our mortality liberates us from the pang of death. There is no refuge from death, but the way to be free from its gnawing burden is to experience it in the abyss of one's own heart. Dickinson's poetry embodies this strategy. The descriptions of personal as well as impersonal death, the dramatization of death as an instrument of release from experiential agony and pathos, the realization of death as a force which enhances man's intensity, passion, and awareness of life—all indicate a daring attempt to master death. By this creative strategy, Dickinson shows her willingness and courage to die. Finding death as one finds the lover, or friend, or God, she affirms life right in the heart of death. She enacts the drama of life and death through various symbolisms, particularly sunrise, sunset, boat, and sea. In her vision of God's playful duplicity (1461), Dickinson discovers the complex meaning of the creator-creation paradox. In the endless continuum of creation and destruction, life and death, heaven and hell, she comes upon the metaphors of poetic resurrection, immortality, and continuity, and thus celebrates the poetic mythology of the eternal return.

By dwelling further on the findings and observations contained in the foregoing paragraph, I hope to show via the interpretation of her poetry the several postures or the many integral phases through which Emily Dickinson experiences the totality or the unity of life-and-death. In this perplexing and soul-searching task, we should begin with the simple though painful hypothesis that human life is mortal, and death, from the viewpoint of the living, is utter silence, darkness, and oblivion from which no return is ever possible. It is true that man has no empirical means to verify the truth or falsehood of this hypothesis, but he can never rest in the conflict between death as terminus and his inner craving for a journey beyond. Dickinson enacts the underlying restlessness and the discomfiture of man caught in the polarity of this situation, doomed to question the why and wherefore of existence till death's finger claps his murmuring lip (56). Death's silence is complete because it utters no syllable; it "only shows his Marble Disc – / Sublimer sort – than Speech" (310). In death's silence, in its "stiff stare," seems to be the place where God "has hid his rare life / From our gross eyes" (338). In one poem, the reality of silence becomes more sharp-edged than the painful fact of death:

> Death's Waylaying not the sharpest
> Of the thefts of Time –
> There Marauds a sorer Robber,
> Silence – is his name –
> No Assault, nor any Menace
> Doth betoken him.
> But from Life's consummate Cluster –
> He supplants the Balm.   [1296]

The contrast between death and silence seems purposeful and deliberate. We know that death in itself is silence. But the point of contrast is that death's robbing is less painful than its ensuing silence. Silence becomes a "sorer Robber." It is like suspense which is "Hostiler than Death" (705). Death assaults man, and it poses a constant threat to his existence. Silence shows no such outward signs of violence, and yet it plunders man's peace which prevails over his "Life's consummate Cluster," connoting the forces which mean life's fulfillment. Silence horrifies man because it deepens the mystery of death. It is silence which makes death final and irrevocable. The dying persona of "Because that you are going" (1260) will never come back; for "Death is final, / However first it be." Dickinson writes with a certain uneasiness: "The Things that never can come back, are several – / Childhood – some forms of Hope – the Dead" (1515). And sometimes

> We never know we go when we are going –
> We jest and shut the Door –
> Fate – following – behind us bolts it –
> And we accost no more –   [1523]

We go from the earth as quietly as the dew, but not like the dew, do we "return / At the Accustomed hour!" (149). Once we leave, we are never seen again "Upon the mortal side" (150). "In dying – 'tis as if Our Souls / Absconded – suddenly" (645). There is no hope to revive us from "A long – long Sleep – A famous – Sleep – / That makes no show for Morn – / By Stretch of Limb – or stir of Lid" (654). We simply disappear into the "Regions wild" (1149) where "The quiet nonchalance of death – / No Daybreak – can bestir" (194). When one perceives that one is dying, and dying without any hope of returning to life, the agony and anxiety take the forms of questions which have no answers:

> Still own thee – still thou art
> What surgeons call alive –
> Though slipping – slipping I perceive
> To thy reportless Grave –
>
> Which question shall I clutch –
> What answer wrest from thee
> Before thou dost exude away
> In the recallless sea?   [1633]

The persona of the poem, represented through thee, thou, and thy, is integral to the perceiving "I" who contemplates the experience of dying by instalments, who in the very moment of being alive feels the sensation of slipping to the "reportless Grave." Death seems to be curiously woven into the fabric of life. Even though the reportless grave is outside man, the sensation of slipping into it is perfectly inside the living being.[3] But this does not help man to know the precise questions that he should clutch at when dying. His sense of being oozed out to the "recallless sea" is too overwhelming to spare him for any answer that he would otherwise like to extract from the moment and experience of death. He seems to be thwarted in his effort to grapple with the mystery of death. After death, his corpse personifies the epitaph:

> Sweet hours have perished here;
>   This is a mighty room;
> Within its precincts hopes have played, –
>   Now shadows in the tomb.   [1767]

Death "nails the eyes" of man (561). He cannot see the path of his journey which takes him toward this utter darkness. He can only cry:

> Dying! Dying in the night!
> Wont somebody bring the light
> So I can see which way to go
> Into the everlasting snow?   [158]

Once he is lost in the night, or when his body becomes a part of the everlasting snow, oblivion overtakes him. In due course of time, he is completely forgotten:

> After a hundred years
> Nobody knows the Place
> Agony that enacted there
> Motionless as Peace   [1147]

The peace which is associated with oblivion has a touch of irony about it. The enactment of the agony of existence which indicates man's tragic vision, passes into a motionless state. Memory, desire, love—all fail to fill the gap between the dead and the living:

> Ambition cannot find him.
> Affection does'nt know
> How many leagues of nowhere
> Lie between them now. [68]

The oblivion of death enhances the mystery of the unknown. However much the human mind may try to unlock the secret of death, the effort is ultimately bound to fail:

> Dust is the only Secret –
> Death, the only One
> You cannot find out all about
> In his "native town." [153]

Death is "the Tomb, / Who tells no secret" (408). Its manner is very obscure: the "Agile Kernel" of life goes out without showing any sign of "Contusion," and what remains is only death's own "Asterisk" (1135). Even when we think that the dead go to "places perfecter," any true knowledge about the realm of death remains "Beyond our faint Conjecture – / Our dizzy Estimate" (499). Like the moon in "I watched the Moon around the House" (629), death is the enigma of life, which has "finer Gravitations – / Than bind Philosopher." The basic problem is the lack of human grasp of death's mystery: "Life – is what we make it – / Death – We do not know" (698). Human knowledge fails before the riddle of death:

> How the Waters closed above Him
> We shall never know –
> How He stretched His Anguish to us
> That – is covered too – [923]

No one has ever returned from the abode of death to tell us his or her experience of it: "None who saw it ever told it" (1110). We can only surmise with a big perhaps: "Went to Heaven perhaps at Death / And perhaps he did'nt" (1201).

The alarming strangeness of frost can be felt in the death of
flowers, but it is beyond analysis: a "Labor vaster than myself / I find it to infer" (1202). We can never guess the secret
of the "gallant sea"; we can only discover that the little boat is
lost (107). In death, adieu is written large on our faces, but

> Adieu for whence
> The sage cannot conjecture
> The bravest die
> As ignorant of their resumption
> As you or I –   [1497]

We can only slowly ford the mystery which the dead have
leaped across (1564). But we can never fully understand the
mystery as we do our conscious experiences. The realm of the
dead is always

> Further than Guess can gallop
> Further than Riddle ride –
> Oh for a Disc to the Distance
> Between Ourselves and the Dead!   [949]

The contrast between life's closeness and death's remoteness is
brought out in the following verses:

> To-day or this noon
> She dwelt so close
> I almost touched her
> To-night she lies
> Past neighborhood
> And bough and steeple
> Now past surmise   [1702]

Death is a subtle, sublime theme which cannot be explored
through conjecture. As the dead can never become alive, or as
the sound of drums can never reach the dead ears in the
tomb, man's attempt to grapple with the secret of the grave,
the "Grate inviolate" (1385) is an exercise in futility:

> Some we see no more, Tenements of Wonder
> Occupy to us though perhaps to them

Simpler are the Days than the Supposition
Their removing Manners
Leave us to presume

That oblique Belief which we call Conjecture
Grapples with a Theme stubborn as Sublime
Able as the Dust to equip it's feature
Adequate as Drums
To enlist the Tomb.   [1221]

What happens after death is certainly beyond human grasp
and knowledge, but death's obscurity should not deter us
from talking about it. Even when our talk and conjectures are
doomed to failure, the failure is human; it is ours, as death is
ours. We cannot leave death out of the discourse of life.[4] We
may regard it as a witchcraft (1708), or call it by the name of
"esoteric belt" (1717), but we must continue our exploration
and dialogue about it. Dickinson considers death a foe whom
she has never seen, but she does not wish to be forgotten by it
(1549). She draws portentous inference from its secrecy, as
she does from the leaves which "like Women, inter-
change / Sagacious Confidence" (987). She likes it better than
suspense, although sometimes "Suspense is neighborly"
(1285):

Fraud of Distance – Fraud of Danger,
Fraud of Death – to bear –
It is Bounty – to Suspense's
Vague Calamity –   [971]

However, these postures do not minimize her sense of awe
and tragedy at the spectacle of human death, which is symbolized for her in the setting sun (231). An acute sense of the
human predicament dawns upon her mind when she visualizes the sun having gone to the west:

But when the Earth began to jar
And Houses vanished with a roar
And Human Nature hid
We comprehended by the Awe

> As those that Dissolution saw
> The Poppy in the Cloud   [1419]

An equally intense and painful awareness of life's triviality
overwhelms her when she sees the dew at the point of vanishing:

> A Dew sufficed itself –
> And satisfied a Leaf
> And felt "how vast a destiny" –
> "How trivial is Life!"
>
> The Sun went out to work –
> The Day went out to play
> And not again that Dew be seen
> By Physiognomy
>
> Whether by Day Abducted
> Or emptied by the Sun
> Into the Sea in passing
> Eternally unknown
>
> Attested to this Day
> That awful Tragedy
> By Transport's instability
> And Doom's celerity.   [1437]

The tragedy abides, though it remains unknown whether the
dew is taken away by the playful day or emptied by the sun
into the sea in passing. At any rate, it is noteworthy that the
dew has the intimation of a vast destiny even in such a brief
course of life. Paradoxically, the sense of the vastness of destiny grows from the realization that life is so trifling and short.
Dickinson is deeply concerned with this life and its gifts. Death
too may have its own gifts, but

> With Gifts of Life
> How Death's Gifts may compare –
> We know not –
> For the Rates – lie Here –   [382]

Our ignorance of death's paradise or hell remains pervasive, and we cannot do anything to mitigate the darkness. Dickinson is quite aware of the limits of the human condition, but when she loses to death her "priceless Hay," symbolic of love that does not fade, or a fruitful life that one values above all other gifts, she dares

> Whether a Thief did it –
> Whether it was the wind –
> Whether Deity's guiltless –
> My business is, to find! [178]

While death continues its paradoxical dance all around her, Dickinson persists in her search into this baffling phenomenon. Death comes and goes simultaneously. It comes like "A Visitor in Marl / Who influences Flowers – / Till they are orderly as Busts," and who caresses them in the night

> But whom his fingers touched –
> And where his feet have run –
> And whatsoever Mouth he kissed –
> Is as it had not been – [391]

Death's sway is so strong and overpowering that whatever comes under its spell drops like flakes or "Like Petals from a Rose – / When suddenly across the June / A Wind with fingers – goes" (409). Describing the death-dance, Dickinson further notes:

> They perished in the Seamless Grass –
> No eye could find the place –
> But God can summon every face
> On his Repealless – List. [409]

Only God knows the secret of the seamless grass. The repealless list indicates the absolute power of the death-God who is the supreme destroyer. Curiously enough, the images of rose, June, and grass, symbolizing life and fertility, are evenly balanced by images signifying death and destruction. The life-death relationship is felt in the sense that death depends upon life for its food. The life-death continuity is, however, not even vaguely suggested here. The whole scene dramatizes merely "Mortality's old Custom" in which everything appears "Just locking up – to Die" (479). Nothing stirs in the "Forest of the Dead" (615). Death is motionlessness personified. It is absolutely changeless:

> All but Death, can be Adjusted –
> Dynasties repaired –
> Systems – settled in their Sockets –
> Citadels – dissolved –
>
> Wastes of Lives – resown with Colors
> By Succeeding Springs –
> Death – unto itself – Exception –
> Is exempt from Change –   [749]

Dickinson finds herself utterly helpless in the presence of death. In this posture, she feels that the lifeless old dynasties can be renovated with life. The systems or traditions which have outlived their use, and the citadels of belief and power, can be dissolved in order to be created anew. Even the wastes of lives can be replanted and revitalized with colors from new springs. But the heart of death cannot be changed because it is "exempt from Change." In other words, all the external forces of man will fail to implement a change in the structure of death. Death asserts itself, for no power can punish it:

> The Frost himself so comely
> Dishevels every prime
> Asserting from his Prism
> That none can punish him   [1236]

Poetizing her experience, Dickinson finds the metaphor of the prism useful in communicating the symbolic relations and interpenetrations of the themes of love, death, and self. The metaphor connotes here death's constant movement. However, in the present context, Dickinson seems to be emphasiz-

ing death's sweeping power over man, as well as man's mortal
fear and trembling in the face of death's disheveling energy.
Dickinson also finds death prompter than love: prompter, because love is hard to come by, whereas death always hovers
over man. Death can cut short man's search for love. In keeping the date, death overtakes every other thing toward which
man moves:

> It came at last but prompter Death
> Had occupied the House –
> His pallid Furniture arranged
> And his metallic Peace –
>
> Oh faithful Frost that kept the Date
> Had Love as punctual been
> Delight had aggrandized the Gate
> And blocked the coming in. [1230]

Once death has arrived and settled in the house of man, love
cannot disturb its "metallic Peace." In the presence of death,
mortal man has no need of love. But if love comes to man
before the frost touches him, he can find some assistance from
love in blocking the way of death, or in stopping death from
coming in. Dialectically speaking, love can help man transcend
death. But, when death becomes a reality, man's yearning for
love is merely a source of anguish. Man cannot win over
death's flight. In the presence of death, man faces only defeat,
agony, and shock:

> I meant to find Her when I came –
> Death – had the same design –
> But the Success – was His – it seems –
> And the Surrender – Mine –
>
> I meant to tell Her how I longed
> For just this single time –
> But Death had told Her so the first –
> And she had past, with Him –
>
> To wander – now – is my Repose –
> To rest – To rest would be

A privilege of Hurricane
To Memory – and Me.   [718]

Death is the great devourer-wooer in this poem. Death seems
to have destroyed and ravished the beloved before the lover
could reach out for her. Death wins, the lover loses. The lover
has not been able to express his longing to see the beloved
even for "just this single time." And now the lover's fate is to
wander, and to make wandering his repose. The only rest that
he can ever hope to know now is the rest that comes as a "privilege" of the violent storm within, meaning that the rest is possible if the hurricane subsides. But the inner storm will only
subside when everything else subsides: "Memory – and Me."
The lover, then, is condemned by death to wander unto
death. When the inner fury becomes a permanent part of life,
and when there is no respite from wandering, death seems to
be the only possibility for release from the fret and fever of
existence. Paradoxically, death becomes our only hope, the
only thing that can free us from the existential pathos. The
"Alabaster Chambers" seem safe, and death provides a
"Rafter of Satin" (216). The graves look like "Sweet – safe –
Houses – / Glad – gay – Houses" (457). We tend to think:

To die – takes just a little while –
They say it does'nt hurt –
It's only fainter – by degrees –
And then – it's out of sight –   [255]

Considering death as a source of release from existential suffering, Dickinson writes:

'Tis not that Dying hurts us so –
'Tis Living – hurts us more –
But Dying – is a different way –
A Kind behind the Door –   [335]

In this mood, living seems to constitute more hurt than dying.
Dickinson finds death a kind being. She feels that when people die

> The Earth lays back these tired lives
> In her mysterious Drawers –
> Too tenderly, that any doubt
> An ultimate Repose – [423]

The dead are beyond human strife. They are carefree; they have no concern for day, summer, or winter (592). They are above this our baffling earth where many things are fruitless, and for them "there is no Gratitude / Like the Grace – of Death" (614). The best men always die of the "Sickness of this World" (1044). The pain of existence can be relieved only by death:

> Pain has but one Acquaintance
> And that is Death –
> Each one unto the other
> Society enough. [1049]

The human heart seeks "Excuse from Pain / And then – those little Anodynes / That deaden suffering" (536). Sometimes, suicide seems to be the only solution for man's agonized self, though legally he "cannot even die" (1692). He gropes a little to see if God is watching, but eventually caresses "a Trigger absently" and wanders out of life (1062). In death alone can the bleating of the tired flocks cease to repeat and in death alone can their wandering be over. They can thus sing:

> Thine is the stillest night
> Thine the securest Fold
> Too near Thou art for seeking Thee
> Too tender, to be told. [1065]

Reviewing her slightest position "in the House," Dickinson writes: "I had often thought / How noteless – I could die" (486). On another occasion, she says: "On such a night / How proud to shut the eye!" (120). But, in spite of the mood in which one seeks death as a form of liberation from the drudgery and morass of existence, the act of dying or the state of being-in-death constitutes man's greatest anxiety and puzzle-

ment. The anxiety about death is paradoxical because it lasts
while one lives. The creative man learns to live with this anxiety and to continue his dialogue with death. Dickinson moves
from one angle of the problem to the other, and goes back
and forth, in a quick succession. If she considers death as "A
Kind behind the Door" (335), she also regards death as incon-
siderate, even callous: it is the "White Exploit" which "annuls
the power / Once to communicate" (922). It does not grieve
for anyone. It has no sentiment for the dying or for the one
who is groping deliriously for light:

> Ah, Brig – Good Night
> To Crew and You –
> The Ocean's Heart too smooth – too Blue –
> To break for You –   [723]

Death bequeaths man "to the night / Extinct by every hum"
(1724). Death is a stupendous tomb which proclaims how dead
we are, and in its closed room

> Not any sunny tone
> From any fervent zone
> Find entrance there   [1674]

Dickinson feels the strangulation and suffocation of death,
and it compels her to raise one of the most piercing cries
against its ruthlessness:

> The Frost of Death was on the Pane –
> "Secure your Flower" said he.
> Like Sailors fighting with a Leak
> We fought Mortality.
>
> Our passive Flower we held to Sea –
> To Mountain – To the Sun –
> Yet even on his Scarlet shelf
> To crawl the Frost begun –
>
> We pried him back
> Ourselves we wedged
> Himself and her between,

Yet easy as the narrow Snake
He forked his way along

Till all her helpless beauty bent
And then our wrath begun –
We hunted him to his Ravine
We chased him to his Den –

We hated Death and hated Life
And nowhere was to go –
Than Sea and continent there is
A larger – it is Woe –   [1136]

The poem epitomizes man's vain struggle with death. In telling man that he should secure his flower, death plays a cruel joke on him, because death knows that man cannot eventually escape the limits of mortality. The flower of life cannot elude the freezing hands of the frost of death. The sea, the mountain, the sun, and even man's own "Scarlet shelf," which symbolizes the height of intensity and passion, cannot save him from the frost which forks its way along like "the narrow Snake," which is a symbolic instrument of man's fall from life into death. Man's wrath against death is impotent, and his search and chasing are futile. Caught up in the net of crippling inability to challenge death, man simply hates death and hates life. He has nowhere to go, except that he must compromise himself with the continent of woe, which is larger than the sea and the earth. The pattern of imagery throughout is very subtle. The images of life and death are perfectly balanced, indicating on the one hand a constant struggle between life and death, and on the other, a sort of relationship between them. But the final tone is that of anguish and woe. There is no sense of relief here; there is only the agony and pathos of dying:

Two swimmers wrestled on the spar –
Until the morning sun –
When One – turned smiling to the land –
Oh God! the Other One!

> The stray ships – passing –
> Spied a face –
> Upon the waters borne –
> With eyes in death – still begging raised –
> And hands – beseeching – thrown!   [201]

This poem records a conscious wrestling and struggle of the two swimmers with the night of death on the sea. One swimmer survives the onslaught of the wave of death, the other succumbs to it. The one turns smiling to the shore, the other floats upon the waters with eyes in death. The whole scene depicting the still-begging eyes of the dead, carrying in them the desire to live, and the beseeching hands as if waiting to be rescued is soul-stirring. The smile of the living seems to fade before the begging eyes of the dead. The scene creates in the reader a sense of pathos which is identical with the despair of living through the experience contained in these verses:

> No lodging can be had
> For the delights
> That come to earth to stay,
> But no apartment find
> And ride away.   [1186]

The sense of futility at the spectacle of death, at man's vain attempts to survive in the heart of death, is sharply felt in these verses:

> Drowning is not so pitiful
> As the attempt to rise.
> Three times, 'tis said, a sinking man
> Comes up to face the skies,
> And then declines forever
> To that abhorred abode,
> Where hope and he part company –
> For he is grasped of God.
> The Maker's cordial visage,
> However good to see,
> Is shunned, we must admit it,
> Like an adversity.   [1718]

Death is the abhorred abode where no one wants to go; even a beggar would not accept it "Had he the power to spurn" (1307). The relationship between God the maker and death the destroyer is obvious here. But when we find the maker's cordial visage associated with death's indifference, we shun it "Like an adversity." The death-god grasps man and conceals him forever. The human consciousness refuses to accept such a god and defies him with all the strength that it is capable of. Dickinson experiences the sensation of dying with a sense of consternation:

> Consulting summer's clock,
> But half the hours remain.
> I ascertain it with a shock –
> I shall not look again. [1715]

She loves the summer of life, and considers that it is an affront to human dignity to concede the presence of the autumn and "of Life's Declivity" (1346). But she is painfully conscious of death's dominance over life when she writes to Mrs. Henry Hills: "The only Balmless Wound is the departed Human Life we had learned to need. For that, even Immortality is a slow solace" (L597). She evinces mental agitation and a sense of weariness over man's mortality when she says: "That *Bareheaded life* – under the grass – worries one like a Wasp" (L220). In sheer anguish and anger, she portrays the death of a bird:

> His Bill is clasped – his Eye forsook –
> His Feathers wilted low –
> The Claws that clung, like lifeless Gloves
> Indifferent hanging now –
> The Joy that in his happy Throat
> Was waiting to be poured
> Gored through and through with Death, to be
> Assassin of a Bird
> Resembles to my outraged mind
> The firing in Heaven,

On Angels – squandering for you
Their Miracles of Tune –   [1102]

The bird's organs of perception and communication are paralyzed and broken by death. The source of its flight is withered.
The claws that clung to existence are lifeless now. The happy
melody that was waiting to be poured from its throat is throt-
tled and clotted. The bird in the poem can also be viewed as
the persona of the poet. Dickinson seems to imagine her own
eventual mutilation at the assassinating hands of death. Her
outraged mind finds a resemblance between death's cruelty
and the "firing in Heaven, / On Angels." The angels, in the
context of this poem, put up with the wrath of God who con-
dones the firing, and still keep on squandering for God "Their
Miracles of Tune." In any case, the angels do not get upset
about the conduct of God, as Dickinson is troubled by the cold
manner of death. The angels in the poem seem to know the
relationship between life and death, love and wrath. In a symbolic sense, this relationship is implied in the image of fire
which consumes and re-creates. But Dickinson, the supposed
speaker of the poem, is still bewildered at the coldness of
death whom she calls assassin. Perhaps both the angelic peace
and the existential agony are necessary for the apprehension
of the reality of death. Paradoxically, the experience of being
outraged at the spectacle of destruction is an essential qualifi-
cation for comprehending what is on the other side of death.
The greatest peace becomes possible only through the greatest
crisis.

For Dickinson, the way of peace lies through the way of
storm. Her buffeting by the tempest of death continues in
many contradictory ways. In terms of poetry, which Stéphane
Mallarmé describes as "the language of a state of crisis," [5]
Dickinson establishes many perspectives in order to delineate
the nature of death. She considers death as a source of human
passion for life. She also visualizes death as a source of dignity
even for the meek and poor of this world: "One dignity delays

for all" (98). Death confers equal rank upon the dead. Even "a powdered Footman" can touch the majesty of death and be dressed like a democrat in "Everlasting Robes" (171):

> Death is the Common Right
> Of Toads and Men –
> Of Earl and Midge
> The privilege –   [583]

In death's graveyard, the poet says, "all mankind deliver here / From whatsoever sea" (1443). Death does not make distinctions between human beings:

> As in sleep – All Hue forgotten –
> Tenets – put behind –
> Death's large – Democratic fingers
> Rub away the Brand –   [970]

Death is the leisure which "equal lulls / The Beggar and his Queen" (1256). "Death warrants are supposed to be / An enginery of equity" (1375). Death is hospitable and friendly toward all:

> No Life can pompless pass away –
> The lowliest career
> To the same Pageant wends its way
> As that exalted here –
>
> How cordial is the mystery!
> The hospitable Pall
> A "this way" beckons spaciously –
> A Miracle for all!   [1626]

But, however cordial the mystery of death may be, it does not alleviate the pain one experiences at the thought of personal death. The idea of death as a universal phenomenon cannot camouflage the bitter reality of one's own death. As Frederick Hoffman puts it, "one's death is a uniquely individual experience. No one can die my death nor can I die anyone else's." [6] Dickinson voices a personal sense of despair at the very thought of death:

I can't stay any longer in a world of death. Austin is ill of fever.
I buried my garden last week – our man, Dick, lost a little girl
through the scarlet fever. I thought perhaps that *you* were dead,
and not knowing the sexton's address, interrogate the daisies.
. . . Ah! democratic Death! . . . Say, is he everywhere? Where
shall I hide my things? Who is alive? The woods are dead. [L195]

Dickinson's mental engrossment in the subject of death does
not indicate any morbid taste for the macabre. By being intensely aware of death, she learns to be intensely aware of life's
possibilities. To her, the concern with death means a search
for meaning, to use Anderson's phrase.[7] She writes to Mrs.
Holland: "I suppose there are depths in every Consciousness,
from which we cannot rescue ourselves – to which none can go
with us – which represent to us Mortally – the Adventure of
Death" (L555). Dickinson's descriptions of the dead and the
dying are metaphorical explorations into "the first form of
Life" (PF70). Even when the descriptions are external or
about other deaths, they are internalized, because death is
meaningful only when it takes place within the inner room
(45) of one's own heart. Describing the features of the dying,
Dickinson captures the physical and emotional response to the
presence of death in these lines:

> A throe upon the features –
> A hurry in the breath –
> An extasy of parting
> Denominated "Death" –   [71]

In "How many times these low feet staggered" (187), the sensation of being dead flows through the images of "soldered
mouth," "awful rivet," "hasps of steel," "cool forehead," "list-
less hair," and "adamantine fingers." Death, says Dickinson,
cannot be feigned:

> The Eyes glaze once – and that is Death –
> Impossible to feign
> The Beads upon the Forehead
> By homely Anguish strung.   [241]

Describing the death of a friend or the lover, Dickinson records:

> 'Twas like a Maelstrom, with a notch,
> That nearer, every Day,
> Kept narrowing it's boiling Wheel
> Until the Agony
>
> Toyed coolly with the final inch
> Of your delirious Hem –
> And you dropt, lost,
> When something broke –
> And let you from a Dream –   [414]

Death envelops man in its own whirlpool. It presses upon him its wheel of fire until his sense of agony merges playfully with "the final inch" of his delirious, hesitating mind. Man drops out of existence as suddenly as one drops out of a dream. The images of the notch and the final inch indicate that death is the boundary of human consciousness. The symbolism of water and fire, contained in the images of maelstrom and boiling wheel, suggests the extreme nature of the experience of death, as well as the process of continuation. Both water and fire are symbolic of destruction and re-creation. Wheel is symbolic of movement and continuity. "And let you from a Dream" seems to imply that existence is a dream, but one which is necessary because without this the "final inch" experience is not possible.[8]

Death is "A Chill – like frost upon a Glass – / Till all the scene – be gone" (519). In "A Dying Tiger – moaned for Drink," Dickinson observes:

> His Mighty Balls – in death were thick –
> But searching – I could see
> A Vision on the Retina
> Of Water – and of me –   [566]

Dying is "From Blank to Blank– / A Threadless Way" (761). In its process, death is a murder by degrees:

> The Cat reprieves the Mouse
> She eases from her teeth
> Just long enough for Hope to teaze –
> Then mashes it to death –   [762]

In the crisis of the moment of death, a soul escapes the house
unseen (948). "Death leaves Us homesick, who behind, / Except that it is gone / Are ignorant of it's Concern" (935). In a
comparatively less agitated and mute tone, Dickinson describes one death scene in these words:

> We waited while She passed –
> It was a narrow time –
> Too jostled were Our Souls to speak
> At length the notice came.
>
> She mentioned, and forgot –
> Then lightly as a Reed
> Bent to the Water, struggled scarce –
> Consented, and was dead –
>
> And We – We placed the Hair –
> And drew the Head erect –
> And then an awful leisure was
> Belief to regulate –   [1100]

Our emotional state while we attend to the dying person is
delineated with deep psychological insight. The fear of personal death disturbs us greatly when we watch someone dying.
The moment of this experience is justly characterized as "a
narrow time," a time of inner affliction. Our souls are too
jostled to speak, for the real struggle is going on within us.
The dying person, however, indicates the moment of death by
some bodily gesture and then bends like a reed to the water
without any outward sign of resistance. We perform the ri-
tualistic acts of placing the dead person in a proper physical
posture. But after this is done we find that our free time is
awful, since it is extremely difficult to regulate our belief
about our own existence. In such tense moments, the only
comfort in the room can be the ticking of the "the living

Clock" (1703). The "belief" could also mean to refer to the orthodox notion of peaceful death as contrasted with the turmoil we experience within ourselves at someone else's death. However contented the dying person may look, it is hard to alleviate our fears to the contrary when we contemplate our own death. In nature, death seems to hang "his Granite Hat / Upon a nail of Plush" (1140). Death is indeed a hard rock pressed against our soft lives. In death, we are like flowers at fall of frost (1667). However, this does not deter Dickinson from asking more about death and the dying:

> To know just how He suffered – would be dear –
> To know if any Human eyes were near
> To whom He could entrust His wavering gaze –
> Until it settled broad – on Paradise –   [622]

She continues with her long list of questions which concludes: "Was He afraid – or tranquil – / Might He know / How Conscious Consciousness – could grow." She is surmising here that one attains a high level of consciousness in the moment of death. This notion is linked with the problem of the self or being, to which I shall return later in this study. Dickinson also feels jealous of the dead, because a dead person symbolizes a rare detachment from the ways of the world:

> So proud she was to die
> It made us all ashamed
> That what we cherished, so unknown
> To her desire seemed –
> So satisfied to go
> Where none of us should be
> Immediately – that Anguish stooped
> Almost to Jealousy –   [1272]

Dickinson contemplates with rare adroitness the moment of her own death, and in her imaginative enactment of this moment, she personalizes death in the most daring and self-destroying terms. This is what eventually provides her with the sense of meaning in life—life which is in and toward death. "I felt a Funeral, in my Brain" (280) may be cited as an example of the process in which Dickinson makes concrete the spiritual experience of death. She imagines herself to be in her coffin, lying numb. The coffins expands into an infinity of space where bells are ringing all over:

> As all the Heavens were a Bell,
> And Being, but an Ear,
> And I, and Silence, some strange Race
> Wrecked, solitary, here –
>
> And then a Plank in Reason, broke,
> And I dropped down, and down –
> And hit a World, at every plunge,
> And Finished knowing – then –   [280]

In this death vision, all the heavens are a bell, and the ear which is attuned to the music of the spheres represents the being of the persona whose relationship with the heavens, like the ear-music relationship, is that of perfect silence. The persona and silence are one, as death and the "I" are one in the solitude of the coffin: a perfect situation for the realization of relationship between "I" and silence. This relationship causes the destruction of the "strange Race," perhaps a race of life against death. After long or short alienation, as the case may be, life meets with death. Once this union takes place, a plank in reason breaks. The whole situation parodies the realm of human knowledge rooted in reason. In this relationship, the human consciousness dives down, and down, and at every plunge discovers a new world. The scene epitomizes a primordial journey into death, which when completed leaves nothing else for knowing. Imaginative and spiritual as this downward plunge is, it is not tantamount to escape from the world of human reality which the truly creative person accepts as necessary to his vision. The poet sees everything happening in the now and here of time and space. The downward plunge, then, constitutes the upward lift, or as Heraclitus puts it: "The way up and the way down are one and the same." [9] For Dickinson, the plunge represents an onward journey, just as the upward rise does, though this is not explicit in the poem under discussion.

The scene of death, with people rustling in and out, the milliner to prepare the mourning veils, the undertaker taking the measure of the house, and the coaches getting ready to go, can mean to Dickinson no more than the abrupt mechanical movements, the "Appalling Trade," and the "Dark Parade" (389). She can even sarcastically remark that

> The Bustle in a House
> The Morning after Death
> Is solemnest of industries
> Enacted upon Earth –   [1078]

But the spiritual experience of death itself, and not the shallow concern of the onlookers, is a grievously serious business with her:

> There is a Languor of the Life
> More imminent than Pain –
> 'Tis Pain's Successor – When the Soul
> Has suffered all it can –
>
> A Drowsiness – diffuses –
> A Dimness like a Fog
> Envelopes Consciousness –
> As Mists – obliterate a Crag.   [396]

Death causes a special type of inertia or loss of vitality. It is more dangerous than pain. It is a condition in which the soul has suffered all it can. It is a drowsiness which numbs consciousness, "As Mists – obliterate a Crag." In this poem, the consciousness does not grow conscious (622); even the soul suffers. But the languor is of the life, meaning that the entire experience of death is integral to life. The images of fog and mists indicate both stasis and movement. The crag is obliterated in the sense in which the consciousness is diffused. However, the light concealed in dimness does not shine here very clearly. In "A Clock stopped," Dickinson handles the theme somewhat differently:

> An awe came on the Trinket!
> The Figures hunched, with pain –
> Then quivered out of Decimals –
> Into Degreeless Noon –   [287]

The experience of dying is awesome, as shown here on the face of the trinket, symbolizing man's trifling existence. The anguish of death is presented through the figures hunching with pain. As the trinket refers to man's temporal clock-existence, the figures refer to the numerical symbols of hours in man's transient show on earth. But then, dying means quivering "out of Decimals," out of the narrow arithmetic of life, into "Degreeless Noon," the noon in which clock-time does not exist.[10] But again the vision of degreeless noon is missing from "I heard a Fly buzz – when I died":

> With Blue – uncertain stumbling Buzz –
> Between the light – and me –
> And then the Windows failed – and then
> I could not see to see –   [465]

Death seems to mean here the total loss of perception: the windows fail and the persona cannot see to see. The last conscious link with reality is established through the buzz of the fly. The humming of the fly or the song of death unsettles the relationship between the dying person and the light. In death, then, the dying person does not experience anything at all concerning life after death. The blue, which is Dickinson's symbol for eternity, becomes here the symbol of complete extinction. "Death's tremendous nearness" is felt by her as "An Omen in the Bone" (532). In spite of the several contradictory sensations of life and death, she feels as if her "life were shaven, / And fitted to a frame" (510). The choice of life (468) seems to elude her at every step. Her existence looks like a living corpse: " 'Twas just this time, last year, I died" (445). But

it is through death she realizes that "in going is a Dram
/ Staying cannot confer":

> I'd rather recollect a setting
> Than own a rising sun
> Though one is beautiful forgetting –
> And true the other one.   [1349]

In "I've dropped my Brain – My Soul is numb" (1046), Dickinson demonstrates that death cannot exhaust the possibilities of
being; rather, it is in itself one of the possibilities of being.
Even when she is palsied and her whole body is caught in a
marble mold by witchcraft or death, the "Instincts for Dance"
and an "Aptitude for Bird" remain intact. Even when her
vitality is carved and cool, she feels there is still a chance to
strain:

> To Being, somewhere – Motion – Breath –
> Though Centuries beyond,
> And every limit a Decade –
> I'll shiver, satisfied   [1046]

In Dickinson's imagination, the question of death is tied
with the ultimate meaning of the whole of existence. She
craves the roses that never fade (L86), but knows that death
precedes and follows her wherever she goes (784). Realizing
that the enigma of death can be solved only by spiritually
going through it, Dickinson experiences death in numerous
ways. In one of her poetic postures, she regards death as an
instrument of heightened awareness, passion, and power. The
constant presence of death in life increases her intensity for
living. In her imagination "A *Wounded* Deer – leaps highest,"
which is "but the Extasy of *death*" (165). Without death, life
would lose its charm:

> Uncertain lease – developes lustre
> On Time
> Uncertain Grasp, appreciation
> Of Sum –

> The shorter Fate – is oftener the chiefest
> Because
> Inheritors upon a tenure
> Prize –   [857]

Death's bold exhibition reveals to us our true nature, "Preciser what we are," and enables us to infer the "Eternal function" of the whole creation (856). "Crisis is a Hair / Toward which forces creep," says Dickinson (889). Death indicates the "Maturity of Fate," whether it comes early or late (990). Death makes nature look different to us by throwing a "great light upon our Minds" (1100). Dickinson declares:

> To disappear enhances –
> The Man that runs away
> Is tinctured for an instant
> With Immortality   [1209]

By dying, we make a "light escape / Into the Beautiful" (1540). The fact that from death we "will never come again / Is what makes life so sweet" (1741). Death is the "Human Nature's West" in which softly sinks the "trembling sun" (1478). To those who are attuned to death, "Winter is good – his Hoar Delights" (1316). Death also increases our power to sacrifice the world outside us, though for that purpose we must first learn to annihilate our own narrow self:

> When One has given up One's life
> The parting with the rest
> Feels easy, as when Day lets go
> Entirely the West
>
> The Peaks, that lingered last
> Remain in Her regret
> As scarcely as the Iodine
> Upon the Cataract.   [853]

By contemplating death as an integral part of life, one gains in self-perception and learns the art of living. To experience death within our own selves in each moment of life is to arrive at "life's meaning in all its depth," to use Nicolai Berdyaev's expression.[11] Emily Dickinson is not afraid of the worst: "At least, to know the worst, is sweet," she says (172):

> Tell that the Worst, is easy in a Moment –
> Dread, but the Whizzing, before the Ball –
> When the Ball enters, enters Silence –
> Dying – annuls the power to kill. [358]

Death heightens our awareness of silence and freedom. Once we acquire this inner silence, death becomes ineffective in its power to kill. Dickinson tells us that even the flowers pass "Through the Dark Sod – as Education," and feel no fear or trepidation (392). She insists that death should be our immediate concern: "Too little way the House must lie / From every Human Heart" (911). In the midsummer of mind, death is like "The Summer closed upon itself / In Consummated Bloom" (962). Dickinson feels that death reveals the dimensions of life's adventure, as "The Hills in Purple syllables / The Day's Adventures tell" (1016). She wins the "privilege of dying" through "transports of Patience" (1153). Death confers upon man the secret of the womb; through death one reaches the origin of one's consciousness:

> The Doom to be adored –
> The Affluence conferred –
> Unknown as to an Ecstasy
> The Embryo endowed – [1386]

For Dickinson, death also symbolizes the moment in which she can find the roots of her vocation, meaning that death is a necessary ingredient in the integer of her being:

> Why Birds, a Summer morning
> Before the Quick of Day
> Should stab my ravished spirit
> With Dirks of Melody
> Is part of an inquiry
> That will receive reply

> When Flesh and Spirit sunder
> In Death's Immediately –   [1420]

The time of action is when the day begins, meaning the dawn
of creation. It is the time when her spirit is ravished, meaning
that it is fully prepared for the process of reception which
leads to creation. But why the birds stab her with dirks of melody at such a time will be answered "When Flesh and Spirit
sunder / In Death's Immediately." Death seems to be the teller
of the secret of her poetic creation which for the poet is syn-
onymous with creation itself. This constitutes for her "One Joy
of so much anguish" (1420). The terror of creation, which is
the terror of one's whole being, surpasses all fears of mortality.

Realizing life's eternal process, Dickinson suggests that "We
wear Mortality / As lightly as an Option Gown" and we take it
off when death or God intrudes upon the scene, in the same
manner that life does (1462). Creator, creation, and life are all
identical. Mortality is the condition through which we can apprehend these relations. But before we can arrive at this
awareness, we must first wear mortality as a garment, so that
we may be able to take if off without much dismay: "What if I
file this Mortal – off" (277). However, the conception of wearing mortality as optional attire is paradoxical, because

> We knew not that we were to live –
> Nor when – we are to die –
> Our ignorance – our cuirass is –   [1462]

In her death-vision, which is spiritually apprehended and
metaphorically rendered, Dickinson does not show any out-
right fear of death. She likes to think of it in terms of
sweetness and flow:

> Of Death I try to think like this –
> The Well in which they lay us
> Is but the Likeness of the Brook
> That menaced not to slay us,

> But to invite by that Dismay
> Which is the Zest of sweetness
> To the same Flower Hesperian,
> Decoying but to greet us –   [1558]

Death becomes here the well or the flowing brook which threatens but does not slay us. The dismay of dying is converted into the zest of sweetness. Death allures us in order to greet us. By one bold leap one can grasp the flower which is symbolic of creativity and growth. Hesperus, the western, evening star, represents light in darkness. The directive of the poem, then, is that death is the well into which we must plunge. It is the water with which we must flow. It is in this sense that death is the "Rendezvous of Light" (1564). Death comes and goes like the seasons: "In snow thou comest / Thou shalt go with the resuming ground," and "men anew embark to live / Upon the depth of thee" (1669). We should be as dauntless in the house of death as if it were our own (1752). Only then we can contemplate the journey with unpuzzled heart (43). "The seeds of smiles are planted – / Which blossom in the dark" (55). By venerating the simple days or the seasons which symbolize life and death, we can liberate ourselves from the "trifle / Termed *mortality*" (57). We should fight "like those Who've nought to lose" (759). With death's nearness, a further force of life develops from within (795). "Death is potential to that Man / Who dies" (548). Dickinson's poetry embodies death as an inner force. Death is at the heart of the poet: "Death is the Wealth / Of the Poorest Bird," and it is death which helps her to show the passion and life of her poetry— contained in the color symbolism of red, cochineal, and vermillion (1059). Dickinson finds in death the source of her true identity, and feels that if there were no death, human existence would be deprived of all meaning. By going through the spiritual experience of the continual process of creation and destruction, the poet achieves the ideal, and stands undefeated before death:

> "Surrender" – is a sort unknown –
> On this Superior soil –
> "Defeat", an Outgrown Anguish –
> Remembered, as the Mile   [325]

Dickinson believes that "Life is Miracle, and Death as harmless as a Bee, except to those who run" (L294). Describing a love scene between the bee and the rose, she writes: "Sweet is it as Life, with it's enhancing Shadow of Death" (L446 and 1339). In her letter to Mrs. Joseph A. Sweetser, Emily Dickinson expresses her thought about death in these words: "Death is perhaps an intimate friend, not an enemy. Beloved Shakespeare says, 'He that is robbed and smiles, steals something from the thief' " (L478).[12] Dickinson recommends smiling in the face of death. She meets death as one meets a lover or a friend or God: "The first We knew of Him was Death" (1006). Through the lover or the persona of death, she knows the secrets of the "Morning's Nest," and of the "Rope the Nights were put across" (446). "Death is the supple Suitor" who takes Dickinson in his coach to "Troth unknown" (1445). In one of her best death-love poems, Dickinson dramatizes the role of death as a kind, civil lover who takes her out for a carriage ride toward eternity:

> Because I could not stop for Death –
> He kindly stopped for me –
> The Carriage held but just Ourselves –
> And Immortality. . . .
>
> We paused before a House that seemed
> A Swelling of the Ground –
> The Roof was scarcely visible –
> The Cornice – in the Ground –
>
> Since then – 'tis Centuries – and yet
> Feels shorter than the Day
> I first surmised the Horses' Heads
> Were toward Eternity –   [712]

It is interesting to note that the experience of death and immortality is simultaneous in this journey. Immortality is not beyond death (a religious promise to be fulfilled after death), but an accompaniment of death. The carriage symbolizes onward movement and continuity. The element of time is superbly controlled in the poem. The movement seems to be both within and beyond time. It is within time as the lovers pause "before a House that seemed / A Swelling of the Ground." This house is the grave, a familiar sight. But it is beyond time in the sense that the "Horses' Heads / Were toward Eternity." Eternity, as embodied in Dickinson's poetry, however, is not an object to be realized beyond time. In being "toward Eternity," the lovers are still in the process and not at the end of their journey. Immortality which is realized as an integral part of life and death is also a process, because it is held in the carriage which is moving. Pause before the grave also indicates movement and not cessation: it is a pause and not a stoppage. Metaphorically speaking, the grave is the condition of immortality and not immortality itself. Thus Dickinson affirms life and its continuity, or to put it this way, life as continuity. Death is merely a pause.

Dickinson finds life and death as simultaneous realities: "How dumb the Dancer lies – / While Color's Revelations break – / And blaze – the Butterflies!" (496). Death confers a new perspective upon man in which he can listen to the "Dialogue between / The Spirit and the Dust" (976). "To die is not to go – / On Doom's consummate Chart" (1295), says Dickinson. "Existence has a stated width / Departed, or at Home" (1308). Life is like the "summer too indelible / Too obdurate for Snows" (1444). In life, "much can come / And much can go, / And yet abide the World!" (1593). Dickinson says:

> Advance is Life's condition
> The Grave but a Relay
> Supposed to be a terminus
> That makes it hated so –   [1652]

She proposes life-in-death and death-in-life in a highly paradoxical way:

> To die – without the Dying
> And live – without the Life
> This is the hardest Miracle
> Propounded to Belief.   [1017]

The suggestion here is, as it seems to me, that one can die
without really physically dying, meaning that one can experience death in the spiritual sense, and one can live without living in the ordinary sense. But, dying to the world and yet living in it "is the hardest Miracle" that challenges one's belief.

Emily Dickinson's death-vision embodies a world of creative
continuity. This dialectic can be shown through a detailed examination of several other symbolic structures. For this purpose, I shall first deal with some of those poems which contain
the sea as their central metaphor. As already pointed out, the
sea symbolizes simultaneous creation and dissolution. In the
symbolic context, the flow and flux of the sea constitute eternal process; in the creative vision, death does not imply the
end:

> Those not live yet
> Who doubt to live again –
> "Again" is of a twice
> But this – is one –
> The Ship beneath the Draw
> Aground – is he?
> Death – so – the Hyphen of the Sea –
> Deep is the Schedule
> Of the Disk to be –
> Costumeless Consciousness –
> That is he –   [1454]

Those who disbelieve the possibility of living "again" are not
even alive in the real sense. This "again" is not "of a twice," as
Dickinson puts it, but "is one." This is her metaphor for continuity and renewed life, which becomes concrete in the human
imagination. The imaginative awareness of life's continuity

places death in the right perspective and liberates one from the anxiety of dying. In this symbolic context, the ship of life is never really aground even when it is apparently beneath the drawbridge. Life's discontinuity or death is only "the Hyphen of the Sea." Sea serves here as the connecting link between man's mortality and eternal life in the now and here of existence, between life which is lived with all the fears of dying and the imaginative life which shatters these fears by illuminating the true nature and purpose of man's creation. The sea-ship relationship highlights the deep schedule or the ambivalent program of the "Disk to be." Death itself becomes involved in the process through which man comprehends his own *becoming*. By confronting death with creative imagination, which Dickinson calls "Costumeless Consciousness," one can achieve an intense awareness of life and a heightened sense of being. This intensity entitles one to live "again" in the Dickinsonian sense. Without the awareness of the deep plan of the sea, the little boat, which is a human body, seems to us to have been lost to the greedy wave of the "gallant sea" (107). By depicting such scenes or by calling the sea recall-less (1633), Dickinson shows us on the one hand the fearful reaction to death of ordinary human beings, and on the other, the fundamental ambiguity and paradox involved in man's creative effort to transcend the anxiety of his own death. This also points out that human consciousness must strive constantly and creatively in order to overcome the debilitating fear of dissolution and destruction. In the creative vision, the sea, which ordinarily devours, becomes the source of regeneration and rebirth. In "I started Early – Took my Dog" (520), the sea follows the persona of the poem as if he would eat her up, but finally "bowing – with a Mighty look" at her, the sea withdraws. In another poem "a shining Sea" becomes the end of the journey of two butterflies, and "never yet, in any Port – / Their coming, mentioned – be" (533). Both the situations are ambivalent. However, the sea brings a promise of life, as seen through the creative imagination:

A soft Sea washed around the House
A Sea of Summer Air
And rose and fell the magic Planks
That sailed without a care –
For Captain was the Butterfly
For Helmsman was the Bee
And an entire universe
For the delighted crew.   [1198]

When the ship of life is captained and steered by the butterfly
and the bee—Dickinson's metaphors for freedom and imagination as well as vigor and hard work—the sea does not pose
any threat. It becomes the soft sea washing around the house
of existence, and producing summer air, which is the breath
of life. In the creative imagination, life sails without a care,
and it is summer all over:

My Garden – like the Beach –
Denotes there be – a Sea –
That's Summer –
Such as These – the Pearls
She fetches – such as Me   [484]

The garden of Dickinson's poetry contains the sea within itself, and it is the source of pearls and summer to her. Summer
is her favorite metaphor for life, and pearls stand for everything that is precious; they symbolize the condition of the
human soul passing through water and fire at once. In and
through her imagination, Dickinson dares to travel "To Evening's Sea" by "routes of ecstasy" (1513). She plays with the
sea of death-and-life, but life remains her primary concern:

Three Times – the Billows threw me up –
Then caught me – like a Ball –
Then made Blue faces in my face –
And pushed away a sail

That crawled Leagues off – I liked to see –
For thinking – while I die –

> How pleasant to behold a Thing
> Where Human faces – be –
>
> The Waves grew sleepy – Breath – did not –
> The Winds – like Children – lulled –
> Then Sunrise kissed my Chrysalis –
> And I stood up – and lived –   [598]

The billows of the sea toss the persona up three times. The persona feels the impact of the enormous energy of the billows which push "away a sail." But the entire play of the billows seems to be a game of movement. The billows embody back-and-forth motion. Pushing away also implies going onward. While thinking that death is close at hand, the persona wishes to see the crawling sail in order to behold in it the human faces. In this life-death drama, the persona breathes and remains conscious of the human faces while the waves grow sleepy and the noisy sea-winds are lulled like children. The image of children affirms the playfulness of the whole act between the billows and the "I" of the poem. The night of play passes, and with the sunrise the persona comes back to a renewed life: "And I stood up – and lived." This is what I call the creative rebirth which one experiences after going through the stormy waves of the sea, or by confronting death face to face. In this symbolic vision, the image of sunrise is perfectly harmonized with the death-dance of the sea.

The symbolism of sunrise and sunset also provides the aesthetic basis for creative continuity. The sunset, which is symbolic of death, baffles Dickinson and challenges her poetic imagination as much as any other symbol of death. But she does not consider the sunset without referring to the sunrise, because sunset and sunrise represent to her two movements of a single dance. The movements are integral and simultaneous in the imagination, though sequentially they are set apart from each other. The landscape of death is ultimately merged with the landscape of life. Dickinson understands the creative function of death and expresses it in many ways: "There's that

long town of White – to cross – / Before the Blackbirds sing"
(221). To her, the sun is "the Juggler of Day" who leaps "like
Leopards to the Sky" and when the day is over lays "her
spotted Face to die" at the feet of the old horizon (228). The
sun in this case represents both creation and destruction. Life
must be understood in terms of both sunrise and sunset, because it is neither only sunrise nor only sunset. The recognition of this life-death dance is essential to the harmony of our
being. Sunset is the "Western Mystery" which closes upon us
night after night (266). But the "Day's superior close" (268)
does not imply any change or alteration; rather, it carries
within itself a revelation of continuity:

> An ignorance a Sunset
> Confer upon the Eye –
> Of Territory – Color –
> Circumference – Decay –
>
> It's Amber Revelation
> Exhilirate – Debase –
> Omnipotence' inspection
> Of Our inferior face –
>
> And when the solemn features
> Confirm – in Victory –
> We start – as if detected
> In Immortality –   [552]

The "ignorance" that an imaginative person experiences at
sunset is dialectical; it refers to a condition of mind that moves
one toward a supreme understanding of life's mystery. Hence
the exhilaration, and a feeling of debasement in the presence
of the infinite. The creative person earns the ethereal gain by
"measuring the Grave – / Then – measuring the Sun" (574).
Sun is the source of life's continual motion: " 'Tis His to stimu-
late the Earth – / And magnetize the Sea," and "To interrupt
His Yellow Plan / The Sun does not allow" (591). Sunset, then,
should be experienced with a sense of equanimity, as "the
Mountain to the Evening / Fit His Countenance – / Indicating,

by no Muscle – / The Experience" (667). At the end of "The Sun kept setting – setting – still," Dickinson writes: " 'Tis Dying – I am doing – but / I'm not afraid to know" (692). Dickinson's "Ancient fashioned Heart" moves "as do the Suns – / For merit of Return – / Or Birds – confirmed perpetual / By Alternating Zone" (973). She describes the sun as both the yellow man of the east and the purple man of the west, signifying that east and west, life and death are symbolized in the rotatory motion of the sun (1032). Like the sun, Dickinson is "A Candidate for Morning Chance / But dated with the Dead" (1194). She experiences death or the sunset with a sense of peace and a feeling of ecstasy:

> A Sloop of Amber slips away
> Upon an Ether Sea,
> And wrecks in Peace a Purple Tar,
> The Son of Ecstasy – [1622]

In another poem, Dickinson regards the sun simply as an instrument of the life-death process, which is controlled by the creator himself:

> Apparently with no surprise
> To any happy Flower
> The Frost beheads it at it's play –
> In accidental power –
> The blonde Assassin passes on –
> The Sun proceeds unmoved
> To measure off another Day
> For an Approving God. [1624]

But the process never ends. At sunset it seems as if life is gone westerly (950), but the sun daily "rises – passes – on our South / Inscribes a simple Noon – / Cajoles a Moment with the Spires / And infinite is gone" (1023).

Through the symbolism of sunrise and sunset Dickinson succeeds in defeating the curse of mortality. By capturing the experience of creation and dissolution in her poems, she proposes a metaphoric way of apprehending the mystery of creation and human destiny. In her finest poem on the sun, she dramatizes the simultaneity of her vision of life and death, and suggests the way in which we should go through the creative experience:

> I'll tell you how the Sun rose –
> A Ribbon at a time –
> The Steeples swam in Amethyst –
> The news, like Squirrels, ran –
> The Hills untied their Bonnets –
> The Bobolinks – begun –
> Then I said softly to myself –
> "That must have been the Sun"!
> But how he set – I know not –
> There seemed a purple stile –
> That little Yellow boys and girls
> Were climbing all the while –
> Till when they reached the other side,
> A Dominie in Gray –
> Put gently up the evening Bars –
> And led the flock away –   [318]

The sunrise and the sunset are instantaneously present in the poet's vision. They refer to the totality of experience in which the light and the dark exist simultaneously. The light and the dark symbolize life and death, movement and stasis. Every image contributes to the thematic pattern of the poem. In the early hour of the dawn, the whole world, with its spiry towers and lofty buildings, bathes and swims in amethyst, which represents a variety of colors, lights, and shades. The whole animal world which is represented here by the squirrels and bobolinks moves and sings, and by juxtaposition intensifies the area of human activity. The hills unveil themselves; all of external nature comes out of the garb of night and silence into the light of the day. In this moment of ceaseless music and motion, the poet speaks to herself softly: "That must have been the Sun!" The ambivalence of this soft utterance merges with the strangeness of the metaphoric scene depicting sunset or death. The purple and yellow gradually fade into gray. We die in the very act of living: the yellow boys and girls continue climbing the purple stile to cross the fence of life till they reach the other side. Climbing embodies an act of living. But since in this drama we are climbing over to death, we are living-in-death. When we reach the other side, the evening bars are put up gently by a dominie in gray; the moment of darkness or death does not cause any emotional upheaval. In this life-death process, we experience the twilight of the morning and the evening at once. We rise continuously like the sun, and continuously untie the bonnets of the night. All this happens on a spiritual level of apprehension. We experience within ourselves, and consummate through our being, many a death and many a birth. And this continuity is what the poem achieves for us in its sensuous and concrete form. Clark Griffith observes: "The poet's failure to say how the sun set reflects her failure to see beyond life: her confusion about an action in Nature registers her inability to fathom death or to justify it philosphically." [13] I think Griffith has missed the whole point. The ambiguity involved in the last eight lines beginning with "But how he set – I know not" is an integral part of the metaphoric design of the whole poem. The nature of the experience is such as cannot be known intellectually or rendered in the form of a direct statement. The inner apprehension cannot be communicated in scientific or precise terms. Hence the expression "There seemed a purple stile." Edward Rose has aptly remarked that "in reading the poem, we see what it is to *see*. By describing the sunrise and the sunset, the poet tells us what life and death are, tells us what there is to a *day*." [14] In her creative perception, Dickinson sees life and death as a unity. The sunset is followed by the sunrise: life follows death, death follows life:

> The Sun went down – no Man looked on –
> The Earth and I, alone,
> Were present at the Majesty –
> He triumphed, and went on –

> The Sun went up – no Man looked on –
> The Earth and I and One
> A nameless Bird – a Stranger
> Were Witness for the Crown –   [1079]

"He triumphed, and went on" shows the sun's victory over the realm of darkness and death, though it must go down to death in order to triumph over it. It also indicates that by going down, the sun can move *on*. This forward movement brings the sun *up*. In this sense, "the sun went down" and "the sun went up" are integral. The sun's movement, then, serves as a paradigm of our own symbolic plunge into and emergence from death. Jung refers to this plunge in these words:

> Out of the unfolding embrace, the enveloping womb of the sea, the sun tears itself free and rises victoriously, and then, leaving the heights of noonday and all its glorious works behind it, sinks back into the maternal sea, into the night which hides all and gives new birth to all.[15]

It is in this sense that Dickinson's suns go down, and the darkness is always about to pass (764). The darkness moves onward and never stops. It is like "Death's Experiment – / Reversed – in Victory" (550), and we hear "The Proclamation of the Suns / That sepulture is o'er" (1519).

Dickinson continues to poetize the never-ending dance of life-and-death. It is in this dance that she comes upon the metaphors of poetic immortality and continuity. Even when her robin is gone, she says:

> Yet do I not repine
> Knowing that Bird of mine
> Though flown –
> Learneth beyond the sea
> Melody new for me
> And will return.   [5]

In the darkness of night, the little boat of her life seems to give up its struggle and gurgle down and down into the sea. But with the new dawn

> – o'erspent with gales –
> Retrimmed it's masts – redecked it's sails –
> And shot – exultant on!   [30]

In the process of life and death, Dickinson perceives everything as being continually renewed:

> New children play upon the green –
> New Weary sleep below –
> And still the pensive Spring returns –
> And still the punctual snow!   [99]

In spite of the snow, or perhaps because of it, Dickinson shows
her confidence in rebirth: "My flowers from a hundred
cribs / Will peep, and prance again" (133). Death continues
"Humming the quaintest lullaby / That ever rocked a child,"
but the bumble bees wake everything up when April woods
are red (142):

> I know a place where Summer strives
> With such a practised Frost –
> She – each year – leads her Daisies back –
> Recording briefly – "Lost" –   [337]

In Dickinson's poetic eschatology, death is merely a brief
pause; her winters do not stay long:

> Myself – for scarcely settled –
> The Phebes have begun –
> And then – it's time to strike my Tent –
> And open House – again –   [403]

In "A Night – there lay the Days between" (471), Dickinson uses
night and day as symbols of recurrence. Ceasing in the grave
which is "a Summer's nimble mansion," is the way of fulfillment, embodied in the metaphor of the "Oriental Circuit"
(813). Touched with a "Compound manner," Dickinson becomes the bride of dust and day (830) and sings:

> With Us, 'tis Harvest all the Year
> For when the Frosts begin

> We just reverse the Zodiac
> And fetch the Acres in.   [1025]

In this creative vision death comes and goes, and becomes intimate like "a Tempest past" (1134). One feels that "finer is a going / Than a remaining Face" (1422) because this going is *forever* which is "deciduous," and hence repeats itself. The poet experiences this going and coming, the autumn and the spring at once:

> The ones that disappeared are back
> The Phebe and the Crow
> Precisely as in March is heard
> The curtness of the Jay –
> Be this an Autumn or a Spring
> My wisdom loses way
> One side of me the nuts are ripe
> The other side is May.   [1690]

In the poetic imagination or intuition all things are possible: things disappear and come back simultaneously. The spring gets mixed up with the autumn, as life gets mixed up with death. But all this baffles the human mind: "My wisdom loses way." The poetic knowledge, however, is also *wisdom* but of a different sort; it cannot state itself as an argument, it lacks evidence. The awareness that "Life is death we're lengthy at, death the hinge to life" (L281), or that "This World is not Conclusion" must remain a paradox which beckons and baffles, and which

> Philosophy – dont know –
> And through a Riddle, at the last –
> Sagacity, must go –
> To guess it, puzzles scholars –
> To gain it, Men have borne
> Contempt of Generations
> And Crucifixion, shown –
> Faith slips – and laughs, and rallies –
> Blushes, if any see –

> Plucks at a twig of Evidence –
> And asks a Vane, the way –
> Much Gesture, from the Pulpit –
> Strong Hallelujahs roll –
> Narcotics cannot still the Tooth
> That nibbles at the soul – [501]

Death flows into life, but it does not conclude either life or it-self. Paradoxically, it means a fresh start, a new awareness. This vision, however, does not take away the anguish of exis-tence; it simply tells the way to live with the anguish. This anguish is integral to the process of the eternal return:

> The longest day that God appoints
> Will finish with the sun.
> Anguish can travel to its stake,
> And then it must return. [1769]

The anguish here is not an ordinary despair or nausea. It is an active partner in man's destiny; it accompanies him to the end of the longest day and then returns, in order to strive with man toward the process of continuity. It is the source of man's tragic vision. When the sense of death creates "the awful Vac-uum" in our lives, the only way to challenge the emptiness of life is to *create* life. Dickinson performs this feat through her art:

> I worried Nature with my Wheels
> When Her's had ceased to run –
> When she had put away Her Work
> My own had just begun. [786]

This is not to deny the reality of death, but a creative way of defeating death by affirming life and creativity. Dickinson's poetry subsumes many a noon and many a night (960). She writes: "Night is the morning's Canvas" (7). The morning sky and the evening sky are eternally present in the colors of her perception (204). She celebrates the breath of life, which she calls her crown, and says "No Wilderness – can be / Where this attendeth me" (195).

The symbolic constructs of the main body of Dickinson's death poetry fully embody the idea of creative immortality. The final direction of her death poetry does not lead toward any mystical or traditional resurrection; in her poetic system, eternity lies in the creative moment itself. Dickinson's forever is composed of nows (624), although she is quite aware of the orthodox religious notions of such matters. Occasionally she writes about the traditional ideas of hell and heaven, death and immortality, and life beyond the grave. But whenever she makes these the subjects of her poetry, her tone is almost invariably ironic and skeptical, and her mood is often that of inquiry rather than metaphoric assertion. In one poem she asks: "Is Heaven then a Prison?" (947). In another she writes: "We pray – to Heaven – / We prate – of Heaven – / Relate – when Neighbors die" (489). She tells us that "Parting is all we know of heaven, / And all we need of hell" (1732). Her treatment of heaven and hell is surely skeptical when she writes: "the Sepulchre / Defies Topography" (929). Her eyes are always set upon the earth: "That Heaven if Heaven – must contain / What Either left behind" (933). She mentions: "The Lark is not ashamed / To build upon the ground / Her modest house" (143). In "You're right – 'the way *is* narrow'," Dickinson ends by saying:

> And after *that* – there's Heaven –
> The *Good* Man's – *"Dividend"* –
> And *Bad* Men – "go to Jail" –
> I guess –   [234]

Concerning the religious notions of death and immortality, she puts the question in this manner: "Is Immortality a bane / That men are so oppressed?" (1728). And she says: "We are molested equally / by immortality" (1646). On the authority of Jesus, Dickinson writes:

> I need no further Argue –
> The statement of the Lord

Is not a controvertible –
He told me, Death was dead – [432]

She also writes about the stimulus, beyond the grave (1001), but when she considers the question of journey after death, her manner becomes ironic and sarcastic:

Those – dying then,
Knew where they went –
They went to God's Right Hand –
That Hand is amputated now
And God cannot be found –

The abdication of Belief
Makes the Behavior small –
Better an ignis fatuus
Than no illume at all – [1551]

A total loss of belief in the existence of God makes the behavior small. Therefore, it is better to have "an ignis fatuus / Than no illume at all." By showing belief in ignis fatuus, Dickinson is undercutting the roots of puritan orthodoxy. Ignis fatuus refers to the flickering flames of heaven and hell, the world of light and of shadows, and God and the devil at the same time. Ignis fatuus also implies delusive hope, and will-o'-the-wisp.

It should be obvious, then, that Dickinson is not looking for the right hand of God. Religious or theological notions do not satisfy her until they are transformed into the symbols of her art. She is not working for immortality beyond life, as most religious people seem to do. She is concentrating on that immortality which is present in each moment of her creative life:

Some – Work for Immortality –
The Chiefer part, for Time –
He – Compensates – immediately –
The former – Checks – on Fame –

Slow Gold – but Everlasting –
The Bullion of Today –
Contrasted with the Currency
Of Immortality – [406]

Dickinson belongs with the chiefer part, the best and the choicest of humanity, who work for time and achieve immortality in time. She is concerned with the bullion of today, and not with the currency of immortality beyond time. She is a beggar who is "gifted to discern" the difference between the two types of immortality. She receives "Bulletins all Day / From Immortality," and the only God she meets is the God of existence:

> The Only One I meet
> Is God – The Only Street –
> Existence – This traversed   [827]

It is this creative immortality which she calls the flood subject (L319). Even a letter feels to her like immortality (L330). She calls the "promised Resurrection" a "conceited thing" (L184). Eternity, she thinks, will be velocity or pause (1295). Motion being fundamental to her creative life, Dickinson eludes stability (1682); she seeks it only as a pause in order to begin anew. This is how she achieves her victory over mortality and comprehends the nature of life and death. And thus she claims:

> Behind Me – dips Eternity –
> Before Me – Immortality –
> Myself – the Term between –
> Death but the Drift of Eastern Gray,
> Dissolving into Dawn away,
> Before the West begin –   [721]

This seems to represent the culmination of her aesthetics of continuity. In this particular mood, Dickinson becomes the dancer and the dance, and death as we know it is no more present in the life of a "loosened spirit" (1587). Her aesthetics absorbs the typology of the "Duplicate divine," the creator and the destroyer, and contains the miracle of the forward movement, which is like a "Crescent in the Sea" and a "Maelstrom in the Sky" (721).[16]

6

Self

THE QUEST FOR IDENTITY

> Lonely one, you are going the way to yourself. And your way leads past yourself. . . . You must wish to consume yourself in your own flame: how could you wish to become new unless you had first become ashes!
>
> Lonely one, you are going the way of the creator: you would create a god for yourself.
>
> —Nietzsche, *Thus Spake Zarathustra*

Self is the matrix of creation; it refers to the sense of being that envelopes man's whole existence. It is the center to which each life converges (680), the sea toward which every river runs (162). It is the ultimate of wheels (633), which governs man's destiny and forward movement. It subsumes all the dimensions of possibility (1208). "Without this – there is nought" (655): it is the source of the human imagination which gives order and form to man's chaotic perceptions; it is the secret of man's freedom. It intensifies man's experience of love and generates spiritual strength to meet the challenge of death. It communicates through its essential silence; at times it seems still, but its stillness is volcanic (175). It is the *presence* which asserts itself more by being invisible. Dickinson's poetry fully dramatizes the ontological necessity of realizing this "seraphic self" (1465), and proposes this "as a continuous adventure and a perpetual crisis," to use Glauco Cambon's expression.[1]

The realization of this self or identity is an endless process; it involves total commitment and a constant striving on the part of one who seeks to merge with his or her being. In this quest, one is always haunted by the notion of ourself behind ourself (670). This engenders a deep sense of loneliness or solitude in which one experiences the "final inch" (875) of one's consciousness. The sense of suffering ripens to such an extent that "A nearness to Tremendousness – / An Agony procures" (963). Dread and danger (974) become the sources of spiritual revelation. Terror remains pervasive in a being which is "impotent to end – / When once it has begun" (565); creation (724) and dissolution (539) seem to represent the prismatic motion of existence.

That Dickinson's poetry embodies the process and the tendencies necessary for the condition of the essential self has been shown in the preceding pages of this study. It has also been observed that by plunging into the abyss of her own being, Dickinson discovers the secret source of her vocation and destiny. It should be reiterated here that she encounters the spiritual terror and silence of the abyss most daringly. In the darkness of the abyss or the realm of the unconscious, she finds the light by which she sees death as the source of renewed life, or what she calls "the first form of life" (PF70). By fitting her "Vision to the Dark" (419), she proclaims that consciousness is noon (1056). She describes the apocalypse of the spirit or identity in terms of the ample images of thunder, lightning, and fire. She shows perfect awareness of the paradox that the realization of the essential self demands the negation of self, and that the achievement of identity costs man "Precisely an existence" (1725) because "All – is the price of All" (772). Also in her aesthetics of the "I-thou" relationship, Dickinson lays stress on the creative ability to lose one's self in order to find one's self; it is only by losing one's narrow or egocentric self that one can discover the larger self.

In the following pages, I propose to elaborate the assumptions and observations contained in the opening paragraphs of this chapter, and to show through the reading of Dickinson's poetry that the human body is not an impediment in the process of self-awareness but if creatively apprehended it becomes an integral part of the human psyche. I also hope to demonstrate that the "I-thou" relationship is not antagonistic to pure and dynamic subjectivity or inwardness; rather, it is integral to the self or being.

For Dickinson, the greatest crisis of existence is the everlasting problem of one's identity. She finds her "Soul condemned to be– / Attended by a single Hound / It's own identity" (822). Paradoxically, it is the "Hound within the Heart" (186) which no one can resist. The realization of self or identity in time constitutes man's ultimate struggle *to be himself*: identity is "Time's sublimest target" (8). The quest for identity entails infinite venture and infinite suffering. To fail in this venture is to remain in one's finitude only: "Finite–to fail, but infinite to Venture – / For the one ship that struts the shore" (847).

In her quest for identity, Dickinson shows a unique sense of pain and suffering. She thinks that "At leisure is the Soul / That gets a Staggering Blow" (618). Since "Garrisoned no Soul can be / In the Front of Trouble," Dickinson affirms: "Safe Despair it is that raves – / Agony is frugal" (1243). To be alienated from one's identity is to face "the Sovreign Anguish" and the signal woe (167). But she deliberately invites woe because "It sets the Fright at liberty" (281):

> The Morning after Wo –
> 'Tis frequently the Way –
> Surpasses all that rose before –
> For utter Jubilee –   [364]

Woe sharpens her imagination:

> Must be a Wo –
> A loss or so –

> To bend the eye
> Best Beauty's way –   [571]

She knows that those "who have the Souls– / Die oftener"
(314). She suffers the "Bandaged moments" of the soul, faces
the ghastly fright of existence, but with her spiritual power
converts suffering into ecstasy: "What Exultation in the Woe"
(1642), and transmutes the stirless, bound moments of the
soul into its moments of liberty and escape in which the soul
knows nothing but noon and paradise (512). She undergoes
the lacerative experience of living when the soul is in pain
(244), and writes:

> The Moments of Dominion
> That happen on the Soul
> And leave it with a Discontent
> Too exquisite – to tell –
>
> The eager look – on Landscapes –
> As if they just repressed
> Some Secret – that was pushing
> Like Chariots – in the Vest –   [627]

Dickinson does not deny the pervasiveness of existential pain
and anguish, but she suggests a creative strategy for contemplating the discontent of the soul which becomes too exquisite to tell. She knows the art of doing "Sickness over / In
convalescent Mind," and "rewalks a Precipice," so that her suffering may prove the existence of her identity (957). The pain
of life prepares her for peace (63). She learns "the Transport
by the Pain – / As Blind Men learn the sun!" (167). However
titanic the pain may be, her "Features keep their place" (175).
She learns to live with pain, and it is this pain which she wants
to instil into us through her art (177), so that we may be able
to cope with it in our own lives. In this way, pain becomes the
source of her power:

> I can wade Grief –
> Whole Pools of it –

I'm used to that –
But the least push of Joy
Breaks up my feet –
And I tip – drunken –
Let no Pebble – smile –
'Twas the New Liquor –
That was all!

Power is only Pain –
Stranded, thro' Discipline,
Till Weights – will hang –
Give Balm – to Giants –
And they'll wilt, like Men –
Give Himmaleh –
They'll Carry – Him!   [252]

The human spirit must be disciplined through pain to carry out the arduous task of grasping the experience of existence as a whole. "So – many – drops – of vital scarlet – / Deal with the Soul" (269), says Dickinson. She weeps not for the sorrow, done her, but the push of joy (276). She cries "at Pity – not at Pain" (588). She envisions that through pain goes the old road "That unfrequented – one – / With many a turn – and thorn – / That stops – at Heaven" (344), and "A piercing Comfort it affords / In passing Calvary" (561). She holds that even "Delight – becomes pictorial – / When viewed through Pain" (572). On being acquainted with no less than boundaries of pain (644), Dickinson regards pain as a primordial condition of existence:

Pain – has an Element of Blank –
It cannot recollect
When it begun – or if there were
A time when it was not –   [650]

A creative apprehension of the mystery of pain and suffering leads toward the road of identity. Suffering brings spiritual awareness—the deeper the suffering, the richer the awareness of being. This is particularly true of those who have the tragic vision of life; this cannot be affirmed of life in general.[2] Dickinson specializes in pain and suffering as the minute particulars of existence, and not as merely philosophical concepts. For her, pain expands the time and contracts the time (967): it is at once the now and the eternity. It is through pain that she realizes her identity, which is eternally on the way. Out of her pride in the sense of pain, she utters: "See! I usurped *thy* crucifix to honor mine!" (1736). She wears the thorns till sunset (1737); pain becomes the source of her freedom, and charts for her the route to the paradise of her love and being:

> Joy to have merited the Pain –
> To merit the Release –
> Joy to have perished every step –
> To Compass Paradise –   [788]

Dickinson's spirit feeds on awe (1486), and she dares every anguish that life can threaten her with. Even the impending moment of her own death does not upset her plans of self-realization. She views her own death with perfect calm and evenness of mind:

> This Me – that walks and works – must die,
> Some fair or stormy Day,
> Adversity if it may be
> Or wild prosperity   [1588]

She reveres the agony caused by love:

> I've got an arrow here.
> Loving the hand that sent it
> I the dart revere.   [1729]

Through suffering Dickinson comes to know that the soul contains fortitude and can endure felicity or doom (1760). She undertakes the task of realizing her identity through the art of poetry, with full awareness of the rigors and personal deprivations involved in the creative process. Her surefootedness is expressed in these lines:

> To undertake is to achieve
> Be Undertaking blent
> With fortitude of obstacle
> And toward encouragement [1070]

The sense of fortitude is fundamental to self-discovery. If identity is the goal, the anguish of existence becomes transporting (148). When anguish becomes absolute (301), its excess or "Avalanches" lead toward the eternal silence and peace of one's self which makes "no syllable – like Death – / Who only shows his Marble Disc – / Sublimer sort – than Speech" (310). Dickinson is wrung with anguish (497) in order to experience the depth of her identity, and she sings in the moment of pain: " 'Tis Anguish grander than Delight / 'Tis Resurrection Pain" (984). In her creative imagination, "Mirth is the Mail of Anguish" (165). This anguish abides in the crisis of the soul, and it is through this crisis that one achieves spiritual ripeness or transcendence over the limitations of the empirical ego, or the created self, or what the Hindus call *Jivatman*. In this mental state, one moves toward the awakened soul or the *Atman*, without ever wholly abandoning the ego or the body.[3] In order to realize the center of her being, Dickinson goes through the ordeal of fire. She sees a soul at the white heat, and consummates herself in "the finer Forge" of her own creativity (365). In her vision the fire ebbs like billows (291), and thus, in the symbolic sense, it consumes and re-creates simultaneously. This creative fire burns her every day and night (362), and she believes that a bird, her metaphor for the poet, "Though Winter fire – [sings] clear as Plover – / To our – ear" (495). This fire brightens up the house of her identity, and she feels sunrise all over, and the noon without the news of night (638). It is the fire that lasts (1132), and Dickinson literally plays with it:

> The embers of a Thousand Years
> Uncovered by the Hand

> That fondled them when they were Fire
> Will gleam and understand   [1383]

Fire is symbolic of light and vision. It is the instrument which
"searches Human Nature's creases" (1678), its secrets, and its
mysteries. It reveals the topography of our spiritual home, our
true self or identity:

> I learned – at least – what Home could be –
> How ignorant I had been
> Of pretty ways of Covenant –
> How awkward at the Hymn
>
> Round our new Fireside – but for this –
> This pattern – of the Way –
> Whose Memory drowns me, like the Dip
> Of a Celestial Sea –
>
> What Mornings in our Garden – guessed –
> What Bees – for us – to hum –
> With only Birds to interrupt
> The Ripple of our Theme – . . .
>
> This seems a Home –
> And Home is not –
> But what that Place could be –
> Afflicts me – as a Setting Sun –
> Where Dawn – knows how to be –   [944]

In the presence of the new fireside of her creative vision,
Dickinson finds herself ignorant of the ways of covenant, and
feels awkward at the hymn. Established religious practices do
not seem to interest her. The fire which burns within her and
brightens her up imposes its own pattern upon her mind. It is
the pattern of the way to self whose memory drowns her.
Memory implies a remembrance or an awareness of the eternal existence of self in the unconscious. Remembering the way
to self is like the dip of a celestial sea. In this dip one drowns
in order to be reborn, as one consumes one's self in the fire in
order to be born anew. In this new birth, Dickinson remains
conscious of the mornings only in the garden of her identity.

The bees hum, and the birds touch the ripple of the theme of self—the all-inclusive subject of her poetry. But the process of identity does not end here: "This seems a Home– / And Home is not." This represents the paradox of continuity; in the very moment of realization we experience the sense of loss of identity, so that we may endeavor to realize it persistently in each moment. The eternal possibility of knowing one's identity—"what that Place could be"—afflicts her "as a Setting Sun – / Where Dawn – knows how to be." As the setting sun poses a challenge for the dawn *to be,* the perpetual loss of identity works as a spiritual spur for a man of destiny to continue finding his identity forever. One deserves identity only by constantly seeking it. Identity is man's freedom and his true existence, and "None is of freedom or of life deserving / Unless he daily conquers it anew," to use Goethe's insight.[4]

To venture upon the ontological problem of identity is to come to terms with the negation of egocentric self, to bear utter loneliness or spiritual isolation, and to undergo the experience of sacrifice and renunciation of all that one normally prizes in life. The accomplishment of identity or the self reflects the most difficult aspiration of man, because the stakes are staggeringly high. It calls for virtual self-abnegation and, in the process, one "perishes – to live anew – / But just anew to die" (705). Annihilation increases at every step toward identity: one faces miles on miles of nought (443):

> Just Infinites of Nought –
> As far as it could see –
> So looked the face I looked upon –
> So looked itself – on Me –   [458]

But, the poet, like a child, is the "Ruler of Nought, / Yet swaying all" (637). Like the spider, the poet plies from nought to nought (605); by becoming nothing, the poet becomes everything. In the creative imagination, one contemplates the ultimate nothing as a contemporaneous reality and thereby reduces the mortal consequence of existence (982). However,

the theme of nothingness is paradoxical because it represents
the source from which all life springs, and a rock on which all
life subsists. Dickinson displays the sense of self-negation also
through the metaphors of the pebble and the stone. She becomes a timid pebble in order to prove worthy of her lover
(966), or a pebble which safely plays in droughtless wells (460).
Stone signifies to her a "Quartz contentment" (341), the lid on
grave's mystery, the silence behind every speech, the
congealed eyes (519), palsy or paralysis (1046), a face devoid
of love or grace (1711), and so on. In the context of identity,
however, the stone symbolizes happiness and the fulfillment of
self:

> How happy is the little Stone
> That rambles in the Road alone,
> And does'nt care about Careers
> And Exigencies never fears –
> Whose Coat of elemental Brown
> A passing Universe put on,
> And independent as the Sun
> Associates or glows alone,
> Fulfilling absolute Decree
> In casual simplicity –   [1510]

The stone in this poem symbolizes a perfect degree of freedom. It rambles without any regard for worldly careers, and it
does not suffer from any urgent human needs. It glows alone,
and as independently as the sun. Its elemental brown color is
symbolic of the earth into which every living phenomenon
merges in the end. Its posture is casual and simple, but in
being alone in the road, the stone represents the harmony and
integration within the self. Spiritual aloneness or solitude is a
fundamental condition of identity: "A pensive Custom it becomes / Enlarging Loneliness" (1068), but "The Soul's Superior
instants / Occur to Her – alone" (306). The growth of man takes
place only when he is essentially alone and silent (750). Dickinson feels "It might be lonelier / Without the Loneliness" (405).
The sense of loneliness is not free from despair and horror:

one shudders as if one is in a cavern's mouth (590). But loneliness is the maker of the soul (777). This loneliness is rare to achieve, and many die without it (1116). Loneliness is the gain and a bliss (1179):

> It is a lonesome Glee –
> Yet sanctifies the Mind –
> With fair association –
> Afar upon the Wind   [774]

Lonesomeness or solitude determines man's inner quality. It is the source of man's courage to choose himself and to put up with the abyss of his own being. This courage is "not courage before witnesses but the courage of hermits and eagles, which is no longer watched even by a god," to use Nietzsche's insight.[5] In this state of being, the created self is completely merged with the spirit or the essential self, and its finitude becomes an integral part of the soul's infinity:

> There is a solitude of space
> A solitude of sea
> A solitude of death, but these
> Society shall be
> Compared with that profounder site
> That polar privacy
> A soul admitted to itself –
> Finite Infinity.   [1695]

Spiritual solitude is profounder than the solitude of space, sea, and even death. The inner space contains the sea of life and death. Dickinson calls it her polar privacy, a thematic symbol signifying the union of the finite self and the infinite self. Without this relationship the created self or ego remains estranged from its identity, and without a creative perception of solitude, our true self remains a stranger to us (L348).

The soul's privacy enhances our power to sacrifice and to renounce what is otherwise valued most highly by the human beings caught up in the web of worldly circumstances. Dickinson considers all "Dominions dowerless" beside the gift of her being, and describes the reward of identity in terms of the images which integrate royalty and poverty:

> My Reward for Being, was This.
> My premium – My Bliss –
> An Admiralty, less –
> A Sceptre – penniless –
> And Realms – just Dross –   [343]

The reward is indeed paradoxical. In the state of being, one has to lose one's outward bliss in order to find it within one's self. One feels royal without any external authority or richness; one rules over wilderness. The things that one likes to possess in life are money and power over others. But, authentic living denies these things and confers upon the person the ability to feel rich in spite of his penniless state or realms of dross. In this sense, then, by choosing one's being one chooses against one's narrow self. This choice constitutes the agony of the "straight renunciation" which only the son of God (527) can experience to the fullest extent. Dickinson expresses the virtue of renunciation in these lines:

> Renunciation – is a piercing Virtue –
> The letting go
> A Presence – for an Expectation –
> Not now –
> The putting out of Eyes –
> Just Sunrise –
> Lest Day –
> Day's Great Progenitor –
> Outvie
> Renunciation – is the Choosing
> Against itself –
> Itself to justify
> Unto itself
> When larger function –
> Make that appear –
> Smaller – that Covered Vision – Here –   [745]

At first glance, the word "piercing" seems to imply some ambiguousness in Dickinson's attitude toward the value of renunciation, and she seems to be somewhat critical of the motives behind it in the first three-quarters of the poem. But on a closer look, it becomes clear that the word is used to enhance the quality and value of the experience of deprivation. In order to realize being, one must go through the penetrating virtue of renunciation. One has to will the crucifixion of the narrow self which is a felt presence, and anticipate the birth or discovery of that self which does not seem to manifest itself in the temporal now. By putting out the earthly eyes one experiences the sunrise on the inner landscape, with which even the sun, the "Day's Great Progenitor," cannot contend. By renunciation, one chooses against one's mortal longings, and against the ego which is bound to the external world and its reality. This choosing reflects its own justification "unto itself," meaning that the awakened soul is autonomous in denying an independent reality to the created self. The larger function of the enlightened self triumphs over the egocentric self and makes the latter look smaller by comparison. Unless the self or being dominates the human ego, man's true identity remains a covered vision here, it remains hidden or veiled within the human psyche. It is an existential imperative to unveil the inner regions of one's own being, and realize their abiding truth in contrast to the transiency of one's temporal desires. A continuous realization of one's identity implies a challenge to one's self-centered condition.

The movement toward the self implies a spiritual thrust into one's interiority or withinness. It embodies a journey toward the inner paradise. For Dickinson, self is "the little Bird / Within the Orchard," or a king of the parlors, shut by day (103). The day in this context signifies the noise and humdrum of daily life. She refers to self by the name of an "intrinsic size" which "Ignores the possibility / Of Calumnies," or the slanders of everyday existence; this "Size circumscribes – it has

no room / For petty furniture" (641). It is a mental form
which expands as the mind does. It is the "Diviner Crowd at
Home" which obliterates the need for going "abroad" (674). It
is the site of the kingdom of heaven (959). Dickinson writes
about the relationship between the soul and silence in these
words:

> To own the Art within the Soul
> The Soul to entertain
> With Silence as a Company
> And Festival maintain
>
> Is an unfurnished Circumstance
> Possession is to One
> As an Estate perpetual
> Or a reduceless Mine.   [855]

The soul's only company is silence, and yet it is the festival
within by which the soul is entertained. To own the art of en-
tertaining the soul through silence is to be in possession of "an
Estate perpetual," or the mine which never diminishes. The
apprehension of silence within the soul is the prerequisite for
our encounter with the self.[6] True transport and agony—the
everlasting conditions of the soul—are always understood in
terms of their muteness. In the ultimate sense, silence defines
every existing phenomenon. Everything seems to sweep by
our heads without a syllable (282). Silence is the "phraseless
Melody" of our inner life (321). It is the source of genuine
fear and dread. Dickinson says:

> I fear a Man of frugal Speech –
> I fear a Silent Man . . .
> Of this Man – I am wary –
> I fear that He is Grand –   [543]

She observes that

> Silence is all we dread.
> There's Ransom in a Voice –

> But Silence is Infinity.
> Himself have not a face.   [1251 and L397]

But she shows great courage by plunging into the "Cellars of the Soul" (1225), and living in their utter silence, in order ultimately to transcribe the experience in the metaphors of her art:

> It's Hour with itself
> The Spirit never shows.
> What Terror would enthrall the Street
> Could Countenance disclose   [1225]

The spirit's monologue with itself is a mystery, which if disclosed would enthral us with terror. It is the reality of the deepest cellar (1182) of one's being. Dickinson respects the muteness of the human psyche, which she finds analogous to the "inaudibleness" of flowers (L388). She is aware that "little of our depth we tell" (L955), and that the depth of the self contains enormous issues (42), even embarrassments and awes (1214). The soul's function is to comprise (1533) everything and reject nothing. The soul's manner is all-inclusive: it can be slow, rapid, timid, and bold at once (1297). But its center defies direct expression; its riddle abides. It is like the "brook within the breast" (122). It is the "appalling Ordnance" within (175). It is also the lamp that "burns sure" within (233). It is the brain, within its groove (556). But, in spite of the terror inherent in the self, Dickinson shows no fear in its presence; the self means to her the summum bonum of existence. And since her experience of existence is contained in her art, she associates identity or the self with the act of creation. She is prepared to risk everything in order to be worthy of her destiny and vocation:

> *One Life* of so much Consequence!
> Yet I – for it – would pay –
> My Soul's *entire income* –
> In ceaseless – salary –

One Pearl – to me – so signal –
That I would instant dive –
Although – I *knew* – to *take* it –
Would *cost* me – *just a life!*

The Sea is full – I know it!
That – does not blur *my Gem!*
It burns – distinct from all the row –
Intact – in Diadem!

The life is thick – I know it!
Yet – not so dense a crowd –
But *Monarchs* – are *perceptible* –
Far down the dustiest Road!   [270]

Dickinson shows readiness to invest the spiritual earnings of her lifetime in order to gain one pearl, which symbolizes the precious gift of her art and identity. She is only too willing to dive into the sea of life and death to procure this gift, although this action would cost her *"just a life."* Her eyes are so intently fixed on the gem of her creativity, or the diadem of her own identity that her vision does not get blurred by the presence of innumerable other pearls or identities: her own "burns – distinct from all the row." Dickinson understands the predicament of life in general: she knows that a purely vegetative life lacks luster and vision; it is indistinct and dull. But she can visualize her own "monarchs," her poetic perceptions which contain the secret of her own existence, identity, and freedom, from far down the dustiest road. In her quest for identity, she transmutes the dust of existence and achieves through it a firelike clarity of perception. Once she perceives the self, Dickinson consecrates herself to the vision. In this posture, she experiences the sense of power and spiritual elation which she conveys in terms of her color-symbolism:

Purple – is fashionable twice –
This season of the year,
And when a soul perceives itself
To be an Emperor.   [980]

Dickinson's response to the self or identity is so complete
that in her creative system the human body, which is normally
thought of as an obstacle in the way of spiritual realization,
becomes a perfect container of the being. In her imagination
the spirit turns "unto the Dust," and says: " 'Old Friend, thou
knowest me' " (1039). But when the dust or the human body
merely impedes the process of the soul.

> The spirit looks upon the Dust
> That fastened it so long
> With indignation,
> As a Bird
> Defrauded of it's song.   [1630]

The spirit or the self is essentially free; in the ultimate sense,
the body cannot check the course of the spirit. Moreover, to
retard the movement of the self is not a determined function
of the body; this is just one of its finite possibilities. A creative
apprehension of the body, however, reveals its infinite quality,
its inseparable relationship with the spirit. In this later sense,
the self cannot be conceived without the body. The body provides an existential mold for the being. Dickinson views the
body in its creative form and visualizes it as a bird with wings
(430) which symbolize its freedom. Flesh is the door through
which one can watch the movement of the soul (292), says
Dickinson. In the existential sense, it is true that "A single
Screw of Flesh / Is all that pins the Soul" (263), but the flesh is
a sharer of the soul's destiny. The flesh puts up with a
"Weight with Needles on the pounds," and reveals the
strength of the compound frame (264), signifying the flesh-
soul relationship. The flesh or the body provides shelter for
the soul and becomes the latter's temple:

> The Body grows without –
> The more convenient way –
> That if the Spirit – like to hide
> It's Temple stands, alway,

> Ajar – secure – inviting –
> It never did betray
> The Soul that asked it's shelter
> In solemn honesty   [578]

The body stands ajar and invites the soul to stay in its secure abode. The body also meets the challenge of the self, which is like an "Assassin hid in our Apartment"; the body bolts the door and encounters the horror of the self in all its nakedness (670). The relationship between the spirit and the body is fraught with dialectical dangers and perils. In the process of meeting the terror of the spirit, the body is transformed; the flesh loses its fleshliness. The body becomes bodiless in the paradoxical sense (524); it becomes a body that stands without a bone (780). The body takes off its earthly filaments, "And during it's electric gale – / The body is a soul" (1431). The finite is furnished with the infinite (906). Of this body, Dickinson is as afraid as she is of the soul:

> I am afraid to own a Body –
> I am afraid to own a Soul –
> Profound – precarious Property –
> Possession, not optional –
>
> Double Estate – entailed at pleasure
> Upon an unsuspecting Heir –
> Duke in a moment of Deathlessness
> And God, for a Frontier.   [1090]

Dickinson equates the body with the soul and fears both. This fear is not any physical fright; it is the spiritual terror at apprehension of the "profound – precarious Property," the possession of which is not optional. Both the body and the soul are man's permanent conditions of being. Both jointly make the "Double Estate" to which man is an unsuspecting heir. By possessing this estate, one becomes like the duke who experiences a moment of everlasting life, and one becomes one's own God, ever ready for a frontier which defines the final boundary of human consciousness. The battle of existence can be fought and won by contemplating both the body and the soul. In the *Isha Upanishad,* it is stated: "To darkness are they doomed who worship only the body, and to greater darkness they who worship only the spirit. Worship of the body alone leads to one result, worship of the spirit leads to another. So have we heard from the wise. They who worship both the body and the spirit, by the body overcome death, and by the spirit achieve immortality." [7] Dickinson meditates upon both the body and the soul as the symbols of being. She believes that the spirit alone has no meaning. The body houses the soul, and the soul illuminates the house (1492). The eyes express the spirit, and the spirit inflates the countenance (1486). The two are coeval:

> The Spirit lasts – but in what mode –
> Below, the Body speaks,
> But as the Spirit furnishes –
> Apart, it never talks –
> The Music in the Violin
> Does not emerge alone
> But Arm in Arm with Touch, yet Touch
> Alone – is not a Tune –
> The Spirit lurks within the Flesh
> Like Tides within the Sea
> That make the Water live, estranged
> What would the Either be?   [1576]

The body is the incarnation of the spirit, and the spirit is the vital force of the body. The spirit lasts only in the mold of the body, and the body speaks only when the spirit furnishes it with the sound. The relationship between the spirit and the body is analogous to the relationship between the musical instrument and the human touch, or between the tides and the sea. Without the human hand the musical instrument cannot dilate into musical sound. But the touch alone is not a tune or harmony. The two must remain arm in arm, in order to be meaningful. As one cannot conceive the sea without the tides or the tides without the sea, one cannot think of the spirit

without the flesh, or vice versa; they cannot be estranged from
each other. In the Christian context, God or the ultimate truth
is also apprehended in terms of the body of Jesus Christ in
time, as he was "made flesh and dwelt among us" (1651). The
flesh is generally liable to a great deal of existential suffering,
but when the flesh is understood as eternally intertwined with
the spirit its suffering becomes highly symbolic; it clarifies the
self. By knowing Christ as the paradigm of man's ultimate
limit of suffering and sorrow, one gains the sense of suffering
and its value. "Only God – detect the Sorrow," says Dickinson
(626). She does not feel concerned about the suffering of the
flesh. In a letter to Austin Dickinson, she writes: "Give me the
aching *body,* and the spirit glad and serene, for if the gem
shines on, forget the mouldering casket!" (L54). She also
writes that the

> Best – must pass
> Through this low Arch of Flesh –
> No Casque so brave
> It spurn the Grave –   [616]

The spirit is the reservoir of sound by which man truly communicates, and it is also the conscious ear by which we actually
hear (733). For Dickinson, the spiritual sense of the body embodies the courage which is instrumental in all forms of revolution, and which prompts one to face even one's own death
with a sense of victory:

> Such spirit makes her perpetual mention,
> That I – grown bold –
> Step martial – at my Crucifixion –
> As Trumpets – rolled –
>
> Feet, small as mine – have marched in Revolution
> Firm to the Drum –
> Hands – not so stout – hoisted them – in witness –
> When Speech went numb –
> Let me not shame their sublime deportments –
> Drilled bright –

> Beckoning – Etruscan invitation –
> Toward Light – [295]

In this movement, one breaks the shackles of ignorance, leaves the darkness of the dungeons, and walks freely toward the open light of the spirit. In this sublime manner, the mere flesh with all its infirmities crawls "centuries" from the soul (1686), or, to put it differently, the corporeality of the flesh is infinitely transcended, and it is "The soul there – all the time" (1727)—the soul or the self which contains the terror of the abysmal sea and the ecstasy of the sunny sky. Dickinson finds the self by going through the flesh in her own creative way.

Without identification with the spirit or the self, the body is a sheer bondage, whereas in conjunction with the soul the body becomes an emblem of freedom. The self, in its moments of freedom, bursts all the doors and "dances like a Bomb, abroad, / And swings upon the Hours" (512). In terms of Dickinson's aesthetics, this dance of the self can be best described through the metaphor of thunder, which, among other things, means the poet's creative power (1581) "to illuminate endlessly the interior life" or the landscape of absence.[8] In nature as well as in the self, Dickinson finds thunder and harmony juxtaposed. But thunder is paradoxical: "Thunder's Tongue" is loud (276), and its "gossip" is low (824). Dickinson clasps her identity with all her spiritual force, and thereby apprehends the storm and the tranquillity of her being at once.

The self in Emily Dickinson's poetry cannot be indiscriminately equated with the transcendent self or the Over-Soul in Emerson's thought.[9] Nor can her problem of identity be examined in terms of the mystical self of Meister Eckhart or the highly metaphysical self of Shankara.[10] In Dickinson's poetry, the self is proposed as an artistic principle. It dominates creativity, and its awareness occurs not through religious meditation or mystical vision but through the very creative act. Dickinson's self, then, constitutes what Rollo May calls the *"creative consciousness of self.*" [11] As pointed out earlier, this self entails a continual search, even doubt in its presence. One perceives it in the state of paradoxical ignorance, and perceives it by the constant questionings of the heart:

> Not knowing when the Dawn will come,
> I open every Door,
> Or has it Feathers, like a Bird,
> Or Billows, like a Shore –   [1619]

The dawn symbolizes the culmination of self-consciousness. Dickinson keeps every door or every pore of her being open so that this consciousness shall not escape her. She asks the questions—though the questions contain the answers— whether the self is like a bird, or like the billows of the sea, symbolizing its essential freedom and violence, which become manifest only when man has achieved necessary liberation and boldness within himself. The metaphoric dawn instigates constant exploration of one's inner life where alone can be found the hidden continent of the self:

> Soto! Explore thyself!
> Therein thyself shalt find
> The "Undiscovered Continent" –
> No Settler had the Mind.   [832]

The sense of self-exploration causes inner expansion, and the self is obtained at the cost of one's spiritual energy. There is no other way to discover it; those who keep it buried within themselves without ever trying to realize it never know its true worth:

> I cannot want it more –
> I cannot want it less –
> My Human Nature's fullest force
> Expends itself on this.
>
> And yet it nothing is
> To him who easy owns –

> Is Worth itself or Distance
> He fathoms who obtains. [1301]

The self is present all the time, but the one "who easy owns" it never really knows its true nature, and thus exists without meaning. To be unaware of the scope of one's self is to be hollow and worthless. The meaning and the value of one's existence is known in proportion to one's awareness of one's being. Only he fathoms the worth or the inner distance of the self who obtains it by spending his human nature's fullest force, by straining to the utmost his physical and spiritual capabilities. Only then can one experience the freedom that a bird knows:

> It soars – and shifts – and whirls –
> And measures with the Clouds
> In easy – even – dazzling pace – [653]

The bird is Dickinson's favorite metaphor for the poet. She renders the experience of the self in terms of her poetry and the essential freedom of the poet. Poetry is the gift given to her by the gods when she was a little girl, and she gives it the name of gold (454). But it is not the gold in solid bars, which symbolizes materiality and captivity; rather, it is the gold which she calls "myself" and which makes her bold and free. The metaphors and the images of gold, dawn, feathers, billows, and shore, to mention only a few, delineate the phenomenology of being or the self in its most concrete and sensuous form.

Emily Dickinson does not evince any interest in the being which a mystic experiences as a result of his metaphysical union with God or the maker. For Dickinson, the maker's ladders stop, but she feels perfectly happy in the realm below where she distinctly hears the voice of her being:

> A Solemn thing within the Soul
> To feel itself get ripe –

And golden hang – while farther up –
The Maker's Ladders stop –
And in the Orchard far below –
You hear a Being – drop –

A Wonderful – to feel the Sun
Still toiling at the Cheek
You thought was finished –
Cool of eye, and critical of Work –
He shifts the stem –a little –
To give your Core – a look –

But solemnest – to know
Your chance in Harvest moves
A little nearer – Every Sun
The Single – to some lives.   [483]

The process of spiritual ripeness takes place within the human soul. Therefore, the being must be experienced within the realm of existence where it eventually belongs, and not beyond the maker's ladders where one cannot reach. It is in the orchard far below, or in the inner Eden, where the sun, a symbol of vision, toils endlessly at the cheek of the self. The sun appraises his work quite critically and perceives it with coolness, and then, slightly moves the stem of being to give the core or the center of the self one perceptive and enquiring look. Insofar as the sun is the persona of the poet, Dickinson seems to visualize her chance of harvest, which is symbolic of fulfillment, through her own development of the self. The process of fulfillment, however, never completes itself; it only draws a little nearer "every sun" or every day. But this in itself means "The Single," a symbol of unity or oneness within the self, to some lives. It is evident from the poem under discussion that Dickinson stresses the importance of realizing the self creatively here and now, and not somewhere beyond the periphery or circumference of existence. She toils toward the harvest of her own being, and remains bound to the moving wheel of time, indicated by the constant going and coming of

the sun. And she feels her identity or being in a fully sensuous
and concrete manner:

> I felt my life with both my hands
> To see if it was there –
> I held my spirit to the Glass,
> To prove it possibler –
>
> I turned my Being round and round
> And paused at every pound
> To ask the Owner's name –
> For doubt, that I should know the Sound –
>
> I judged my features – jarred my hair –
> I pushed my dimples by, and waited –
> If they – twinkled back –
> Conviction might, of me –   [351]

The sensuous and the psychic are interfused in the process of
the poem. Dickinson draws upon almost all the senses in order
to convey the experience which is essentially mental or spiritual. She mentions her being as a physical and existential entity. She feels her life with her hands and sees if it is there. She
holds her spirit to the glass, in order to prove it "possibler,"
meaning that the degree of awareness heightens by visualizing
the spirit or the visage of the soul (1311), through the spar-
kling clarity of the mirror. In a much more subtle sense it
means the viewing of the spirit through the imagination or
consciousness, symbolized here by the glass: it is like proving
the mirror through the mirror, or showing the mirror to the
mirror, so that the reality of the mirror or the spirit may not
be distorted. She turns her being round and round, and
pauses to ask the owner's name, not so much for the sake of
the name, as for the sake of affirming the being through its
own sound. The being thus becomes the object that one can
touch, see, hear, and feel in all its concreteness. Dickinson examines her features, strikes her hair, pushes her dimples, and
waits to find out if they gleam back to her. For her, their

twinkling means the conviction of her essential self. To realize
one's self creatively, and through one's own creativity, is the
greatest battle fought in Dickinson's life. This battle constitutes man's war against the formless abyss of his own psyche in
which lies hidden the mystery of being:

> The Battle fought between the Soul
> And No Man – is the One
> Of all the Battles prevalent –
> By far the Greater One –
>
> No News of it is had abroad –
> It's Bodiless Campaign
> Establishes, and terminates –
> Invisible – Unknown –
>
> Nor History – record it –
> As Legions of a Night
> The Sunrise scatters – These endure –
> Enact – and terminate –   [594]

In this battle, man undergoes a metamorphosis; he cannot be
understood entirely in terms of his physical existence. The
whole campaign is bodiless and invisible: the awareness of the
inner struggle takes place in the existential realm, but the
struggle itself cannot be verified physically or empirically. The
battle between the soul and no man is greater than all other
battles; cultural or political wars are insignificant in comparison with this spiritual battle which begins and terminates
within the abyss of one's being. But in the moment of vision or
self-discovery, the darkness of the abyss becomes translucent
and the armies of night disperse in the sunrise. Since the entire drama is enacted and terminated within the self, each ter-
mination means a new beginning. This continuity is loaded
with spiritual terror. Dickinson faces the horror of this battle
most courageously. She believes that the creative reality of the
self can be discovered only by going through the tension that
exists between night and day. Day-night symbolism, like life-
death symbolism, defines the continuity of being:

> The first Day's Night had come –
> And grateful that a thing
> So terrible – had been endured –
> I told my Soul to sing –
>
> She said her Strings were snapt –
> Her Bow – to Atoms blown –
> And so to mend her – gave me work
> Until another Morn –
>
> And then – a Day as huge
> As Yesterdays in pairs;
> Unrolled it's horror in my face –
> Until it blocked my eyes –
>
> My Brain – begun to laugh –
> I mumbled – like a fool –
> And tho' 'tis Years ago – that Day –
> My Brain keeps giggling – still.
>
> And Something's odd – within –
> That person that I was –
> And this One – do not feel the same –
> Could it be Madness – this? [410]

Dickinson meets the terror of the night with equanimity and tells her soul to sing. This also explains her "terror – since September" (L261). The soul in passing through the night of dissolution and chaos finds that her strings or musical cords are rudely pulled, and that her bow is "to Atoms blown." The persona in the poem mends the soul, because the power of the soul is not permanently impaired; it is only scattered for a short while, "Until another Morn." For Dickinson, the day, which is symbolic of light and the beginning of creation, also holds horror, equaled only by the terror of the night in which one cannot perceive anything. When the day unrolls its horror in her face, her eyes are blocked. But, paradoxically, it is out of this darkness that light is born. The paradox reveals itself to the poet in the moment of the latter's encounter with the creative reality of the day and the night, or as she puts it, the

day's night. In this vision, the brain of the poet laughs, and
the poet mumbles like a fool. The brain laughs with "Glee intuitive and lasting" (L472), and the poet mumbles like a fool
because the poet's wisdom cannot be translated into discursive
prose. Even long after the initial experience, the "Brain keeps
giggling – still." In this state of giggling and dialectical foolery,
Dickinson finds the extraordinary difference between the person that she was and the one that she is now. She becomes
aware of the present state of her being and asks: "Could it be
Madness – this?" The interrogatory form of the last line does
not mean that Dickinson has no answer to the question. The
awareness of being or identity is indeed a dialectical madness
with which she is so intimate (1284). She knows only too well
that the poetic vision itself is madness or a paradoxical state of
insanity, and writes:

> Much Madness is divinest Sense –
> To a discerning Eye –
> Much Sense – the starkest Madness –
> 'Tis the Majority
> In this, as All, prevail –
> Assent – and you are sane –
> Demur – you're straightway dangerous –
> And handled with a Chain –   [435]

But this type of insanity or foolery is the poet's mask. It is only
by becoming the clown that the poet can ponder "this tremendous scene – / This whole Experiment of Green – / As if it
were his own!" (1333). The poet views the whole creation
through the eye of divine madness, and thus in the state of
spiritual exuberance caused by this madness he assimilates in
his own being the terror and the ecstasy of simultaneous creation and dissolution. In this situation, the sense of being is
understood as pure subjectivity which "is realized in the moment of passion," to use Kierkegaard's expression.[12] Passion is
the source of the poet's imagination and creativity; rather, it is
the imagination. Since man's being or self is realized through

the imagination, it can be rendered only imaginatively. Dickinson chooses the self or subjectivity, and renders the experience in these words:

> The Soul selects her own Society –
> Then – shuts the Door –
> To her divine Majority –
> Present no more –
>
> Unmoved – she notes the Chariots – pausing –
> At her low Gate –
> Unmoved – an Emperor be kneeling
> Upon her Mat –
>
> I've known her – from an ample nation –
> Choose One –
> Then – close the Valves of her attention –
> Like Stone – [303]

The soul is the persona of the poet: by choosing her own society, Dickinson shuts her door to the outside world. In this state of withdrawal, she dedicates all her attention to the chosen one. This one is no other than the art of poetry through which she contemplates the meaning of existence. This irrevocable choice reflects the level of her spiritual maturity or the state of her being. She does not show any interest in the external symbols of royalty and power: she remains unmoved in the presence of the pausing chariots of her lovers or social aspirants, and shows complete indifference to the kneeling emperor. The valves of her attention are closed to everything except the creating self or her creativity, which she calls an ample nation—the kingdom of her poetic vision. By turning a heart of stone to all worldly pleasures or by assuming the form of a stone, which symbolizes perfection and harmony, Dickinson achieves the inner self. This self is reflected as an existential inwardness, the inner paradise or heaven that exists only so long as the mind or the soul exists. The apprehension of its beauty and depth is dependent upon our own spiritual or psychic capacity:

> Heaven is so far of the Mind
> That were the Mind dissolved –
> The Site – of it – by Architect
> Could not again be proved –
>
> 'Tis vast – as our Capacity –
> As fair – as our idea –
> To Him of adequate desire
> No further 'tis, than Here –   [370]

The human mind is the container of the heaven which is man's identity. If the mind is dissolved or disintegrated, the being or identity cannot be located by any means, no matter how professional. The dimensions of the self are as vast as the limits of man's ability to perceive. Its fairness is equal to the power of human conception. It defines the adequacy or limits of our desire, meaning that we must have sufficient desire or passion or creativity to possess it. And it is no further than here; it is eternally present in the here and now of existence. Because of the essential inwardness of the self or subjectivity, the being is infinitely tied down to the mind or psyche or consciousness: "Of Consciousness, her awful Mate / The Soul cannot be rid" (894). It is like the secret which should not be told, because

> A Secret told –
> Ceases to be a Secret – then –
> A Secret – kept –
> That – can appal but One –   [381]

The secret or the mystery of the self ceases to be a secret if told. The mystery must appall the one to whom it belongs. This mystery belongs eternally to each existing individual, and yet no one can share one's terror of it with another. Each person's awareness of the essential horror of the self or existence is unique and subjective. However, the sharing is possible only if the "other" is integrated into the structure of one's own being. Dickinson does not tell her secret to anyone in the ordinary sense; she sings her secret out in the form of her poetry, and thus shares it with her readers through the metaphors of her art. In this manner of sharing, it is necessary for the reader to identify himself or herself spiritually with the haunted house of her art (L459a), in order to apprehend fully the meaning of her poetry. At any rate, Dickinson continues to believe in the autonomy of the soul or the self, and she understands the self in terms of its own inner mood and circumstance:

> The Soul unto itself
> Is an imperial friend –
> Or the most agonizing Spy –
> An Enemy – could send –
>
> Secure against it's own –
> No treason it can fear –
> Itself – it's Sovreign – of itself
> The Soul should stand in Awe –   [683]

The soul embodies all the contradictions of life: it is its own "imperial friend" and the most agonizing "Spy." In being "unto itself," it is its own defender and the enemy. Outside danger or treason cannot threaten it because it contains enough terror of its own. It is complete in itself: "Itself – it's Sovreign." Dickinson says that the soul should experience no other terror or awe except what is integral to itself. However, Dickinson's autonomous self is not exclusive of the "other"; rather, it includes the "other," though only as an "I-thou" identity. In this identity, the "other" does not belong outside herself; she internalizes the "other" into the being that she is. As pointed out in chapter four, the daemon of the "other" is an integral part of the self. Dickinson conveys this theme in many paradoxical ways. The "other" may be identified as the lover or her image of God who seems to influence the fructification of her being: "He found my Being – set it up – / Adjusted it to place – / Then carved his name – upon it" (603). It is by merging with the "other" that the individual grows in self-awareness. The "I-thou" relation or identity cannot be empirically objectivized; it is realized only in dynamic subjectivity. In "The look of thee, what is it like" (1689), Dickinson seeks to affirm the "other" or "thou" as a "Mansion of Identity." She proposes "thou" as identity through the indirect method of imaginative rendering. The relations of identity are the existential realms, themes, delight, fear, longing, and values. The existential domains and subjects define the "pursuit" of identity. Delight and fear define its mood, and longings and values determine its character. Viewing identity through the flux of time, Dickinson aims to show it as untouched by the change which transfuses all other traits, and enacts all other blame, signifying time's censure of everything except identity: "thou shalt be the same." A constant pursuit of identity is the source of man's victory over the sense of impermanence. Although the "other" is proposed as identity, man's search for being does not take place outside himself. The outward forms simply serve as symbolic representations of what is existentially and essentially within man himself. In this sense, the "I-thou" relationship may be described as a projection of the self. Through this relationship, the created self loses its egocentricity and advances toward the larger self. This particular drama of the "I-thou" relationship has been rendered by Dickinson in these verses:

> The Drop, that wrestles in the Sea –
> Forgets her own locality –
> As I – toward Thee –
>
> She knows herself an incense small –
> Yet *small* – she sighs – if *All* – is *All* –
> How *larger* – be?   [284]

By wrestling in the sea, the drop merges with the sea, and forgets her own locality. By losing her narrow identity, the drop finds her true identity. She forgets from where she started. The "I" also moves toward "thee" in the same manner. The created self or the "I" of the poem grows conscious of her insignificant size in the presence of the vastness of the

sea or "thee." But in the very moment of encounter with the
sea, the drop visualizes herself as *all,* and wonders at the
largeness of her identity. On being exposed to the size of the
true self or the sea, the created self enters the process of
becoming the sea. In this "I-thou" encounter one discovers
that the egocentric self contains the possibility of being the
self. That is why the created self can never be wholly aban-
doned; the being is born of an existing being. In the aesthetic
sense, the drop contains the sea, and the "I" contains the
"thou." In Dickinson's poetry the drop and the sea are dimensions of the self, and the "I" and the "other" are interfused
with the oneness of the being. In the structure of her imagination, the guest and the host are one:

> He was my host – he was my guest,
> I never to this day
> If I invited him could tell,
> Or he invited me.
>
> So infinite our intercourse
> So intimate, indeed,
> Analysis as capsule seemed
> To keeper of the seed.   [1721]

In this inner dialogue, "he" or the "other" is merged with the
larger identity of the relationship which is beyond rational
analysis—the analytical approach can deal merely with the surface or outer layer of the relationship; it cannot touch the
center or the seed of this unity. The intercourse between host
and guest, or between "he" and "me" is so infinite and intimate that it is difficult to tell who is who. The sexual symbolism also refers to the basic oneness of the relation in which
the "I-thou" identity is fully realized. The "thou" does not
remain thou any more. Like the being or the self, "I" and
"thou" are referred to as one and one:

> One and One – are One –
> Two – be finished using –

> Well enough for Schools –
> But for Minor Choosing –
>
> Life – just – Or Death –
> Or the Everlasting –
> More – would be too vast
> For the Soul's Comprising –   [769]

"One and One – are One" symbolizes the fundamental unity of the two. In the ultimate sense, the being or the self can be apprehended only in terms of the creative monad which subsumes the polarity of the subject-object relationship. The being is essentially one, and yet it contains everything that is outside itself. It gives perspective to the contradictions of existence without ever denying the tension and irony that stem from the paradox of ever-abiding unity in polarity. The authentic self or the soul comprises "Life – just – Or Death – / Or the Everlasting." "More would be too vast" is ironic, because there is nothing beyond the reality of life and death. To comprise the "Everlasting" or the endless process of life and death is to comprise all.

The authentic self generates the sense of self-sufficiency within one's own being, which is reflected through one's individuality. This determines the spiritual health of the existing being. In his essay on self-reliance, Ralph Waldo Emerson succinctly remarks: "Nothing is at last sacred but the integrity of your own mind. Absolve you to yourself, and you shall have the suffrage of the world." [13] Dickinson poetizes her own sense of self-reliance and inwardness, and thereby celebrates in her art "the greatness of man." [14] She keeps company with herself, because she knows that "the Man within" never experiences satiety, and

> Never for Society
> He shall seek in vain –
> Who His own acquaintance
> Cultivate –   [746]

She firmly believes that

> The Soul that hath a Guest
> Doth seldom go abroad –
> Diviner Crowd at Home –
> Obliterate the need – [674]

The guest refers to the solitary self for which the poet has made a conscious choice. In the existential realm, life in general is full of deprivations and denials. The only way to cope with this agonizing situation is to withdraw spiritually from the cold, indifferent look of the world into one's self. However, the world's indifference is paradoxical insofar as it cultivates in some the urge *to become themselves.* Dickinson writes:

> Deprived of other Banquet,
> I entertained Myself –
> At first – a scant nutrition –
> An insufficient Loaf –
>
> But grown by slender addings
> To so esteemed a size
> 'Tis sumptuous enough for me –
> And almost to suffice [773]

On being deprived of the outer banquet or the feast, Dickinson learns to entertain herself with herself. The process is gradual: at first it seems a scant nutrition and an insufficient loaf to depend exclusively upon one's own inner resources. But by slender addings of inwardness, the self grows to such an esteemed size that it becomes sumptuous and is sufficient to the need. Dickinson's "almost" indicates that we can never really know the end of the experience; we must continue to add to the holdings of the self, which is a vast sensibility, and entertain ourselves with the everlasting process. Dickinson receives her nutrition from the ever-growing self which is her inner banquet. The self is her "Banquet of Abstemiousness" which "Defaces that of Wine" (1430). This is "That indestructible estate" which no one can steal "From any Human soul" (1351). It is like the light which is sufficient to itself (862). Dickinson feels that

Who Court obtain within Himself –
Sees every Man a King –
And Poverty of Monarchy
Is an interior thing –   [803]

By relying on the self, and by creatively visualizing the visage
of the soul (1311), one prepares one's self to meet all the ex-
tremities and perils of existence:

On a Columnar Self –
How ample to rely
In Tumult – or Extremity
How good the Certainty

That Lever cannot pry –
And Wedge cannot divide
Conviction – That Granitic Base –
Though None be on our Side –

Suffice Us – for a Crowd –
Ourself – and Rectitude –
And that Assembly – not far off
From furthest Spirit – God –   [789]

In symbolic terms, a "Columnar Self" implies spiritual stability; its vertical structure represents an upward push of self-affirmation, and its circular form symbolizes a continual state of
being. To depend on this self is certainly ample for a lifetime.
The one who relies on his own being can go through the
tumult or extremity of existence with a peaceful demeanor.
Perilous storms and uprooting commotions cannot disturb the
individual who has the certainty that "Lever cannot pry,"
meaning that no external force, however powerful, can peer
into the self impertinently. "And Wedge cannot divide" indicates that the conviction of the self is impervious to the
splitting energy of the wedge. The mechanical images of lever
and wedge point out the ruggedness of existence, and symbolize a brute material force. But the self in being columnar is far
above the brutality of the existential scene, although it is
rooted in existence. The conviction of the self is the "Granitic

Base" which strengthens man. Even when no one is on our side and we are all alone, the self secures us against the challenge of a crowd. Dickinson suggests that a perfect awareness of the self leads toward fulfillment: the self brings us close to the "furthest Spirit – God." It is the abiding spirit or soul that she cannot see empirically, but knows it is there (1262). For Dickinson, man's perpetual creation of his own being or self is identical with God's own act of creation. As God manifests himself in his creation, man manifests his true self through his creativity. Dickinson embodies herself in her poetry, which is her real identity. Roy Harvey Pearce has observed:

> Writing poems, she writes herself. She claims to do nothing more and dares do nothing less. She must know as much of the world as she can, yet in the end know it only as it serves to shape her knowledge of herself. Her words are exact: She is hounded by her own identity. The most apt analogy is Melville's Ishmael, insisting that he is writing his novel after the fact, urging our assent to his utter freedom to adduce material from whatever quarter he wishes and to write from various points of view and in various forms, just so he may understand what has happened to him, just so he may create himself, or at least the possibility of himself.[15]

Dickinson's conception of the creating self is indeed individualistic, but it is not empty of interest in others. It is through this self or her creativity that she brings "an unaccustomed wine" to "lips long parching" next to hers, and summons them to drink (132). Her art contains innumerable windows of perception which, if entered, can satiate the human hunger:

> I found
> That Hunger – was a way
> Of Persons outside Windows –
> The Entering – takes away – [579]

She takes her power or the creative energy in her hand, which is symbolic of the state of spirituality, and goes against the world (540) in a highly paradoxical sense. For she suffers for us in the process; by enacting the inner drama of existence, and by going against the purely material world, she exhausts herself. In her state of withdrawal from the world she shows great anxiety for the world, and writes

> This is my letter to the World
> That never wrote to Me –
> The simple News that Nature told –
> With tender Majesty   [441]

By emphasizing the importance of creative self-reliance through the metaphoric and metamorphic structures of her art, Dickinson teaches us that before we can be useful to others we must first become meaningful to ourselves; that before we can help others to choose for themselves we must first choose for ourselves; and that before we can show any genuine compassion for others we must first feel concerned about ourselves. By following this strategy we can participate in the spiritual growth of a society. In the context of this experience which pertains to her social vision, Dickinson's poetry can be called the "poetry of concern," to use Northrop Frye's phrase.[16] In her revolutionary message of self-reliance, Dickinson proposes the self for every existing individual, and proposes it as the house that ultimately stands on its own:

> The Props assist the House
> Until the House is built
> And then the Props withdraw
> And adequate, erect,
> The House support itself
> And cease to recollect
> The Augur and the Carpenter –
> Just such a retrospect
> Hath the perfected Life –
> A past of Plank and Nail
> And slowness – then the Scaffolds drop
> Affirming it a Soul.   [1142]

The house is assisted by the supporting poles and structures until it is built. Once it is complete, the supports are withdrawn, and it stands erect and adequate by itself. Man's life is like this house: in the process of self-making, one needs and accepts the props, symbolizing the forces of culture and tradition and all other forms of external assistance. Once it has been shaped, the self becomes sufficient, robust, and assertive. In due course, the self ceases to recollect, retaining no memory of the tools and the artificer who were instrumental in its making. The perfected life or the authentic self has just such a retrospect or view of its past. The images of plank, nail, and carpenter allude to the life of Jesus—his youth spent in the carpenter's workshop. In this dimension, the suffering involved in the process of self-finding comes to mind as a past yet contemporaneous event. The images also indicate that the self-finder should lead a life of humility, face whatever suffering is there with cheer, and then transcend the external poles and planks of existence. This posture expresses the amplitude of the self.

The creative self is the paradigm of man's wholeness—the totality of his being. It refers to the perfection which is perpetually realized or perfected. It is not subject to public opinion or censure. It is the truth that outlasts the sun (1455). The person who experiences this self stands on the tops of things; he sees mirrors on the scene, and no lightning can frighten him away:

> Just laying light – no soul will wink
> Except it have the flaw –
> The Sound ones, like the Hills – shall stand –
> No Lightning, scares away –
>
> The Perfect, nowhere be afraid –
> They bear their dauntless Heads,
> Where others, dare not go at Noon,
> Protected by their deeds –   [242]

The self is like the spring which through its inundation "Enlarges every soul– / It sweeps the tenement away / But leaves the Water whole" (1425). Dickinson plays with the waters of the flood and feels that "we part with the River at the Flood through a timid custom, though with the same Waters we have often played" (L466). The water makes us whole in the symbolic sense, and the self is the whole to which nothing can be added:

> Unto the Whole – how add?
> Has "All" a further Realm –
> Or Utmost an Ulterior?
> Oh, Subsidy of Balm!   [1341]

The self is the all. It is the last kingdom or realm in man's journey through existence. It is the utmost, which has no beyond or future but itself. It is the subsidy of balm, the gift of peace that springs from within yourself. Out of this peace grows the eye of perception which makes Dickinson sing:

> The Meadows – mine –
> The Mountains – mine –
> All Forests – Stintless Stars –
> As much of Noon as I could take
> Between my finite eyes –
>
> The Motions of the Dipping Birds –
> The Morning's Amber Road –
> For mine – to look at when I liked –   [327]

And out of this peace grows love which "nought can supersede" (L357). The self is "without the date, like Consciousness or Immortality" (L356). Its beginning and end are the same:

> The Opening and the Close
> Of Being, are alike
> Or differ, if they do,
> As Bloom upon a Stalk.
>
> That from an equal Seed
> Unto an equal Bud
> Go parallel, perfected
> In that they have decayed.   [1047]

The bloom upon a stalk symbolizes the creative perfection of the being. A flower is perfect in the moment of creation. The stalk is the axis or center from which a flower stems and to which it goes. The being opens and closes in the same endless manner. The seed becomes the bud, the bud becomes the seed, and in this continuous metamorphosis they "decay" into perfection. The being is both the seed and the bud, and as a flower withers or decays in order to be born afresh, the being eternally renews itself. This shows the ultimate unity of life and death, creation and destruction within the self.

CONCLUSION

What poetry expresses is neither the mythic word-picture of
gods and daemons, nor the logical truth of abstract determina-
tions and relations. The world of poetry stands apart from both,
as a world of illusion and fantasy—but it is just in this mode of
illusion that the realm of pure feeling can find utterance, and
can therewith attain its full and concrete actualization.
—Ernst Cassirer, *Language and Myth*

In this study, I have paid little attention to Emily Dickinson's
prosody,[1] because my chief concern has been the exploration,
via imagery and symbolism, of her *meanings* and not her met-
ric patterns. In commenting upon Dickinson's metaphoric
structures, I have dealt thoroughly with the nature of her poetic language, but it has not been within the scope of the
present work to take "account of the theories and methods of
modern linguistics" [2] in literary criticism. Dickinson's manner
of writing evinces her essential freedom from the burden of
rules of grammar and syntax: her poetic utterance constitutes
her revolt against the traditional techniques of verbal art.
Dickinson's frequent use of the dash has been accepted as in-
dicative of a pause, a suspense, or a mark of musical notation.
To my mind, the use of the dash also represents the open-
ended or "inconclusive" form of her poetry. The free use of
capital letters—other than the opening letters of the verses—
often signifies Dickinson's mode of emphasis, as well as her

concern to express a certain nuance of meaning in the images and metaphors of her poetry. For Dickinson, the act of poetry is the act of living; the creative process is the way of self-realization which she embodies in her poetic images and symbols. My primary concern, then, has been with the expanse and depth of Dickinson's poetic vision which is also her vision of life.

I think it is in order here to recapitulate the essential features of the way in which this study unfolds. Chapter one, "Center of the Sea: The Aesthetics of Terror," delineates the nature of Dickinson's "terror – since September" in juxtaposition with her aesthetics of suffering, dread, danger, and despair, and charts the relationship between "terror" and Dickinson's consecration to poetry as vocation and destiny. It deals with Dickinson's penetrating sense of earth, time, and body, indeed her ontological response to all of existence, and brings out the primordial—mythic and religious—character of her poetry. In short, it proposes Dickinson as a mythopoeic, ontological, tragic, and existential poet, and provides a basis for an encounter and dialogue with her creative mind. Chapter two, "The Landscape of Absence: Mansions of Mirage," continues the *dialogue,* and examines the paradox of absence-presence through its several modes and relationships. Absence is considered as *experience* which defines itself through silence, stillness, and the darkness of the human heart. It is viewed as *being* which contains the primeval magic and terror of existence. It is looked at as *distance* or *beyond* which metaphorically represents inwardness, and which highlights the notions of instress and inscape. It is regarded as *withdrawal* from the world, which carries its own mode of encounter with the world. It is treated as *deception* which affirms reality as dream and dream as reality. It is contemplated as *perception* which is the angle of vision, and which reveals an instant relationship between the perceiver and the perceived in the act of creation. It is felt as *love* which increases one's capacity to annihilate one's self and the ability to remain in uncertainties. It is apprehended as *death* which negates and intensifies life at once. And it is identified as *time* and *deity* which remain ever present, though ever hid. All these forms of absence are proposed as metaphoric and ambivalent, and as referring to the condition of creation in which all the contradictions and ambiguities of life meet. Chapter three, "Perception: The Billows of Circumference," pertains to Dickinson's theory of perception, which is stated in terms of a fourfold structure of imagination, defining the nature of relationship between the poet and the realm of existential reality, the poet and the poetic experience, the poet and the creative process, and the poet and the poem. It stresses the subjective-objective character of perception, while recognizing the primacy of the creative mind in its search for fullness or identity. Besides pointing out the metamorphic nature of the poetic vision, the archetypes of Dickinson's poetic experience, the solemn role of language in the creative process, and the becoming of the poet through the poem, it deals with the problems of the relationship between the poet and the reader or the critic, and the social function of the poet's art. Chapter four, "Love: The Garment of Fire," explores at considerable length the several aspects of the involute theme of love in Dickinson's poetry. It is shown that many moods and postures are syncretic to the structure of love, as several colors are integral to the prism of existence. Basically, Dickinson's concept of love is apprehended in terms of the tradition in which eroticism merges with asceticism, and in which *Eros* is reconciled with *Agape*. It is also pointed out that in the process of an inward journey of love, Dickinson experiences all forms of contradictory emotions, and by passing through a number of levels or phases of suffering and moral pathos she appropriates and enacts the essential truth of love, which is perennial creativity. The levels or dimensions of love are shown as integral and simultaneous and not as mutually exclusive areas of human commitment. Chapter five, "Death: The Cosmic Dance," inquires into the pervasive theme of death in Dickinson's poetry. It states that death haunts Dickinson in many paradoxical ways, and that before she realizes death imaginatively as a primordial metaphor for survival, before she fathoms tomb as womb, and before she makes it an integral ingredient of her aesthetics of continuity, she undergoes the excruciating experience of knowing death as eternal silence and darkness, as the unknown mystery and oblivion from which there is no return. The paradoxical and ambiguous vision of life-and-death continuity or unity is proposed as man's most stupendous attempt to rescue himself from the human condition of impermanence and transiency, and as a symbolic representation of man's longing for some kind of immortality. Chapter six, "Self: The Quest for Identity," evaluates Dickinson's concern for self or being as the matrix of creation. It shows that Dickinson's poetry fully dramatizes the ontological necessity to realize the "seraphic self." This realization is seen "as a continuous adventure and a perpetual crisis." The quest for identity entails infinite venture and infinite suffering. It is observed that for Dickinson the human body is not an impediment in the process of self-awareness but if creatively apprehended it becomes an integral part of the human psyche; and that the "I-thou" relationship is not antagonistic to pure and dynamic subjectivity or *inwardness*. Dickinson's self is not equated with the transcendent self of Emerson, or the mystical self of Meister Eckhart, or the highly metaphysical self of Shankara. It is studied as a creative principle; for it dominates creativity, and its awareness occurs not through the forms of religious meditation but through the creative act itself. For Dickinson the creator-artist, creative self is the ultimate self, and she realizes it as such by plunging into the abyss of her own being.

Richard Sewall writes:

> My own prediction is that Emily Dickinson will grow stronger with the years as we continue to outdistance the sentimentalities that still cling to her. Her eccentricities will fall into perspective. We will become increasingly aware of the toughness and sinew

of her poetry, its range and versatility, its challenge to our understanding. We will test our knowledge of humanity against
hers and find that we can learn on almost every front. Far from
the little figure of frustrations and renunciations and regrets, we
will come to see her as a poet of great strength, courage, and
singleness of purpose.[3]

My own encounter with Dickinson's poetry, as described in
the foregoing paragraphs, has revealed, in more ways than
one the validity of the basic contentions of Sewall's prediction.
In my reading, I have, in the main, dealt with "the toughness
and sinew of her poetry, its range and versatility, its challenge
to our understanding" from several angles. I hope to have
shown that Dickinson is "a poet of great strength, courage,
and singleness of purpose." But the task is not yet over;
rather, it is a continuing one. Literary commentary on Dickinson's poetry, I believe, has to be a process in itself. Therefore,
I am not implying finality or definitiveness of any sort. As a
matter of fact, the existential or experiential mode of interpretation forbids conclusiveness.

I cannot myself predict future trends in Dickinson criticism,
but in order that we may comprehend the dimensions of her
creative mind in all its subtlety and paradox, its darkness and
illumination, we must confront the whole of her poetry and
examine closely the metaphoric and symbolic structures in
which she presents the drama of her inner life. In suggesting
this, I am fully conscious of the heavy demands that Dickinson's poetry imposes upon the critic. Since the poet "cannot
talk about what he knows," to use Northrop Frye's [4] critical
axiom, the critic's job is to talk *about* the poetic creation and to
make explicit what is implicit in the metaphors of the poet's
art. In this venture of *talking,* the critic has to create the medium through which he can communicate his imaginative perception of the creative work he intends to interpret. In other
words, the critic has the responsibility not only to enhance our
appreciation of the mystery at the heart of the poetic perception but also to rescue his own work from being merely para-

sitic. This position can be further explained in the words of Arturo Fallico:

> the first and most important thing we must understand is that though the artist, in doing art, has no need to do criticism, the art critic, in doing his art criticism, must be able to enact the aesthetic presentation he wishes to talk about. This is a little more involved than it sounds, for the sense in which the art critic must be artist is twofold: he must be able to speak in the manner of the first utterance which is the art work he wishes to talk about and he must also be able to make his own first speech by which to say what he has to say concerning the work of art he wishes to criticize. The work of art speaks for itself in any case, so that the critic's job is never to speak *for,* but only *about* it, and this is the critic's own first utterance. This can only mean that, successful or unsuccessful (in the sense in which such evaluations apply to the art-thing), the work of criticism is, at the same time, a work of art on its own. If it were not, it could not speak at all or say anything.[5]

Emily Dickinson's poetry, then, must be explored and rendered "in the manner of the first utterance." Like Blake, Stevens, and several others, Dickinson is the true "literalist of the imagination." [6] In order that her metaphors should "yield their full meanings," we have to intuit the heart of her perceptions. The voice of her poetry cannot be heard without imagination. The "Scarlet Experiment" (861) of her art, I am afraid, cannot be understood within the limits of judgment, to use Yvor Winters' phrase.[7] Purely rational and pragmatic analyses of her poems will not take us very far. She is not a surface poet, and to evaluate her as such is spiritual lethargy. Douglas Duncan observes:

> Certainly the finest comments on her poetry have come, not from the analysts, but from other poets. When the town of Amherst celebrated its bicentenary in 1959, three distinguished American poets—Louise Bogan, Richard Wilbur, and Archibald MacLeish—were invited to lecture on its most famous inhabitant. Their lectures . . . were illuminating and subtly apprecia-

tive in a way that more severely academic criticism has often
failed to be.[8]

This does not mean that to appreciate poetry is the sole right
of the poets, or that in order to comment on poetry one has to
be a poet in the professional sense of the word. But it certainly
implies that one must have poetic sensibility and a certain
point of view before one assumes the role of critic. I think
these are the necessary qualifications for a critic who undertakes to grapple with the peace and the violence of Dickinson's
poetic vision. In order to perceive the nature of her creative
experience, the critic should also have the ability to see both
the inner and the outer layers of Dickinson's poems, by which
I mean her metaphoric structures or symbolic constructs. Herbert Muller has rightly observed that "the language of a poem
is a continuous reference to things outside itself. Its meaning
is never intact, self-contained, self-explanatory." [9] The metaphor must be explored in all its dimensions, intrinsic as well as
extrinsic. Hence the urgency simultaneously to read the poem
on the page and "to stare a hole in the page." My own interpretation of Dickinson's poetry is, in every sense, an attempt to meet the requirements of the approach that I have
outlined in the foregoing paragraphs. But in no sense can I
claim to have exhausted the inherent possibilities of that approach. There is scope for more rigorous and more imaginative readings of Dickinson's poetry.

NOTES

INTRODUCTION

1   Anderson's book was published in 1960, and it is so far the best critical study of Emily Dickinson's poetry. In his critical method, Anderson considers the work itself as central, and pays negligible attention to Dickinson's biography and her social or historical background. The other full-length study which deserves special mention here is Gelpi's, which appeared in 1965, and is a useful contribution to Dickinson criticism.

2   "Emily Dickinson," *Fables of Identity: Studies in Poetic Mythology,* p. 216.

3   This aspect has not so far been adequately explored by any critic of Dickinson's mind and art. I can only hope that readers will find my treatment of the problem of "terror" rewarding enough to place Dickinson's poetry in a new perspective.

4   For the "sources" of Dickinson's poetry, see Jack Lee Capps, *Emily Dickinson's Reading: 1836–86.* I do not intend to undermine the relative importance of contributory streams of thought, but I wonder if a truly creative mind can be understood wholly in terms of so-called "influences."

5   "Psychology and Literature," *Modern Man in Search of a Soul,* p. 172.

6   *Fables of Identity,* p. 198.

7   Ibid. Also see Martin Buber, *Between Man and Man.* Buber observes (p. 33): "When we really understand a poem, all we know of the poet is what we learn of him in the poem—no biographical wisdom is of value for the pure understanding of what is to be understood: the *I* which approaches us is the subject of this single poem. But when we read other poems by the poet in the same true way their subjects combine in all their multiplicity, completing and confirming one another, to form the one polyphony of the person's existence." I entirely agree with

Buber's insight. Our knowledge of the poet should proceed from our
understanding of his poetry. The real poet is his work.

8   In any case, my study of Dickinson's poetry will be markedly different
    from most other studies which rely heavily on her external biography,
    her literary and social heritage, her immediate ethos, and so on. Some
    of the studies that I have in mind here are: Josephine Pollitt, *Emily
    Dickinson: The Human Background of Her Poetry;* Genevieve Taggard, *The
    Life and Mind of Emily Dickinson;* George Frisbie Whicher, *This Was a
    Poet: A Critical Biography of Emily Dickinson;* Rebecca Patterson, *The Rid-
    dle of Emily Dickinson;* Richard Chase, *Emily Dickinson;* Thomas H. John-
    son, *Emily Dickinson: An Interpretive Biography;* Theodora Ward, *The Cap-
    sule of the Mind: Chapters in the Life of Emily Dickinson;* Polly Longworth,
    Emily Dickinson: Her Letter to the World; Thomas W. Ford, *Heaven Beguiles
    the Tired: Death in the Poetry of Emily Dickinson;* J. B. Pickard, *Emily Dickin-
    son: An Introduction and Interpretation;* John Evangelist Walsh, *The Hidden
    Life of Emily Dickinson;* and John Cody, *After Great Pain: The Inner Life of
    Emily Dickinson.*

9   See William Barrett, *Irrational Man: A Study in Existential Philosophy,* pp.
    120–46.

10 See Henry W. Wells, *Introduction to Emily Dickinson.* Wells seems to me to
    be the pioneer of the idea that Dickinson's poetry can be fruitfully stud-
    ied in relation to the insights of writers who are not American and
    whose cultural backgrounds differ widely from Dickinson's own.

11 Benjamin T. Spencer, "Criticism: Centrifugal and Centripetal," p. 139.
    Spencer observes that there "is the great temptation that centripetal
    criticism confronts us with: to discount literature both aesthetically as a
    value in itself and also cognitively as a unique mode of achieving a kind
    of knowledge. It countenances literature chiefly as a confirmatory or
    illustrative agent of ideas already fully conceived and understood. It
    distrusts the ambiguities of centrifugal reading and prefers the clear-
    cut security of formula, the one-dimensional assurance of a key idea to
    the fuller reality of contradiction and paradox which the greatest works
    seem to hold forever in solution in the name of the widest truth about
    things. In effect, it denies to literature what William Faulkner in
    Knight's Gambit has claimed for it as a raison d'être: '. . . it is only in lit-
    erature that the paradoxical and even mutually negativing anecdotes in
    the history of a human heart can be juxtaposed and annealed by art
    into verisimilitude and credibility' " (p. 149).

12 Thomas H. Johnson, ed., *The Poems of Emily Dickinson.* Johnson must be
    praised for undertaking the monumental task of making available both
    the product and the workshop of Dickinson's creative life. The
    variorum reproduces in one place all the manuscripts—fair copies, fair

with variant readings, semifair drafts, and worksheet materials. This edition is responsible for almost all the textual studies of Dickinson's poetry. But this edition does not bring us anywhere close to a truly definitive edition or what is called the "reader's copy." In this connection, the subsequent findings of Ralph William Franklin, *The Editing of Emily Dickinson: A Reconsideration,* and the arrangement of manuscripts pointed out by Ruth Miller in *The Poetry of Emily Dickinson,* deserve every attention. I am not sure if another, truly definitive, edition of Dickinson's poetry is in the making. But there is an urgent need to settle many 'questions about variant fair copies, worksheets, and semifinal drafts of the poems. For my own purpose, however, I intend to comment on individual poems and / or clusters of poems so as to be representative of the whole of Dickinson's poetic vision. I am mainly concerned with her symbolic structures and not with the number of poems.

13 The word *developmentally* is from Richard B. Sewall's introduction to *Emily Dickinson: A Collection of Critical Essays,* p. 3. For studies based on the chronological order of poems or the theory of periods in Dickinson's poetic life, see David Thomas Porter, *The Art of Emily Dickinson's Early Poetry;* and William R. Sherwood, *Circumference and Circumstance: Stages in the Mind and Art of Emily Dickinson.* However, my own examination of Dickinson manuscripts revealed that an imposed chronological order can even be misleading in so far as we are concerned with the study of Dickinson's mind and her creative method. The manuscripts are undated and they should be allowed to remain so.

14 Sewall, ed., *Critical Essays,* p. 104.

15 Ibid., p. 3.

CHAPTER 1

1 "Burnt Norton," 5. 142–43.

2 For a typology of "the eternal return," the following poems may be read as a single unit: 5, 30, 99, 133, 140, 142, 204, 221, 304, 337, 369, 392, 403, 471, 550, 680, 764, 830, 1025, 1134, 1274, 1320, 1422, 1519, and 1690. The cluster method used throughout this study is based on the related patterns of imagery and common symbolic constructs of the poems.

3 In order to provide a fuller background and context for the discussion of Dickinson's sense of *danger,* I would suggest a close reading of the following poems: 179, 238, 241, 242, 264, 379, 419, 455, 544, 686, 703, 772, 807, 845, 870, 875, 925, 951, 1070, 1109, 1217, 1416, 1487, 1516, 1518, 1563, 1613, 1629, 1642, 1656, 1677, 1678, 1736, and 1758. See *Selected Letters of Rainer Maria Rilke,* ed. Harry T. Moore. Rilke also

expresses his belief in the "difficult," in the aesthetics of danger, when he writes to Emmy Hirschberg in 1904 (pp. 77–78): "What is required of us is that we *love the difficult* and learn to deal with it. In the difficult are the friendly forces, the hands that work on us. Right in the difficult we must have our joys, our happiness, our dreams: there, against the depth of this background they stand out, there for the first time we see how beautiful they are. And only in the darkness of the difficult does our smile, so precious, have a meaning; only there does it glow with its deep, dreamy light, and in the brightness it for a moment diffuses we see the wonders and treasures with which we are surrounded."

4   For a variety of existential moods and postures, read the following poems: 320 (existential learning); 404 and 1293 (existential void and predicament); 301, 669 (existential questioning); 1506 (existential transiency of time and permanency of sorrow); 521 (existential sympathy); 125, 193 (existential anguish and ecstasy); 335 (existential hurt and "kind" death); 344, 1440, 1733, 1769 (continuous existential pain, scar, awe, and anguish); 1350 (existential toil); and 405 (existential fate). For references to existential suffering, also see L30, L33, L56, L278, and L416.

5   *The Poetry of Emily Dickinson,* pp. 69–70. It would have been more plausible to say that the terror is that of Dickinson's own impending death which makes her sing or write poetry with all the more fear and intensity so that she may fulfill her destiny before she dies. But there is no indication of such a premonition in Dickinson's life during the years 1861–62. Also see: "Afraid! Of whom am I afraid? / Not Death – for who is He?" (608).

6   For the theme of the aesthetics of terror, I recommend reading poems 281, 315, 323, 362, 410, 528, 535, 591, 875, 986, 1225, 1486, and 1581 in conjunction with 505, 544, 569, 883, and 919, in which the awe, pain, and terror of the poet are fused in his ultimate role. The theme of the poet is developed further in chapter three.

7   For Emily Dickinson's use of paradox, irony, and opposites, not only as literary devices to accomplish indirection but also as symbolic constructs to portray fulfillment and the syncretic vision, the following poems may be read as a cluster: 7, 21, 22, 67, 125, 135, 175, 256, 276, 281, 299, 313, 329, 353, 355, 364, 384, 385, 451, 572, 599, 684, 689, 738, 771, 791, 816, 834, 838, 910, 1054, 1057, 1093, 1106, 1125, 1168, 1179, 1287, 1439, 1470, 1503, 1562, 1573, 1640, 1642, and 1726. For opposites and paradox, see L34, L874, and PF65.

8   "In Search of Goethe from Within," *The Dehumanization of Art and Other Writings on Art and Culture,* p. 127. For Dickinson's theme of existential courage and sense of danger, read the following poems: 10, 20, 48, 73, 147, 172, 252, 269, 554, 561, 875, and 1113.

9   The following poems refer to Emily Dickinson's celebration of the *here:* 313, 370, 623, 889, 1012, 1118, 1205, 1231, 1370, 1373, 1408, 1544, 1665, and 1775. Linked with the *here* are the poems of the *now,* which refer to her aesthetic treatment of *time* which is the present moment. These are: 434, 624, 672, 765, 825, 1165, 1309, 1367, 1380, 1398, 1631, 1684, and 1734.

10 For references to earth, world, and mortality, see the following letters: L11, L13, L23, L185, L389, and L524.

11 The reference here is to the opening lines of "Auguries of Innocence":

> To See a World in a Grain of Sand
> And a Heaven in a Wild Flower,
> Hold infinity in the palm of your hand
> And Eternity in an hour.

12 *The Selected Poetry and Prose of Shelley,* p. 445.

13 See Jacques Maritain, *Art and Scholasticism and the Frontiers of Poetry,* p. 123. Poetry, according to Maritain, is ontology because it deals with "the roots of the knowledge of Being."

14 "Jerusalem," 1.10:20–21:

> I must Create a System, or be enslav'd by another Mans
> I will not Reason & Compare: my business is to Create

15 In "Out of the Cradle Endlessly Rocking" (lines 144–57), Whitman's exploration of the bird-bard relationship provides an analogous experience.

16 See poems 857, 859, 1329, 1335, and 1411.

17 *The Vision of Tragedy,* p. 6.

18 *Stairway of Surprise,* p. 322.

19 See poems 193, 225, 295, 317, 322, 506, 527, 538, 553, 740, 833, 1487, 1543, and 1736.

20 The other poems that I have in mind to put with this cluster are: 59, 185, 324, 401, 437, 503, 508, 597, 600, 947, 1069, 1144, 1201, 1258, 1317, 1357, 1377, 1412, 1461, 1545, 1551, 1569, 1591, 1639, 1657, 1672, 1718, 1719, and 1751.

21 See Søren Kierkegaard, *Concluding Unscientific Postscript,* pp. 327–29. Kierkegaard questions the validity of baptism in these words: "What is baptism without personal appropriation? . . . Baptism is surely not the slip of paper that the parish clerk issues and which he frequently fills with errors of writing; it is surely not the mere external event that took place at 11 o'clock on the morning of the 7th of November? That time, or existence in time, should be sufficient to decide an eternal happiness is in general so paradoxical that paganism cannot conceive its possibility. But that the whole matter should be decided in the course of five

minutes, two weeks after birth, seems almost a little too much of the paradoxical."

22 *Stairway of Surprise,* pp. 20–21.

23 The quotations in this paragraph are from L389 and L387. Also see Nicolai Berdyaev, *Christian Existentialism: A Berdyaev Synthesis,* p. 225. Berdyaev states the case of religion and existence in these words: "In the objective history of the world there is nothing sacred, only a conditioned symbolization; the sacred obtains only in the world of existence, only in existential subjects. The real depth of the spirit is known existentially in experiencing one's destiny, in suffering, yearning, death, love, creativity, in freedom rather than in objects. Religion is above all existential in its nature, it is rooted in the spirit; it is contact with primal realities."

24 The other poems which have not been cited, but which are necessary to the whole discussion of "What mystery pervades a well!", are: 888, 891, 892, 905, 978, 1172, 1298, 1397, 1558, and 1727. These numbers do not by any means exhaust the list of nature poems.

25 Quoted in Richard B. Sewall, "Emily Dickinson: The Problem of the Biographer," p. 128.

26 See Arturo B. Fallico, *Art and Existentialism,* pp. 91–109. In the entire discussion of art, Fallico links the idea of language as "first utterance" with the notions of "freedom," "aesthetic purposing," "personality," and "existential sharing."

27 For reference to the power of words, see: 952, 1126, 1212, 1261, 1409, 1467, 1563, 1587, and 1651. Also see L374, L379, L791, L797, L873, L946, and L965.

28 For complete understanding of the problem of the inadequacy of language, or the simple human inadequacy of the poet, to communicate the poetic vision, read the following poems together: 407, 581, 797, 1358, 1452, 1472, 1668, 1700, and 1750.

29 The essential inarticulateness of the poetic vision or the dichotomy between communication and original perception is brought out by Thoreau in "Friday" of his *A Week on the Concord and Merrimack Rivers;* by Walt Whitman in "Song of Myself," section 50; and by Shelley in "A Defence of Poetry." On the inadequacy of linear language and the poet's use of it, also see Susanne K. Langer, *Philosophy in a New Key: A Study in the Symbolism of Reason, Rite, and Art,* p. 92; T. S. Eliot, "East Coker," 5.172–82; and George Steiner, *Language and Silence: Essays on Language, Literature, and the Inhuman,* p. 40. In the last cited study, see particularly "The Retreat from the Word," pp. 12–35; and "Silence and the Poet," pp. 36–54. Steiner offers a rigorous analysis of the loosening power of "language," the poet's transcendence of his own medium, and

the final silence which still awaits the word. He writes: "But as the poet draws near the Divine presence, the heart of the rose of fire, the labor of translation into speech grows ever more exacting. Words grow less and less adequate to the task of translating immediate revelation. Light passes to a diminishing degree into speech; instead of making syntax translucent with meaning, it seems to spill over in unrecapturable splendor or burn the word to ash (p. 40) . . . language, when truly apprehended aspires to the condition of music and is brought, by the genius of the poet, to the threshold of that condition. By a gradual loosening or transcendence of its own forms, the poem strives to escape from the linear, denotative, logically determined bonds of linguistic syntax into what the poet takes to be the simultaneities, immediacies, and free play of musical form. It is in music that the poet hopes to find the paradox resolved of an act of creation singular to the creator, bearing the shape of his own spirit, yet infinitely renewed in each listener (p. 43). . . . But there is a third mode of transcendence: in it language simply ceases, and the motion of spirit gives no further outward manifestation of its being. The poet enters into silence. Here the word borders not on radiance or music, but on night" (p. 46). Eliot and Langer also make several references to the power of words in their respective works.

CHAPTER 2

1 See Fallico, *Art and Existentialism.* Fallico explains this inner-outer action in these words (p. 143): "It is, in fact, with such internal *live* sense of my own body—the *thing* that I myself am—that I begin to 'see' the thing which stands before me. But, of course, I have already crossed the line between the obscure, unyielding, positively dumb thing as it first confronted me. . . . A world of transparent qualities is now emerging 'in' and 'outside' my concrete bodily being, gradually supplanting what was there obscurely 'given' to me earlier."
2 For wheel symbolism, see Blake, "Jerusalem," 1.15 : 14–20. Blake contrasts the wheels of Ezekiel with the wheels of vegetable existence.
3 *Romeo and Juliet,* 2.2.85; 2.2.133; 2.1.32 respectively.
4 See Paul Tillich, *The Courage to Be.* Tillich, the noted theologian, describes the relationship between being and nonbeing in these words (p. 34): "If one is asked how nonbeing is related to being-itself, one can only answer metaphorically: being 'embraces' itself and nonbeing. Being has nonbeing 'within' itself as that which is eternally present and eternally overcome in the process of the divine life. The ground of everything that is not a dead identity without movement and becoming; it is living creativity. Creatively it affirms itself, eternally conquering its

own nonbeing. As such it is the pattern of the self-affirmation of every finite being and the source of the courage to be."

5 See "What is Metaphysics?" in *Existence and Being*. Martin Heidegger states the relationship between *being* and the "other" or "nothing" in this manner (p. 353 and p. 360): "This, the purely 'Other' than everything that 'is,' is that-which-is not (*das Nicht-Seiende*). Yet this 'Nothing' functions as Being. It would be premature to stop thinking at this point and adopt the facile explanation that Nothing is merely the nugatory, equating it with the non-existent (*das Wesenlose*). Instead of giving way to such precipitate and empty ingenuity and abandoning Nothing in all its mysterious multiplicity of meanings, we should rather equip ourselves and make ready for one thing only: to experience in Nothing the vastness of that which gives every being the warrant to be. That is Being itself. . . . One of the essential theatres of speechlessness is dread in the sense of the terror into which the abyss of Nothing plunges us. Nothing, conceived as the pure 'Other' than what-is, is the veil of Being. In Being all that comes to pass in what-is is perfected from everlasting."

6 *The Ethics of Ambiguity*, p. 156. For "The Aesthetic Attitude," see pp. 74–78.

7 *Selected Letters of Rilke*, pp. 388–91. The letter is dated 13 November 1925.

8 The images are taken from poems 210, 421, 501, 662, 774, 998, 1051, 1108, 1120, 1195, 1209, 1235, 1245, 1254, 1353, 1382, 1442, 1463, 1468, 1524, 1567, 1740, 1744, and 1746 respectively. Other poems, indicating veil, silence, riddle, and unknowability of the "landscape," are 915, 920, 1118, 1200, 1222, 1417, 1429, and 1490.

9 Gerard Manley Hopkins used the words "inscape" and "instress" in his writings in many different contexts. For sources and full treatment of the terms, see W. H. Gardner, *Gerard Manley Hopkins (1844–89): A Study of Poetic Idiosyncrasy in Relation to Poetic Tradition*.

10 Conrad Aiken, "Emily Dickinson," p. 10. Also see Caesar R. Blake and Carlton F. Wells, eds., *The Recognition of Emily Dickinson: Selected Criticism since 1890*, p. 111.

11 *Walden* ["Solitude"], pp. 122–23.

12 "Emily Dickinson," p. 202. Also see Sewall, ed., *Critical Essays*, pp. 19–20. Tate's essay was written in 1932.

13 See Friedrich Schiller, *On the Aesthetic Education of Man: In a Series of Letters*, pp. 125–132; *The Philosophy of Nietzsche*, pp. 498–543; Susanne K. Langer, *Feeling and Form*, pp. 45–68; and Jung, *Modern Man in Search of a Soul*, pp. 152–72. Also see R. G. Collingwood, *Essays in the Philosophy of Art*, ed. Alan Donagon, pp. 52–72; Herbert Read, *The Forms of Things*

Unknown, pp. 64–65; and Ortega y Gasset, *The Dehumanization of Art,* pp. 3–50.

14 *The Dehumanization of Art,* p. 20.

15 Ibid., p. 29.

16 *Feeling and Form,* p. 68. Langer discusses the "experiential character" of illusion in chapter 13, "Poesis," pp. 208–35.

17 For the power of dream—dream as a metaphor for imagination and perception—see 103, 188, 302, 371, 475, 493, 518, 531, 569, 646, 939, 1291, 1376, and 1592.

18 See Karl Jaspers, *Truth and Symbol.* Jaspers has put forward this point of view with great lucidity and I consider it vital to the acts of true philosophizing and literary criticism: "the being of the subject itself is the necessary condition for the presence of Being through a content which appears from out the depth of subjectivity. Consciousness of Being lies simultaneously in the grasping of the object and in the consummation of subjectivity. . . . In point of fact, however, there is no separated duality of subjectivity and objectivity. Both are inseparably bound together. The presence of Being is in the movement which grasps and permeates subject and object simultaneously. We take possession of Being in the polarity, but in such a way that subject and object mutually overlap. While we are directed towards the object, Being in its essence is not already before our eyes as an object but is present only in the Encompassing, through object and subject simultaneously as that which permeates both. . . . *Existenz* appears in the intertwining of subjectivity and objectivity. . . . Only in the polarity of subject and object is our life. In this polarity the object can attain that suspension which at the same time allows it to exist and elevates it. This suspension makes possible the consciousness of Being; for this the object is imbued from the depths with spirit. From this depth of Being the object obtains an irreplaceable meaning" (pp. 22–24 and 39).

19 Some other poems relevant to the whole discussion of absence as perception and the notion of metaphors as relations and human forms are: 2, 78, 375, 495, 564, 629, 696, 890, 993, 1320, 1559, and 1627.

20 Letter to George and Thomas Keats, 21 December 1817.

21 See Lionel Trilling's introduction to *The Selected Letters of John Keats,* p. 29. The concept of negative capability is highly paradoxical in that it favors selflessness in a creative artist in order that he may discover his true self, his *freedom* through empathy and receptivity.

22 *Stairway of Surprise,* p. 211.

23 *Either / Or,* 1 : 447. Sensuousness is a quality which is defined by its directness, its immediacy, and its spontaneity. It is *intuition* which is most tan-

gible, and yet highly elusive. In music, sensuousness expresses itself fully in the *moment* of performance, which is its eternity. Love shares with music the traits of sensuousness or "spiritual sensation."

24   Jung, "Psychology and Literature," p. 172.

25   See Keats's letter to Richard Woodhouse, 27 October 1818.

26   See Søren Kierkegaard, *Fear and Trembling and the Sickness unto Death.* In *The Sickness unto Death,* Kierkegaard considers despair from several points of view. His treatment of despair under the aspects of finitude / infinitude seems to be relevant to Dickinson's notion of self as a *process:* "The self is the conscious synthesis of infinitude and finitude which relates itself to itself, whose task is to become itself, a task which can be performed only by means of a relationship to God. But to become oneself is to become concrete. But to become concrete means neither to become finite nor infinite, for that which is to become concrete is a synthesis. Accordingly, the development consists in moving away from oneself infinitely by the process of infinitizing oneself, and in returning to oneself infinitely by the process of finitizing. If on the contrary the self does not become itself, it is in despair whether it knows it or not. . . . In so far as the self does not become itself, it is not its own self; but not to be one's own self is despair. . . . For the self is a synthesis in which the finite is the limiting factor, and the infinite is the expanding factor. Infinitude's despair is therefore the fantastical, the limitless. The self is in sound health and free from despair only when, precisely by having been in despair, it is grounded transparently in God" (pp. 162–63).

27   For other interpretations of this poem, see Yvor Winters, "Emily Dickinson and the Limits of Judgment," pp. 149–65; Laurence Perrine, "Dickinson's 'There's a Certain Slant of Light' "; Donald E. Thackerey, *Emily Dickinson's Approach to Poetry,* pp. 76–80; Johnson, *Emily Dickinson: An Interpretive Biography,* pp. 189–90; and Anderson, *Stairway of Surprise,* pp. 245–47.

28   See Paul Tillich, *The Shaking of the Foundations.* In the chapter on "Meditation: The Mystery of Time," Tillich writes (p. 35): "Time is as inexhaustible as the ground of life itself. Even the greatest minds have each discovered only one aspect of it. But everyone, even the most simple mind, apprehends the meaning of time—namely, his own temporality. He may not be able to express his knowledge about time, but he is never separated from its mystery. His life, and the life of each of us, is permeated in every moment, in every experience, and in every expression, by the mystery of time. Time is our destiny. Time is our hope. Time is our despair. And time is the mirror in which we see eternity. Let me point to three of the many mysteries of time: its power to

devour everything within its sphere; its power to receive eternity within itself; and its power to drive toward an ultimate end, a new creation." The concept of time as both creator and destroyer is as old as the *Bhagavad-Gita*, "one of the foundational documents of Hinduism," as described by S. G. F. Brandon. In his *History, Time and Deity: A Historical and Comparative Study of the Conception of Time in Religious Thought and Practice*, pp. 31–64, Brandon offers a brilliant analysis of time as deity.

29 See William F. Lynch, *Christ and Apollo: The Dimensions of the Literary Imagination*, p. 49.

30 Expanded perception is not the same thing as a mystical trance in which one liberates oneself from the tyranny, suffering, and relentless logic of temporal time. The poetic methodology is different from the route of asceticism. See Brandon, *History, Time and Deity* (pp. 102–03). The poet is highly conscious of his *being in time;* the mystic obliterates the sense of self defined by time. For the mystic, time is an illusion, for the poet time is real, though he struggles to achieve timelessness through the creative imagination. Brandon offers a very profound analysis of the notion of time in Indian thought, which one can apply with certain qualifications, to the position of the poet (p. 105): "The conception of deity as ambivalent in character, manifesting itself in both creation and destruction, and the equation of this deity with Time, connotes a realistic appreciation of what existence in time and space must involve. The acceptance of this situation did not, however, remove its dread, and the instinct to escape from it has been, through the centuries, the abiding motive of Indian religious thought and practice. Hence the twofold effort to magnify the suffering caused by the 'sorrowful weary wheel' of Time, and to deny Time's ultimate reality. The solution is essentially an existential one; for it assumes both the reality of empirical existence and the reality of those psychic states that attest an existence beyond Time. In other words, the *nunc fluens* is real for those who accept it and become enmeshed in it, and it is, moreover, for such, endless. But its spell can be ended by the enlightened *Yogin*, who, by meditative techniques, perceives its fundamental illusion and glimpses the *nunc stans* into which he will for ever pass on the extinction of his *Karma*." The poet is certainly a Yogin-artist, but he achieves the goal of timelessness in and through time, and by the creative process of his art, and not by the "Yoga praxis." I must insist that the poet and the mystic are poles apart in their methods, although perhaps not so much in their objectives. Also see William Blake, "The Marriage of Heaven and Hell," plate 14. Blake tells us that "if the doors of perception were cleansed everything would appear to man as it is, infinite. For man has closed himself up, till he sees all things thro' narrow chinks of his cavern."

CHAPTER 3

1   Poetic perception or the poetic experience cannot be understood in
    terms of sense-datum theories or the rational structures of empirical
    knowledge. Poetic knowledge is primarily intuitive and can be rendered
    only in symbols and metaphors, and not in scientific, objective, or one-
    dimensional language. For this contrast, see Robert J. Swartz, ed., *Per-
    ceiving, Sensing, and Knowing: A Book of Readings from Twentieth-Century
    Sources in the Philosophy of Perception;* and Jacques Maritain, *Creative Intu-
    ition in Art and Poetry,* p. 144. Maritain rightly points out that "in poetic
    knowledge things are known as resounding in the subjectivity, and as
    one with it, and this knowledge—essentially obscure—is expressed, not
    through abstract ideas, but through the images awakened by intuitive
    emotion. As a result, science, the kind of science unnaturally required
    of poetic knowledge, is to be ruled by the law of images for which there
    is no principle of noncontradiction, and for which the sign contains and
    conveys the very reality of the thing signified. In other words, poetic
    knowledge transformed into absolute knowledge is magical knowl-
    edge."
2   Seeing, in this context, is inclusive of the other means of perception:
    hearing, feeling, smelling, tasting, etc. Seeing emphasizes the central
    position of the perceiver and the faculty of imagination, which is the
    primary creative organ. Seeing is both contemplation and creation.
3   Paul Tillich, *The New Being,* p. 129. Tillich develops the notion of poetic
    seeing in these words: "We never see only what we see; we always see
    something else with it and through it! Seeing creates, seeing unites, and
    above all seeing goes beyond itself. If we look at a stone we see directly
    only the colors and forms of the side which is turned towards us. But
    with and through this limited surface we are aware of the roundness, of
    the extension and mass of the structure of the whole thing. We see
    beyond what we see. . . . If we look at a human face, we see lines and
    shades, but with it and through it we see a unique, incomparable per-
    sonality whose expressions are visible in his face, whose character and
    destiny have left traces which we understand and in which we can even
    read something of his future. With and through colors and forms and
    movements we see friendliness and coldness, hostility and devotion,
    anger and love, sadness and joy. We see infinitely more than we see
    when we look into a human face. And we see even beyond this into a
    new depth" (pp. 129–30). Whatever theology Tillich's statement might
    adumbrate, it is certainly valid that poetic perception means seeing
    "into a new depth."
4   Fallico, *Art and Existentialism,* p. 60. Fallico comments on this "dream-

like" consciousness and its creative role in these words (pp. 60–61): "In the perfect coalescence of feeling with image, the original aesthetic constructivity accomplishes perfectly what neither waking-state reality nor dream can accomplish separately—it lends wakeful reality to the dream, and dream-like liberating spontaneity to wakeful life. In this sense, the work of art implies that all reality is something that is *made,* or that the possibility of its free and unrestricted making and unmaking stands prior to any and all of its actual formations so that none can have ultimacy of being and meaning for the existent. The very presence of the presence which is art casts a veil of illusion over all the hard, fast, and pressing realities, even if only by comparison. Who in the presence of the artist's vision has not felt the realities of ordinary experience fade away like transient and distorted dream images?"

5 The images refer to poems: 737, 1233, 931, 1556, and 1581. For the power of eyes or seeing, and paradoxical blindness, see: 196, 327, 507, 647, 761, and 1284.

6 Herbert Read, *The Forms of Things Unknown,* p. 134.

7 See Jacques Maritain, *Creative Intuition in Art and Poetry,* p. 296. At the end of "The Three Epiphanies of Creative Intuition: Poetic Sense, Action and Theme, and Harmonic Expansion," Maritain writes: "Creative intuition is the only supreme gift that a poet, in any art whatsoever, ought to seek—in the way in which a gift can be sought: not in the sense that it might be acquired by any effort of the human will, but in the sense that it can be cared for, and protected, and assisted, when it is there. And it is there, perhaps in a humbler way than he believes, in any man who is inclined toward the workings of art by an inner necessity. Sometimes, and in the greatest artists, creative intuition may be at work in darkness and despairing agony. Then they may think of what Pascal felt about another kind of grace, and this holds true for them also: 'Take comfort, thou wouldst not be seeking me, hadst thou not found me.' " This means that the creative intuition is the *presence* in the inmost subjectivity of every man, but the artist *discovers* it, and is impelled by it to create.

8 See M. H. Abrams, *The Mirror and the Lamp: Romantic Theory and the Critical Tradition,* p. 22. I have borrowed the word "reflector" from this study. There are obvious connections between Dickinson's way of perception and romantic poetics. Summarizing the "central tendency of the expressive theory of art," Abrams writes: "A work of art is essentially the internal made external, resulting from a creative process operating under the impulse of feeling, and embodying the combined product of the poet's perceptions, thoughts, and feelings. The primary source and subject matter of a poem, therefore, are the attributes and actions of the

poet's own mind; or if aspects of the external world, then these only as they are converted from fact to poetry by the feelings and the operations of the poet's mind." He continues (p. 60): "As in the English Platonists, so in the romantic writers, the favorite analogy for the activity of the perceiving mind is that of a lamp projecting light."

9   For symbolic reference to "withinness" or the "interior" of the poet, see 383, 395, 526, 579, 636, 803, 903, 1097, 1123, 1223, 1242, 1695, 1712, and 1748.

10 Alfred North Whitehead, *Process and Reality: An Essay in Cosmology,* p. 273.

11 *Emily Dickinson,* p. 135. Also see Anderson, *Stairway of Surprise,* pp. 89–106. Anderson writes (p. 104): "Nature to her is graspless and its meaning unmanifest. God has simply made his experiment and she must make hers. It is the poet's task to create in a similar way, so that his poem also will contain the kind of dual significance he has discovered in nature by coercing the flux of experience into intelligible forms. Since his poems are artifacts rather than natural facts, he must 'try,' as nature does not need to, in order to make them haunted. Nature best serves him, then, not as a source of subject matter nor as a key to meaning but as exemplar. Also as a reservoir of imagery, since through perception he can select certain aspects of nature, or rather define his impressions of them, and give them a quasi-symbolic value that helps him create his own world." I agree with Anderson's insight. But I would like to point out that Dickinson apprehends nature as a haunted house, with all its terror, awe, wonder, freedom, and creativity. The meaning of nature, with all its inherent ambivalence, is manifest to her mind. That is why she wants her art to become both haunted and haunting like nature. I have stressed this point in my discussion of "What mystery pervades a well!" (1400).

12 See José Ferrater Mora, *Being and Death: An Outline of Integrationist Philosophy.* I do not wholly subscribe to Ferrater Mora's highly philosophic, scientific, and rational methodology of knowing the nature of human experience. But I think there is some relevance, in what he regards as "the external" and "the internal," to our examination of Dickinson's theory of perception and to the way Dickinson relates the external to the internal in spite of the seeming or real emphasis on the internal. Ferrater Mora writes (pp. 71–72): " 'The external' and 'the internal' are names of absolute realities, and since the latter do not exist the former do not properly name anything. But by means of them the universe is made intelligible. I have said that every entity *tends to be* more or less external or more or less internal because its being is deter-

mined by *both* poles. I am not affirming that reality is primarily some-thing external, for example, something primarily inorganic, so that the ontological measure of each thing would be determined by its orienta-tion toward that exteriority. Nor am I maintaining that reality is pri-marily something internal, for example, something personal, so that the ontological measure of each thing would be determined by its orienta-tion toward that interiority. I am postulating an ontological succession of entities. *But I assume that this succession cannot be depicted by a single, uninterrupted line having only one direction which, like an arrow, would in-dicate the direction of being toward 'real existence.'* It would be more accurate to represent this succession by a line on every point of which two con-trary and complementary tendencies or polar directions converge. The corresponding ontology can be variously named: the 'ontology of dou-ble direction,' the 'bi-directional ontology,' the 'two-way ontology,' and so on. In any case, it is the 'ontology of integrationism.' "

13 Concerning the ontological as well as the aesthetic problem of subject-object relationship, and its significance for the romantic-existentialist theory of poetry, the insights of Plotinus, Blake, Kant, Fichte, Schelling, Schiller, Keats, Coleridge, Kierkegaard, Thoreau, Emerson, Rilke, Hölderlin, Husserl, Heidegger, Sartre, Merleau-Ponty, Wallace Stevens, Marianne Moore, Hart Crane, and many others come to mind. Some of the useful studies or works which deserve mention here are: Abrams, *The Mirror and the Lamp;* James M. Edie, ed., *Maurice Merleau-Ponty: The Primacy of Perception;* Heidegger, *Existence and Being;* Erich Heller, *The Disinherited Mind;* Frederick J. Hoffman, *The 20's: American Writing in the Postwar Decade;* Joseph J. Kockelmans, ed. *Phenomenology: The Phi-losophy of Edmund Husserl and Its Interpretation;* F. O. Matthiessen, *Ameri-can Renaissance: Art and Expression in the Age of Emerson and Whitman;* Elmer O'Brien, *The Essential Plotinus;* Herbert Read, *The True Voice of Feeling: Studies in English Romantic Poetry;* Rainer Maria Rilke, *Letters to a Young Poet;* Jean-Paul Sartre, *The Psychology of Imagination;* and Oskar Walzel, *German Romanticism.*

14 Letter to the Rev. Dr. Trusler, 23 August 1799. *The Portable Blake,* p. 179.

15 Wordsworth seems to be indebted to Coleridge for the notion of ex-ternal-internal relationship. Coleridge writes much earlier than Words-worth: "In looking at objects of Nature while I am thinking . . . I seem rather to be seeking, as it were asking, a symbolical language for something within me that already and forever exists, than observing anything new." This remark of Coleridge is quoted in M. H. Abrams, "Structure and Style in Greater Romantic Lyric," p. 551. At the above-

noted level of poetic perception, the mind is subconsciously in the possession of the objective experience as a part of its own reality, and thus seems to appropriate the objective reality or nature.

16   "Where I Lived, and What I Lived For," *Walden and Other Writings,* p. 73.

17   "The Inward Morning," ibid., p. 401.

18   Quoted from *American Poetry and Poetics: Poems and Critical Documents from the Puritans to Robert Frost,* ed. Daniel G. Hoffman, p. 338.

19   Eudo C. Mason, *Rilke,* p. 54.

20   Ibid., pp. 54–55.

21   See *The Collected Poems of Wallace Stevens.* For my discussion of Stevens, I am indebted, in general, to: Northrop Frye, "The Realistic Oriole: A Study of Wallace Stevens"; Louis L. Martz, "Wallace Stevens: The World as Meditation"; Ralph Freedman, "Wallace Stevens and Rainer Maria Rilke: Two Versions of a Poetic"; and Frank Kermode, *Wallace Stevens.*

22   I find Merleau-Ponty's point of view of special interest and relevance to our discussion of Dickinson's theory of perception. In his "The Primacy of Perception and Its Philosophical Consequences," Merleau-Ponty writes (p. 16): "Perception is thus paradoxical. The perceived thing itself is paradoxical; it exists only in so far as someone can perceive it. I cannot even for an instant imagine an object in itself. As Berkeley said, if I attempt to imagine some place in the world which has never been seen, the very fact that I imagine it makes me present at that place. I thus cannot conceive a perceptible place in which I am not myself present. But even the places in which I find myself are never completely given to me; the things which I see are things for me only under the condition that they always recede beyond their immediately given aspects. Thus there is a paradox of immanence and transcendence in perception. Immanence, because the perceived object cannot be foreign to him who perceives; transcendence, because it always contains something more than what is actually given. And these two elements of perception are not, properly speaking, contradictory. For if we reflect on this notion of perspective, if we reproduce the perceptual experience in our thought, we see that the kind of evidence proper to the perceived, the appearance of 'something,' requires both this presence and this absence." This view may be applied to Dickinson's "A Something in a Summer's Day" (122).

23   On the need and efficacy of "faith" or poetic fidelity, see the following poems: 81, 260, 387, 440, 455, 497, 637, 702, 792, 797, 912, 969, 972, 999, 1007, 1054, 1152, 1424, 1433, 1766, and 1768. In Dickinson's poetry, faith should be understood as a creative principle and not as a

traditional theological term. Dickinson is quite conscious of the loss of faith or the "tattered Faith" (1442) that happens frequently in day-to-day existence (see, for instance, 145 and 1557). But she suggests that "faith" can be recovered by creative imagination:

> To mend each tattered Faith
> There is a needle fair
> Though no appearance indicate –
> 'Tis threaded in the Air –   [1442]

24   The poems mentioned here are: 288, 779, and 1510 respectively. In his "The Making of a Poem," Stephen Spender has this to say about poetic faith: "The poet's faith is therefore, firstly, a mystique of vocation, secondly, a faith in his own truth, combined with his own devotion to a task. There can really be no greater faith than the confidence that one is doing one's utmost to fulfill one's high vocation, and it is this that has inspired all the greatest poets. At the same time this faith is coupled with a deep humility because one knows that, ultimately, judgment does not rest with oneself. All one can do is to achieve nakedness, to be what one is with all one's faculties and perceptions, strengthened by all the skill which one can acquire, and then to stand before the judgment of time." I have quoted the above from *The Creative Process,* ed. Brewster Ghiselin, p. 123.

25   For the ideas of process or the continuity of creation, see the following poems: 501, 724, 1036, 1073, 1593, 1599, and 1605.

26   For the image of "barefoot" see the following poems as well: 78, 117, 166, 215, 275, 717, 763, and 986.

27   *The Forms of Things Unknown,* p. 132. Read maintains, and rightly so, that psychology has been of little help in exploring the basic problems of creativity: "We have to admit that the illumination cast by modern psychology on these 'fundamental problems' of creativity is almost nil. Myth and dream, symbol and image—all the paraphernalia of depth-psychology—are conceived as shadow play, and it is their analysable signification, and not their sensuous actuality, that attract the analyst. The depth-psychologist may claim that therapy is his only concern, and that the sensuous quality of works of art would merely distract him. That is to misunderstand the nature of art, and precisely its most intrinsic values. It is to disregard the unity of the psyche, which is not a unity of concepts, of spirit or intellect, or even of images, but of sensation. . . . The poem is a sensuous unity, a totality of utterance, and meaningful as unity or totality. . . . Do we then end with a mystery, and a veto on psychological attempts to explain it? Not exactly. We end with the reality of being or existence, and the experience of poetry is a proof of its intrin-

sic originality, of its ceaseless novelty, of its unpredictable form. There is a chain of cause and effect in our practical life, in our intercourse with the external world; but deep within man's subjectivity there is an effect which has no discernible cause, which is a process of discovery, self-realization, a rending of the numinous veil of consciousness. The immediate object of the poetic experience refuses to be identified: it is infinite and eternal, formless and uninformed. In so far as this poetic experience can be described, Francis Thompson described it in these paradoxical words:

> *O world invisible, we view thee,*
> *O world intangible, we touch thee,*
> *O world unknowable, we know thee,*
> *Inapprehensible, we clutch thee!*

View, touch, clutch—these are sensible modes of knowledge, and what we know by these means can be described only by the one simple but ambiguous word: Truth" (pp. 133–35).

28   "Creativity and Encounter," *The Creative Imagination: Psychoanalysis and the Genius of Inspiration*, p. 283. In this brilliant paper, Rollo May proposes a theory: "Creativity occurs in an act of encounter, and is to be understood with this encounter as its center." He explains his theory in these words: "Cézanne sees a tree. He sees it in a way no one else has ever seen it. He experiences, as he no doubt would say, a 'being grasped' by the tree. The painting that issues out of this encounter between a person, Cézanne, and an objective reality, the tree, is literally new. Something is born, comes into being, something which did not exist before—which is as good a definition of creativity as we can get. Thereafter everyone who has the experience of encounter with the painting, who looks at it with intensity of awareness and lets it speak to him, will see the tree with the unique powerful movement and the architectural beauty which literally did not exist in our relation with trees until Cézanne experienced and painted them" (p. 284). The same may be said of Emily Dickinson's poems because they are encounters with the forms of reality, as seen through the creative vision.

29.   "The Birth of a Poem," *The Creative Process*, p. 125. Ghiselin further states (p. 128): "Often a poem is written with the eye intent upon an object that isn't there, before it. Such an object must be excitingly significant, capable of making the mind glow about it. Half the trick then lies in keeping the object spotted in the central furnacelight of the aroused excitement while the construction of the poem goes on in relative shadow, as if it were a thing of slight importance."

30.   "Narcissus as Narcissus," *The Creative Process*, pp. 135–36.

31 Gelpi, *Emily Dickinson*, p. 126. I entirely agree with Gelpi's observation: "There is an alternate last line, and when the poem is made to speak of the knight 'that dares to covet thee' and 'that bends a knee to thee,' it stands even more emphatically as the final testament to the multiple complexities which characterized (for Emily Dickinson at least) the life of consciousness: the ambivalence of the active and passive self in the pain and pleasure of experience. Here is the sublime culmination: within the awesome Circumference she is both bride and knight, each possessing and being possessed" (pp. 126–27).

32 *The Hero with a Thousand Faces*, p. 87, n. 51.

33 "Eternity" is a frequently used image in Dickinson's poetry. She puts it to useful purpose in poems dealing with the themes of love, death, self, and time. The other poems under reference are: 13, 76, 263, 271, 296, 343, 350, 372, 388, 453, 461, 511, 587, 622, 644, 682, 694, 695, 712, 721, 728, 765, 781, 788, 800, 802, 827, 889, 892, 900, 924, 1053, 1078, 1260, 1295, 1380, 1499, 1503, 1668, and 1684.

34 The poems which refer to "awe" directly are these: 287, 525, 575, 609, 683, 732, 829, 1363, 1370, 1394, 1397, 1400, 1419, 1486, 1620, 1678, and 1733. For reference to "awful," see: 160, 187, 198, 505, 506, 609, 786, 894, 1100, 1106, 1134, 1171, 1173, 1204, 1217, 1323, 1347, 1428, 1437, and 1667. For reference to "terror," see: 281, 410, 565, 1124, 1225, 1323, and 1476. A close reading of these and other poems will show that "awe" and "terror" are the creative forces of her poetry.

35 *The Future Poetry*, pp. 39–51. Mantric poetry concerns itself primarily with the discovery of one's being or self, through the metamorphosis of experience. The poet captures his whole being in the form of a poetic transcription. The true poem is always the poet himself, the real source of creative experience. But it happens when the dynamic vision of the poet, his psyche, the illumined mind—all dilate into the form of his creation. In this case, poetry becomes something much more than mere word and rhythm, rhyme and meter; it becomes *Mantra*. To the greatest poets, the power to transcribe the *true* and *vital* experience comes as if in a flash, gleaming intermittently. But when it comes, the vision becomes the mold with supreme inevitability and spontaneity. Think of Keats's "magic casements, opening on the foam of perilous seas, in faery lands forlorn," Shelley's "Life like a dome of many-coloured glass stains the white radiance of Eternity," Shakespeare's "The prophetic soul of the wide world dreaming on things to come!", and Goethe's "Shaping—reshaping—the eternal spirit's eternal pastime." Instances of mantric utterances, in a great variety of styles, can be multiplied. Homer, Dante, Shakespeare—all abound in them. The *Gita* and the *Upanishads* are unsurpassably rich in flights of spiritual vision. Emily

Dickinson possesses the qualities of a great *seer* as well as a great *sayer*. She excels many a great poet in the mode of her *saying*. The nature of her creative experience prompts her to write poetry of lyrical intensity. She has a great sense of poetic austerity (*tapasyâ*); her language is rich in the severity and meditative restraint of expression.

36 *Christ and Apollo,* p. 29.

37 "Psychology and Literature," p. 164.

38 Quoted in Read, *The Forms of Things Unknown,* p. 135. These lines belong to the last section of Lu Chi's essay on literature, the famous poem *Wen Fu.* This section concludes with the following verses (pp. 135–36):

> But there are other moments as though the Six Senses were
>   stranded,
> When the heart seems lost, and the spirit stagnant.
> One stays motionless like a petrified log,
> Dried up like an exhausted river bed.
> The soul is indrawn to search the hidden labyrinth;
> Within oneself is sought where inner light may be stored.
> Behind a trembling veil Truth seems to shimmer, yet ever
>   more evasive,
> And thought twists and twirls like silk spun on a clogged
>   wheel.
> Therefore, all one's vital force may be dispersed in rueful
>   failure;
> Yet again, a free play of impulses may achieve a feat
>   without pitfall.
> While the secret may be held within oneself,
> It is none the less beyond one's power to sway.
> Oft I lay my hand on my empty chest,
> Despairing to know how the barrier could be removed.

My purpose in quoting the above lines is to show that the great poets of all lands pass through a similar experience, and that Emily Dickinson is no exception. In fact, Emily Dickinson must have gone through the entire experience, because the moods described in Lu Chi's poem are integral parts of the human psyche. For instance, see Dickinson's "I felt a Cleaving in my mind" (937).

39 I have borrowed these expressions from Edward J. Rose, "Blake's Milton: The Poet as Poem," p. 20.

40 *Demian: The Story of Emil Sinclair's Youth,* p. 76.

41 The phrases quoted here are from poem 291.

42 The reference is to Thoreau, *Walden,* p. 290. The conception of the art-

ist as both *in* and *beyond* Time, and the conception of the art work as a nonlinear, symbolic process are highlighted in this intensely imaginative parable in *Walden* (pp. 290–91): "There was an artist in the city of Kouroo who was disposed to strive after perfection. One day it came into his mind to make a staff. Having considered that in an imperfect work time is an ingredient, but into a perfect work time does not enter, he said to himself, It shall be perfect in all respects, though I should do nothing else in my life. He proceeded instantly to the forest for wood, being resolved that it should not be made of unsuitable material; and as he searched for and rejected stick after stick, his friends gradually deserted him, for they grew old in their works and died, but he grew not older by a moment. His singleness of purpose and resolution, and his elevated piety, endowed him, without his knowledge, with perennial youth. As he made no compromise with Time, Time kept out of his way, and only sighed at a distance because he could not overcome him. Before he had found a stick in all respects suitable the city of Kouroo was a hoary ruin, and he sat on one of its mounds to peel the stick. Before he had given it the proper shape the dynasty of the Candahars was at an end and with the point of the stick he wrote the name of the last of that race in the sand, and then resumed his work. By the time he had smoothed and polished the staff Kalpa was no longer the pole-star; and ere he had put on the ferule and the head adorned with precious stones, Brahma had awoke and slumbered many times. But why do I stay to mention these things? When the finishing stroke was put to his work, it suddenly expanded before the eyes of the astonished artist into the fairest of all the creations of Brahma. He had made a new system in making a staff, a world with full and fair proportions; in which, though the old cities and dynasties had passed away, fairer and more glorious ones had taken their places. And now he saw by the heap of shavings still fresh at his feet, that, for him and his work, the former lapse of time had been an illusion, and that no more time had elapsed than is required for a single scintillation from the brain of Brahma to fall on and inflame the tinder of a mortal brain. The material was pure, and his art was pure; how could the result be other than wonderful?" There are some marked similarities between Thoreau's aesthetics and Dickinson's view of art. For critical evaluation of Thoreau's mythic passage concerning the "artist in the city of Kouroo," the city of Kurukshetra where Arjuna of the *Bhagavad-Gita* fought his battle against his very kinsmen and destroyed the "night of ignorance," see Edward J. Rose, " 'A World With Full and Fair Proportions': The Aesthetics and the Politics of Vision," pp. 45–53; and Charles R. Anderson, *The Magic Circle of Walden*, pp. 276–78.

43   *Stairway of Surprise,* p. 73. The quotations in this passage are from L900, 430, and 675 respectively. The other poems in which Dickinson uses the word India are: 3, 202, 299, 791, and 1477.

44   For a more detailed discussion of poetic language, its power and tension, as experienced by the poet, see pp. 44–46. Also see L413 and L556 for reference to words and their paradoxical nature.

45   For hand symbolism I am indebted to Edward J. Rose, "Blake's Hand: Symbol and Design in JERUSALEM."

46   For a detailed evaluation of "Of Bronze – and Blaze" (290), see Anderson, *Stairway of Surprise,* pp. 53–65. This is the best critical commentary on the poem that I have read so far, and I find myself unable to improve upon it, though I differ with some of its details.

47   For butterfly symbolism, see: 18, 35, 64, 70, 86, 100, 111, 129, 137, 154, 173, 188, 214, 247, 257, 328, 333, 354, 380, 397, 438, 496, 533, 541, 593, 647, 682, 805, 970, 1058, 1099, 1198, 1246, 1338, 1434, 1521, and 1627.

48   For the bird figure, see: 5, 14, 35, 48, 74, 92, 96, 101, 103, 130, 143, 146, 148, 153, 179, 191, 238, 243, 248, 254, 262, 274, 294, 328, 334, 335, 346, 376, 380, 495, 500, 507, 513, 514, 526, 533, 592, 602, 606, 613, 617, 620, 653, 655, 703, 728, 766, 768, 774, 783, 790, 791, 797, 805, 846, 861, 880, 885, 925, 941, 944, 949, 1012, 1046, 1059, 1079, 1084, 1102, 1107, 1134, 1137, 1155, 1177, 1252, 1259, 1265, 1279, 1304, 1310, 1381, 1389, 1420, 1449, 1451, 1466, 1514, 1530, 1574, 1585, 1600, 1606, 1619, 1630, 1634, 1650, 1655, 1666, 1677, 1723, 1758, 1761, and 1764. The bird symbolizes freedom, imagination, and creativity. In most poems, bird is the persona of the poet.

49   Bee and flower symbolism is quite pervasive in Dickinson's poetry. For bee, bee's, and bees, see: 2, 14, 18, 20, 26, 40, 46, 50, 54, 92, 111, 128, 130, 134, 138, 142, 154, 155, 200, 206, 211, 213, 216, 230, 297, 302, 319, 330, 333, 366, 373, 380, 386, 438, 447, 557, 591, 593, 620, 647, 661, 668, 676, 727, 743, 782, 805, 852, 869, 896, 899, 916, 956, 981, 991, 994, 1042, 1058, 1077, 1107, 1115, 1154, 1198, 1220, 1224, 1338, 1339, 1343, 1381, 1388, 1405, 1522, 1526, 1627, 1628, 1693, 1755, and 1763. For flower, flower's, and flowers, see: 31, 32, 75, 81, 94, 97, 100, 104, 106, 109, 133, 134, 137, 140, 149, 154, 169, 179, 180, 197, 322, 339, 380, 391, 404, 434, 467, 495, 513, 574, 606, 620, 629, 663, 707, 766, 790, 811, 849, 903, 905, 945, 978, 1019, 1026, 1037, 1058, 1136, 1202, 1214, 1224, 1241, 1250, 1310, 1324, 1372, 1423, 1456, 1490, 1519, 1520, 1558, 1579, 1586, 1621, 1624, 1650, 1667, 1673, 1722, 1730, 1734. The following poems may be read for rose symbolism: 5, 12, 19, 34, 35, 44, 46, 56, 93, 100, 110, 163, 179, 208, 339, 342, 409, 442, 500, 512, 517, 620, 656, 675, 876, 880, 930, 956, 991, 994, 1154,

1316, 1339, 1416, 1434, 1444, and 1582. Some poems contain all the symbolisms mentioned here.

50   This is Friedrich Nietzsche's expression, which I have borrowed from "Composition of *Thus Spake Zarathustra*," *The Creative Process*, p. 202.

51   "Psychology and Literature," p. 169. Also see *Psychological Reflections: An Anthology of the Writings of C. G. Jung.* Jung writes (p. 183): "Whether the poet knows that his work is generated in him and grows and ripens there, or whether he imagines that he creates out of his own will and from nothingness, it changes in no way the curious fact that his work grows beyond him. It is, in relation to him, like a child to its mother." On the high office of poetry and the poet, we have Coleridge's famous words in his *Biographia Literaria:* "The poet, described in ideal perfection, brings the whole soul of man into activity, with the subordination of its faculties to each other according to their relative worth and dignity. He diffuses a tone and spirit of unity that blends, and (as it were) fuses, each into each, by that synthetic and magical power, to which I would exclusively appropriate the name of Imagination" (p. 151).

52   "Emily Dickinson," *Fables of Identity*, p. 196.

53   For Dickinson's use of day-dawn symbolism, see: 24, 101, 133, 174, 425, 450, 469, 471, 575, 595, 638, 659, 716, 808, 839, 850, 888, 902, 931, 938, 944, 975, 1018, 1053, 1171, 1289, 1381, 1528, 1542, 1583, 1619, 1675, and 1739.

CHAPTER 4

1   See Kierkegaard, *Concluding Unscientific Postscript.* On the mode of a lover's communication, Kierkegaard writes (p. 68: footnote): "A lover, for example, whose inwardness is his love, may very well wish to communicate; but he will not wish to communicate himself directly, precisely because the inwardness of his love is for him essential. Essentially occupied constantly in acquiring and reacquiring the inwardness of love, he has no result, and is never finished. But he may nevertheless wish to communicate, although he can never use a direct form, because such a form presupposes results and finality. So, too, in the case of a God-relationship. Precisely because he himself is constantly in process of becoming inwardly or in inwardness, the religious individual can never use direct communication, the movement in him being the precise opposite of that presupposed in direct communication. Direct communication presupposes certainty; but certainty is impossible for anyone in process of becoming, and the semblance of certainty constitutes for such an individual a deception." Communication in such matters as-

sumes the paradoxical form because paradox alone can fulfill the role
of joining the contradictory movements.

2   Love is the subject of most of her letters to Susan Gilbert Dickinson.
See, for instance, L38, L73, L74, L77, L85, L92, L93, L94, L96, L102,
and L107. The tone of these letters is intense. For example: "Susie – I
shall think of you at sunset, and at sunrise, again; and at noon, and fore-
noon, and afternoon, and always, and evermore, till this heart stops
beating and is still" (L92). But this mood wanes in L173. The reason for
the rift between Emily Dickinson and Susan Gilbert could have been
"the disagreement on spiritual matters." The letter brings out clearly
Dickinson's power of feeling, her sense of pathos at the loss of persons
whom she deeply loved, her rich experience, and her courage to put up
with "Time's brief masquerade" (70), in order to be able to look forward to something far more abiding than human caprice. The letter
reads:

"Sue – you can go or stay – There is but one alternative – We differ
often lately, and this must be the last.

You need not fear to leave me lest I should be alone, for I often part
with things I fancy I have loved, – sometimes to the grave, and sometimes to an oblivion rather bitterer than death – thus my heart bleeds so
frequently that I shant mind the hemorrhage, and I only add an agony
to several previous ones, and at the end of day remark – a bubble burst!

Such incidents would grieve me when I was but a child, and perhaps I
could have wept when little feet hard by mine, stood still in the coffin,
but eyes grow dry sometimes, and hearts get crisp and cinder, and had
as lief burn.

Sue – I have lived by this. It is the lingering emblem of the Heaven I
once dreamed, and though if this is taken, I shall remain alone, and
though in that last day, the Jesus Christ you love, remark he does not
know me – there is a darker spirit will not disown it's child.

Few have been given me, and if I love them so, that for *idolatry*, they
are removed from me – I simply murmur *gone,* and the billow dies away
into the boundless blue, and no one knows but me, that one went down
today. We have walked very pleasantly – Perhaps this is the point at
which our paths diverge – then pass on singing Sue, and up the distant
hill I journey on."

3   *Emily Dickinson: A Revelation,* pp. 9–10.

4   Ortega y Gasset, *On Love: Aspects of a Single Theme,* p. 7. In this brilliant
study, Gasset writes (p. 13): "Everything I say refers to the act of love in
its psychic inwardness as a process of the soul. You cannot go to the
God that you love with the legs of your body, and yet loving Him means

going toward Him. In loving we abandon the tranquillity and permanence within ourselves, and virtually migrate toward the object. And
this constant state of migration is what it is to be in love." He continues
(pp. 13–14): "Love is prolonged in time: one does not love in a series of
sudden moments or disjointed instants which are ignited and die like
the spark of a magnet, but one loves the beloved with continuity. . . .
love is a flow, a stream of spiritual matter, a fluid which flows continually like a fountain. We could say, in searching for metaphoric
expression to crystallize and qualify intuitively the character of that to
which I now refer, that love is not an explosion, but a continued emanation, a psychic radiation which proceeds from the lover to the beloved.
It is not a single discharge, but a current." The notion of continuity, or
an endless process, is quite relevant to our study of Dickinson's love
poetry.

5   Ibid., p. 18.

6   See Miguél de Unamuno, *Tragic Sense of Life.* Chapter 7 of this study,
"Love, Suffering, Pity, and Personality" (pp. 132–55), is most relevant
to our purpose here. Unamuno remarks (p. 135): "This other form of
love, this spiritual love, is born of sorrow, is born of the death of carnal
love, is born also of the feeling of compassion and protection which
parents feel in the presence of a stricken child. Lovers never attain to a
love of self abandonment, of true fusion of soul and not merely of
body, until the heavy pestle of sorrow has bruised their hearts and
crushed them in the same mortar of suffering."

7   Love, in the ultimate sense, is that choice which man finds ever present
in his own being. It is the existential imperative of the process of becoming, which no human being can deny himself. For this insight, I am
indebted to George Price, *The Narrow Pass: A Study of Kierkegaard's Concept of Man,* pp. 41–42 and pp. 77–79 (Appendix 1, note 39).

8   Buber, *Between Man and Man,* p. 73. Buber is right in pointing out that
"our human way to the infinite leads only through fulfilled finitude"
(p. 84).

9   Other poems in which Dickinson has described the lover-beloved's face
with some deeper meanings are: 461, 463, 474, 506, 640, 663, 754, 788,
881, 1189, and 1499.

10 See Buber, *I and Thou.* Buber clarifies the "I-thou" relationship in these
words (p. 63): "Where there is no sharing there is no reality. Where
there is self-appropriation there is no reality. The more direct the contact with the *Thou,* the fuller is the sharing. The *I* is real in virtue of its
sharing in reality. The fuller its sharing the more real it becomes. But
the *I* that steps out of the relational event into separation and consciousness of separation, does not lose its reality. Its sharing is pre-

served in it in a living way. . . . Genuine subjectivity can only be dynamically understood, as the swinging of the *I* in its lonely truth. Here, too, is the place where the desire is formed and heightened for ever higher, more unconditioned relation, for the full sharing in being. In subjectivity the spiritual substance of the person matures." Buber's position is valid and is fully applicable to Dickinson's poetry of the conjugal as well as the religious dimensions of love.

11   See Mircea Eliade, *Myth and Reality.* In his chapter on eschatology and cosmogony, Eliade writes (p. 54): "Myths of cosmic cataclysms are extremely widespread. They tell how the World was destroyed and mankind annihilated except for a single couple or a few survivors. The myths of the Flood are the most numerous and are known nearly everywhere (although extremely infrequent in Africa). In addition to Flood myths, others recount the destruction of mankind by cataclysms of cosmic proportions—earthquakes, conflagrations, falling mountains, epidemics, and so forth. Clearly, this End of the World was not final; rather, it was the end of one human race, followed by the appearance of another. But the total submergence of the Earth under the Waters or its destruction by fire, followed by the emergence of a virgin Earth, symbolize return to Chaos followed by cosmogony." Eliade further writes (p. 55): "The Flood opened the way at once to a re-creation of the World and to a regeneration of humanity. In other words, the End of the World in the past and that which is to take place in the future both represent the mythico-ritual system of the New Year festival projected on the macrocosmic scale and given an unusual degree of intensity."

12   *The Shaking of the Foundations,* p. 110.

13   In the Greek language both *Eros* and *Agape* mean love. For the Greek conception of Eros, Plato's *Symposium,* Plotinus's *Enneads,* and Plutarch's *Dialogue on Love* can prove highly useful readings. Plotinus's notion of *Caritas* offers a sort of reconciliation between the Greek conception of *Eros* and the Christian ideal of *Agape.* Other studies which deserve mention here are: Søren Kierkegaard, *Works of Love,* and *Edifying Discourses;* Anders Nygren, *Agape and Eros: A Study of the Christian Idea of Love,* part 1; Martin C. D'Arcy, *The Mind and Heart of Love;* Denis de Rougemont, *Passion and Society;* Erich Fromm, *The Art of Loving;* and C. S. Lewis, *The Four Loves.* Of particular interest is Father D'Arcy's *The Mind and Heart of Love.* D'Arcy counters the interpretations of de Rougemont. For instance, he does not consider *Eros* (human passion) and *Agape* (divine love) irreconcilable. D'Arcy also differs with Nygren's standpoint represented in *Agape and Eros.* De Rougemont considers Eros as a "dark passion," but Nygren regards it as a divine passion in the Greek sense. D'Arcy focuses on the sharp contrast between the differing viewpoints

of de Rougemont and Nygren, and takes a position which emphasizes God-man love as a two-way street.

14 Gelpi, *Emily Dickinson,* p. 3. Gelpi begins and ends his study with L93, and I find his analysis of this letter quite interesting. He writes (pp. 2–3): "The passage itself reads as though Emily realized that she had summoned up a frightening, long submerged secret to plain view. However unconscious she may have been of the full implications of her remarks, she was revealing the dilemma that determined her response to experience on all levels. For a few moments and in her own words she is caught hesitating between the desire to be ravished and the fear of being violated, between the need for integration with something else and the assertion of self-contained individuality, between the need for union with or subservience to the not-me and the insistence upon the separate identity of the ego."

15 *Agape and Eros,* p. 85. Nygren further writes (p. 86): "Had we never known the manifestation of love on the Cross, we might have known the meaning of love in general, but we should never have known the Christian meaning of love; we should never have known love in its highest and deepest meaning, God's own love, Agape. The testimony of the Cross is that Agape-love is a love which gives itself, pours itself out, even to the uttermost." According to Nygren, or rather, according to Paul "who first introduces the term Agape in the Scriptures, and thereby hands it down to later generations" (p. 84), God's Agape is a one-way street: "And all things *are* of God, who hath reconciled us to himself by Jesus Christ, and hath given to us the ministry of reconciliation" (2 Cor. 5 : 18). Christ is symbolic of God's *forgiveness* and man's atonement (at-one-ment). In forgiveness God restores man to his *primal state of being.* This we must accept on the authority of Jesus, the God-man. But, since God does not spare man the existential process of becoming *what is being,* the responsibility falls upon man to strive endlessly in order to obtain the condition of God's forgiveness. This brings in the notion of man's love for God, or the Greek conception of heavenly *Eros* in which man constantly strives to ascend to God. The notions of God's love for man and man's love for God need to be understood simultaneously, because man's existential striving is meaningful only in his relationship to God. The seeming polarity between God's descent toward man and man's ascent toward God can be aesthetically resolved. The daring paradox of the knowledge that God *exists* can be stated only in terms of the metaphor. It is Jesus as the "type" who can provide a clue to man's destiny and give meaning to man's otherwise absurd suffering.

16 For a full account of the image of Shiva, see Nancy Wilson Ross, *Three*

Ways of Asian Wisdom, pp. 19, 24, 32, 38, 49, 57, 58, 60–63, and 75. For Dickinson's use of the word "Himmaleh," see 252, 350, 481, and 862. For Dickinson's paradoxical God, see 376, 564, 621, 744, 820, 871, 882, 885, 1145, 1260, 1461, 1487, 1718, and 1719.

17 See *Christian Existentialism.* Nicolai Berdyaev has summed up the relationship between God and man in these words (p. 43): "All the complexity of religious life, the meeting and communion of God and man, is linked with the fact that there are two movements, and not one: from God toward man, and from man toward God. If religious life was based upon only the one movement from God toward man, only upon the will of God, and only upon revelation by God, it would be quite simple, the attainment of the purposes of life in the world would be easy, it would be easy to realize the Kingdom of God. Then there would be no world tragedy. But the birth of man in God, man's answer to God, cannot concern God alone; it is man's affair, a matter of man's freedom. By the nature of God as infinite love, by God's purpose in creation, the Kingdom of God cannot be realized without man, without man's participation in creation. Autocracy in heaven is quite as unjust as on earth. The Kingdom of God is the kingdom of Divine-humanity, in it God is finally born in man and man in God, and this is accomplished in the Spirit" [*Freedom,* 11, pp. 16–17].

18 I have borrowed the phrases "holier love," and "wheel of fire" from Wordsworth's "Tintern Abbey," line 155, and Shakespeare's *King Lear* (4.7.47) respectively.

19 See *The Kama Sutra of Vatsyayana.* In his introduction to this work, K. M. Panikkar tells us (p. 21): "In the *Chandogya Upanishad,* the sexual act is compared to a sacred sacrifice. There it is stated, 'The woman is the fire, the womb the fuel, the invitation of man the smoke. The door is the flame, entering the ember, pleasure the spark. In this fire gods form the offering. From this offering springs forth the child.' " The images of fuel, flame, fire, and spark clearly indicate the process of dying. But this is not the end. From the fire springs forth the child, symbolizing man's rebirth and continuity.

CHAPTER 5

1 See *Selected Letters of Rilke.* In a letter to Witold Von Hulewicz, postmarked Sierre, 13 November 1925, Rilke discusses the unity of life and death in these words (p. 387): "To grant one without the other is . . . a limitation which in the end shuts out all that is infinite. *Death is the side of life,* averted from us, unshone upon by us: we must try to achieve the

greatest consciousness of our existence which is at home in *both un-bounded realms, inexhaustibly nourished from both*. . . . The true figure of life extends through *both* spheres, the blood of the mightiest circulation flows through *both: there is neither a here nor a beyond, but the great unity* in which the beings that surpass us, the 'angels,' are at home."

2　See Unamuno, *Tragic Sense of Life*. In chapter 3 "The Hunger of Im-mortality," Unamuno writes (p. 38): "It is impossible for us, in effect, to conceive of ourselves as not existing, and no effort is capable of en-abling consciousness to realize absolute unconsciousness, its own an-nihilation. Try, reader, to imagine to yourself, when you are wide awake, the condition of your soul when you are in deep sleep; try to fill your consciousness with the representation of no-consciousness, and you will see the impossibility of it. The effort to comprehend it causes the most tormenting dizziness. We cannot conceive ourselves as not ex-isting." He further writes (pp. 38–39): "I want to be myself, and yet without ceasing to be myself to be others as well, to merge myself into the totality of things visible and invisible, to extend myself into the illimitable of space and to prolong myself into the infinite of time. Not to be all and for ever is as if not to be—at least, let me be my whole self, and be so for ever and ever." The cry for personal immortality is rooted in the religious imagination of almost all lands. But, in the context of Dickinson's poetry, I hope to show that for the creative artist, immortal-ity realized through the creative process and in the very now and here of existence is more effective and plausible than the one sanctioned by the religious tradition.

3　See Ferrater Mora, *Being and Death*. On the inside-outside of death, Fer-rater Mora writes (p. 172): "The expression 'the interiority of death' is meant to describe the following state of affairs: death is not simply the end of life but an event which shapes and constitutes life. Corre-spondingly, the expression 'the exteriority of death' is meant to desig-nate the fact that death falls outside the scope of life. Now then, it is my opinion that no matter how much death may belong to man as his 'property,' it is never completely interior (or, as we shall also say, 'inter-nal') to man's life. If such were the case, man's life would be explicable solely in terms of his death. On the other hand, I maintain that a complete exteriority of death with respect to life is most improbable and, indeed, inconceivable, for in this case human death would be an entirely meaningless event. We must assume, then, that death is partly internal, and partly external, to human life. The question is now, to what degree does the interiority of death noticeably prevail over its ex-teriority in human beings? The answer is, to a considerable degree." At this stage in our discussion, Ferrater Mora's observation, though significant in itself, has limited relevance. It explains the character of death as being both *within* and *beyond* man, but it does not answer the predicament of man in the face of death, formulating to himself the questions which will never receive any answer.

4   Ibid. On the paradox of death as being "beyond life" and yet "within life," Ferrater Mora's position is worth recording here. He argues (pp. 170–171): "On the one hand, death seems to make its presence felt only 'at the other end of life'; thus, death emerges truly 'outside of,' and has little to do with, human life. To be sure, some thinkers have surmised that man is, as it were, perpetually dying, for he begins to die from the very moment when he begins to live. Yet once a man is dead, his death is, in fact, 'beyond his life.' Death is not simply dying, but 'that which has died.' Hence to die is, as Paul Ludwig Landsberg has put it, 'to set foot into the ghostly, chilly world of absolute death.' From this point of view, we are able to say little, if anything at all about death. 'Death' is a name which merely designates the complete absence of life. Since the complete absence of life (or, for that matter, of anything) is nothingness, it would seem only wise to abstain from talking about it, for nothingness is not a proper subject of meaningful talk. On the other hand, death 'refers to'—in the senses of 'points at,' 'calls attention to'—life, even if it is only 'a life that was.' Something remains for a time after death which can be regarded as 'that which death has left behind': the 'dead one,' the corpse. Thus, it is hard to believe that death refers to nothing; as the saying goes, it 'preys upon' *living* beings." This argument underlies Ferrater Mora's observation recorded in note 3. But I wish to emphasize here that whatever side of the paradox one might like to examine, any discussion of death is inevitably bound up with the discussion of life. Death has no meaning without life. Concerning its mystery, and man's everlasting question "wherefore," there can be no philosophic or scientific solution. The solution, if any, lies in man's creative apprehension of the eternal presence of death, as intuitively experienced in the depth of his own heart. Dickinson's repeated concern with the problem of death's mystery is a pointer toward man's ultimate need to comprehend death spiritually and come to terms with it, as one comes to terms with existence itself.

5   Quoted from Arthur Symons, *The Symbolist Movement in Literature,* p. 66.

6. *The Mortal No: Death and the Modern Imagination,* p. 430. Hoffman further writes (pp. 430–31): "As a general condition, mortality is of little use beyond the point of establishing the limits of human possibility; that is, the proposition 'all men are mortal' means very little. As a uniquely personal experience, the expectation of death qualifies and differentiates each self, and remains a continuous challenge to it, to make of its

life (and of the ego which lives it) what it can and must. This is the
major 'essence' to which all existentialisms must refer: I exist, that is, in
the sense that I am a being that will some time cease to exist." Human
death is of course a strictly personal event, and no one can die for the
other, except in a very special and complex sense, in the sense in which
one dies at the death of the beloved or someone whose identity is interfused with one's own being.

7 *Stairway of Surprise,* p. 258.

8 The aesthetic implications of the word "dream" have been explored in
chapter two. The conception of life as a dream provokes response of a
somewhat metaphysical nature. If life is a dream, then death which
comes to life must also be a dream. In Oriental thought, or more particularly, Indian thought, the life-death continuum is a process of *Maya*
or illusion. Reality lies beyond *Maya,* though, paradoxically, the only
way to discover reality is to go through *Maya.* One cannot transcend
what one has not seen. In this sense, *Maya* becomes reality for the
human being. For the created being, however, and from the point of
view of aesthetics, even transcendence of *Maya* is paradoxical. For the
man of imagination, transcendence must become possible within existence, that means, he should only comprehend the meaning of *Maya,*
without ever trying to negate it. *Maya* is the realm of his creation.
Dickinson's dream can be understood in the aesthetic as well as the
humanistic context. I think she is raising the same question which is
being raised by Poe in a different manner in his "A Dream within a
Dream":

> I stand amid the roar
> Of a surf-tormented shore,
> And I hold within my hand
> Grains of the golden sand—
> How few! yet how they creep
> Through my fingers to the deep,
> While I weep—while I weep!
> O God! can I not grasp
> Them with a tighter clasp?
> O God! can I not save
> *One* from the pitiless wave?
> Is *all* that we see or seem
> But a dream within a dream?

9 Quoted from Philip Wheelwright, *Heraclitus,* p. 90 (frag. 108).
Wheelwright observes (pp. 91–92): "The most characteristic difficulty in
Heraclitus' philosophy lies in the demand which it makes upon its

hearers to transcend the 'either-or' type of thinking and to recognize in each phase of experience that a relationship of 'both-and' may be present in subtle ways that escape a dulled intelligence. Heraclitus' thought moves not by exclusion but more characteristically by coalescence, and always with a sense of otherness. To him nothing is exclusively this or that; in various ways he affirms something to be *both* of two disparates or two contraries, leaving the reader to contemplate the paradox, the full semantic possibilities of which can never be exhausted by plain prose statements. The upward and downward ways are contrary and yet one; the human soul is destined and yet is faced with the ever-present choice between up and down; the soul originates out of fire (frag. 28) but it originates out of water (frag. 44); time is eternal and yet time, like everything else, must come to a death which is also a rebirth; God is at once universal process, the intelligence that steers the process, the model by which a wise man will guide himself (frag. 106), and a child idly moving counters in a game." What Wheelwright writes about Heraclitus' philosophy can be applied to Emily Dickinson's poetry, because her poetry also deals with the paradox which lies at the very heart of existence.

10   See Anderson, *Stairway of Surprise*. Anderson explains the metaphor of "degreeless noon" in these words (pp. 267–68): "When the hands of the clock have swung full circle around their three hundred and sixty degrees, at the exact moment that they point to the beginning of a new cycle they also strike the hour of 'Noon,' or midnight, which is there mathematically though not registered on the dial, and which is 'Degreeless' because the pointers are superimposed instead of separated at an angle. Twelve o'clock is zero as well as zenith, and if the clock stops then it escapes 'out of Decimals,' hence out of time." Anderson further points out that Dickinson "habitually passed over the conventional middle of the night as the zero hour, when villagers are asleep and unaware of time, preferring midday as the hour when eternity begins." I can add little to this brilliant analysis. But I should point out that in Dickinson's poetry, the image of midnight is full of many subtle and paradoxical meanings. It is the hour of destruction before a new creation, the moment of frost before the sun. It is also the moment of pure eclipse and dissolution (236). The poet, waking at midnight, dreams of the Dawn (450). Dickinson is not afraid of the "midnight's awful pattern" (1171) when she writes: "all my stratagem had been the midnight to confirm" (786). In her imagination, even "midnight's due at noon" (415). For other poems concerning the image of midnight, see: 174, 205, 347, 400, 419, 420, 425, 461, 510, 577, 670, 699, 710, 721, and 1095.

11   *Christian Existentialism*, p. 81. Berdyaev writes: "In order fully to com-

prehend death and to have the right attitude toward it, extraordinary effort and spiritual enlightenment are necessary. We may say that the meaning of man's moral experience throughout his whole life lies in putting him into a position to comprehend death, in bringing him to the proper attitude toward it."

12 *The Letters of Emily Dickinson*, 2 : 479. As pointed out by the editors the quotation in Dickinson's letter is from *Othello*. The Duke of Venice concludes a part of his dialogue with Brabantio in these words: "The robb'd that smiles, steals something from the thief, / He robs himself, that spends a bootless grief" (1.3.208–9).

13 *The Long Shadow: Emily Dickinson's Tragic Poetry*, p. 112.

14 " 'The Ship? Great God, Where Is the Ship?' An Editorial Critique of American Literature," p. 16.

15 *Psychological Reflections*, p. 294. Jung continues (pp. 294–95): "This image was the first to become—and with the most profound justification—the symbolic bearer of human destiny: in the morning of life, man painfully tears himself away from the mother, from the home-hearth, and fights his way up to his full heights, not seeing his worst enemy before him but carrying him within him as a deadly longing for his own abyss, a yearning to drown in his own source, to be engulfed in the mother. His life is a constant battle with death, a violent and transitory liberation from the ever-threatening night. This death is no outer enemy, but his own inner longing for the silence and deep peace of non-existence, that dreamless sleep in the sea of all birth and death."

16 For the conception of "duplicate divine," the God who is both creator and destroyer, see Alan W. Watts, *The Two Hands of God: The Myths of Polarity*. For the idea of "the eternal return," see Eliade, *The Myth of the Eternal Return*.

CHAPTER 6

1 *The Inclusive Flame: Studies in American Poetry*, p. 49.

2 See Richard B. Sewall, *The Vision of Tragedy*. Sewall points out (p. 155, n. 45): "Though the affirmation that suffering brings knowledge seems clearly one of the constants of tragedy, it is by no means true of life in general. All suffering does not lead to knowledge. Suffering leads often to a complete collapse of personality; it can degrade and benumb." I entirely agree with this observation. But Dickinson's sense of suffering does not refer to "life in general." Her sense of suffering is integral to her psychology of being; it is the essence by which she defines existence in its ontological dimension. This is a special kind of suffering. With a great degree of accuracy, this suffering can be defined in Sewall's

words: "This kind of suffering presupposes man's ability to understand the full context and implications of his action, and thus it is suffering beyond the reach of the immature or brutish, the confirmed optimist or pessimist, or the merely indifferent. To the Greek tragedians, as to the Poet of Job, only the strongest natures could endure this kind of suffering—persisting in their purpose in spite of doubts, fears, advice of friends, and sense of guilt—and hence to the Greeks it became the mark of the hero. Only the hero suffers in this peculiar, ultimate way" (p. 47).

3   According to the Hindus, the ultimate reality or identity is the *Parmatman* or *Brahman* which permeates all and is above all. The Hindu *Atman*, or the awakened soul, is not antagonistic to a created self or ego, but is the source of the latter's freedom from earthliness and sheer human bondage. The human ego seeks relation with the enlightened self or *Atman* in order to reach the center of being. In the quest for identity, Dickinson touches the realm of the *Atman* or the spiritual center of her own being.

4   *Faust (part 2)*, p. 269.

5   *The Portable Nietzsche*, p. 400. The quotation is from *Thus Spake Zarathustra* (4th part). Nietzsche writes further (p. 400): "Cold souls, mules, the blind, and the drunken I do not call brave. Brave is he who knows fear but *conquers* fear, who sees the abyss, but with *pride*. Who sees the abyss but with the eyes of an eagle; who grasps the abyss with the talons of an eagle—that man has courage."

6   See Thoreau, *A Week on the Concord and Merrimack Rivers*. On the infinite nature of silence and the human inadequacy to interpret it fully, Thoreau has this to say (pp. 435–36): "It were vain for me to endeavor to interpret the Silence. She cannot be done into English. For six thousand years men have translated her with what fidelity belonged to each, and still she is little better than a sealed book. A man may run on confidently for a time, thinking he has her under his thumb, and shall one day exhaust her, but he too must at last be silent, and men remark only how brave a beginning he made; for when he at length dives into her, so vast is the disproportion of the told to the untold that the former will seem but the bubble on the surface where he disappeared." However, the paradoxical character of silence can be expounded in more ways than one. It can be stated that silence (*Shantam*) is the basis of all speech and communication; that silence and speech are essentially one and it is to silence that all sound returns; that silence is self or soul; and that silence is the transcendent God.

7   *The Upanishads: Breath of the Eternal*, p. 28. The gist of the *Isha Upanishad* is rendered in these words (p. 26): "LIFE in the world and life in the

spirit are not incompatible. Work, or action, is not contrary to knowledge of God, but indeed, if performed without attachment, is a means to it. On the other hand, renunciation is renunciation of the ego, of selfishness—not of life. The end, both of work and of renunciation, is to know the Self within the Brahman without, and to realize their identity. The Self is Brahman, and Brahman is all." Brahman is the being of transcendence toward which the being of existence eternally moves. The world is the body which embodies the self of the existential being. The body in itself is not absolute, but it is indispensable as a medium of self-realization. Dickinson's sense of the body should be understood as a mode of the self and not the self itself. Dickinson's self of existence is interfused with the self of transcendence. But, for her, there is no transcendental self beyond the one which permeates and is permeated by the creative process. In the context of her poetry, the creative self is the ultimate self.

8   I borrow the expression "to illuminate endlessly the interior life" from Charles R. Anderson, "The Conscious Self in Emily Dickinson's Poetry," p. 303.

9   See Hyatt H. Waggoner, "Emily Dickinson: The Transcendent Self." Waggoner seems to me to be overemphasizing Dickinson's debt to Emerson or Emersonian ideas. He writes (p. 305): "What Emerson meant to her is apparent not so much in the *number* of her references to him, despite his position in this respect right after the Bible and Shakespeare, as in the *nature* of them—in their tone, in the contexts in which they appear, and in the uses to which they are put. For the most part, she didn't *need* to quote him: he had been too thoroughly digested for that. But when she did quote, it was from memory, inaccurately, and in a kind of private short-hand language. Even without considering, for the moment, the poems, which provide all the evidence one would need to show that Emerson was essential to her, we can find in the letters alone very strong evidence that Emerson meant very much more to her than any of the writers or works she named to Higginson except the Bible." I am fully aware of Dickinson's admiration for Emerson. It is true that she calls Emerson's *Representative Men* "a little granite book" (L481), that she feels that Emerson "touched the secret spring" (L750) in her, that she shows fascination for Emerson's phrase "tumultuous privacy of storm" (PF116), and that she thinks "as if he [Emerson] had come from where dreams are born" (PF10). But I find it hard to accept "that Emerson meant very much more to her than any of the writers or works she named to Higginson except the Bible." Higginson himself points out that "after long disuse of her eyes she read Shakespeare & thought why is any other book needed" (L342b). It is also on record

that she admired several other writers with equal intensity. However, my point is that Dickinson thoroughly believes that "each mind is itself, like a distinct bird" (L457), and that "there is always one thing to be grateful for – that one is one's self & not somebody else" (note to L405). In these notions, or many others, if Dickinson happens to resemble Emerson, it does not mean that she is under the "influence" of Emerson. Nor does it mean that Emerson has a monopoly over these ideas. Emerson himself does not claim that. In his essay on self-reliance, Emerson makes it clear that "every great man is a unique." For a balanced view of the possible relationship between the ideas of Emerson and Dickinson, as well as between the ideas of Thoreau and Dickinson, see Glauco Cambon, "Emily Dickinson and the Crisis of Self-Reliance."

10   For reference to Eckhart and Shankara, see Alan W. Watts, *The Supreme Identity: An Essay on Oriental Metaphysics and the Christian Religion.*

11   *Man's Search for Himself,* p. 120.

12   *Concluding Unscientific Postscript,* p. 176. The sense in which Kierkegaard uses the word passion is quite relevant to my discussion of the self in Dickinson's poetry. Dickinson emphasizes the creative subjectivity which is realizable within existence; through creativity one can achieve existentially a unity of the finite and the infinite. This unity constitutes true subjectivity which "is realized in the moment of passion." Kierkegaard writes (p. 176): "Passion is the culmination of existence for an existing individual—and we are all of us existing individuals. In passion the existing subject is rendered infinite in the eternity of the imaginative representation, and yet he is at the same time most definitely himself." The word passion, then, should be understood as defining the sense of creativity, because Dickinson knows no other infinity or eternity than the one she creates through her own "imaginative representation."

13   *Essays,* p. 30. In the opening paragraph of his essay, Emerson observes (p. 27): "To believe your own thought, to believe that what is true for you in your private heart is true for all men—that is genius. Speak your latent conviction, and it shall be the universal sense; for the inmost in due time becomes the utmost, and our first thought is rendered back to us by the trumpets of the Last Judgment. . . . A man should learn to detect and watch that gleam of light which flashes across his mind from within, more than the lustre of the firmament of bards and sages." In this revolutionary document, Emerson further notes (p. 32): "What I must do is all that concerns me, not what the people think. This rule, equally arduous in actual and in intellectual life, may serve for the whole distinction between greatness and meanness. It is the harder because you will always find those who think they know what is your duty better than you know it. It is easy in the world to live after the

world's opinion; it is easy in solitude to live after our own; but the great man is he who in the midst of the crowd keeps with perfect sweetness the independence of solitude."

14 I borrow this phrase from Perry D. Westbrook, *The Greatness of Man: An Essay on Dostoyevsky and Whitman*. In the preface to this brilliant study, Westbrook observes (p. 9): "The subject of all great thought, all great art and literature, is the greatness of man. Man attains true greatness in his mind and in his spirit. Art and literature are the records of man's pondering on his greatness, marveling at it more rapturously than on even the sublimest works of mere physical nature."

15 *The Continuity of American Poetry*, p. 179. Pearce concludes his observation with these words (pp. 179–80): "The great conglomeration of Emily Dickinson's poetry is indeed a kind of *Moby Dick*. Her poetry has its own kind of proliferation and plenitude, and likewise its own kind of incompleteness; for the very lack of 'system' in the poetry, the open-endedness of its conception of the creating self, is such that there is, properly speaking, no end and no beginning—simply life being made as it is being lived through."

16 *A Study of English Romanticism*, p. 164. For a full-length treatment of the idea of "concern," see Northrop Frye, "The Knowledge of Good and Evil."

CONCLUSION

1 For Dickinson's poetic techniques, see Gay Wilson Allen, "Emily Dickinson"; and Thomas H. Johnson, "The Poet and the Muse: Poetry as Art." Johnson observes (p. 70): "Her writing techniques were self-taught. She did not follow traditional theories, but developed her own along highly original lines."

2 Brita Lindberg-Seyersted, *The Voice of the Poet: Aspects of Style in the Poetry of Emily Dickinson*, p. 10. I wish to acknowledge here that I have learned a great deal from Lindberg-Seyersted's handling of Dickinson's meter, speech rhythms, rhetorical patterns, and syntax.

3 Introduction, *Critical Essays*, p. 8. Concerning Dickinson's literary status, Sewall observes (p. 4): "There is now little dispute about her stature— we can hardly miss its dimensions—and, given the size of her achievement, there is less inclination to complain about her unevenness." In this context, also see Douglas Duncan, *Emily Dickinson*. Duncan concludes his book with this remark: "We may or may not like the voice we hear, just as we may or may not be able to sympathise with the whole inward direction of her life. But we cannot miss in her the disturbing

presence of genius, or fail to be moved by the thought of the strange guises in which it has walked the earth" (p. 106).

4 *Anatomy of Criticism: Four Essays,* p. 5. Frye observes: "The axiom of criticism must be, not that the poet does not know what he is talking about, but that he cannot talk about what he knows. To defend the right of criticism to exist at all, therefore, is to assume that criticism is a structure of thought and knowledge existing in its own right, with some measure of independence from the art it deals with."

5 *Art and Existentialism,* p. 155.

6 The phrase "literalists of the imagination" is from Marianne Moore, "Poetry," *Collected Poems,* p. 41.

7 See "Emily Dickinson and the Limits of Judgment." For the images and metaphors of "scarlet gown," "scarlet freight," "scarlet rain," and "scarlet log," see poems 12, 404, 656, and 1693 respectively.

8 *Emily Dickinson,* p. 101. Also see Archibald MacLeish, Louise Bogan, and Richard Wilbur, *Emily Dickinson: Three Views.*

9 Quoted in Sewall, *The Vision of Tragedy,* p. 169, n. 100.

A SELECTED BIBLIOGRAPHY

PRIMARY SOURCES

Dickinson, Emily. *Poems,* 1st series. Edited by Mabel Loomis Todd and T. W. Higginson. Boston: Little, Brown, and Co., 1890.
———. *Poems,* 2nd series. Edited by T. W. Higginson and Mabel Loomis Todd. Boston: Little, Brown, and Co., 1891.
———. *Poems,* 3rd series. Edited by Mabel Loomis Todd. Boston: Roberts Brothers, 1896.
———. *Selected Poems.* Edited, with an introduction, by Conrad Aiken. London: Jonathan Cape, 1924.
———. *Bolts of Melody: New Poems.* Edited by Mabel Loomis Todd and Millicent Todd Bingham. New York: Harper & Bros., 1945.
———. *The Poems: Including Variant Readings Critically Compared with All Known Manuscripts.* 3 vols. Edited by Thomas H. Johnson. Cambridge, Mass.: Harvard University Press, Belknap Press, 1955.
———. *Selected Poems.* Edited, with an introduction and notes, by James Reeves. London: William Heinemann, 1959.
———. *The Complete Poems.* Edited by Thomas H. Johnson. Boston: Little, Brown, and Co., 1960.
———. *Poems: Final Harvest.* Selection and introduction by Thomas H. Johnson. Boston: Little, Brown, and Co., 1961.
———. *Letters* (New and Enlarged Edition). Edited by Mabel Loomis Todd. New York: Harper & Bros., 1931 [1894].
———. *Letters.* Edited by Mabel Loomis Todd, with an introduction by Mark Van Doren. New York: World Publishing Co., 1951. [Reprint of the 1894 edition, with an introduction.]
———. *Letters: To Dr. and Mrs. Josiah Gilbert Holland.* Edited by their granddaughter Theodora Van Wagenen Ward. Cambridge, Mass.: Harvard University Press, 1951.

———. *The Letters.* 3 vols. Edited by Thomas H. Johnson; associate editor, Theodora Ward. Cambridge, Mass.: Harvard University Press, Belknap Press, 1958.

WORKS ABOUT EMILY DICKINSON

Books

Anderson, Charles R. *Emily Dickinson's Poetry: Stairway of Surprise.* Garden City, New York: Doubleday & Co., Anchor Books, 1966 [1960].

Bianchi, Martha Dickinson. *The Life and Letters of Emily Dickinson.* London: Jonathan Cape, 1924.

Bingham, Millicent Todd. *Ancestors' Brocades: The Literary Debut of Emily Dickinson.* New York: Harper & Bros., 1945.

———. *Emily Dickinson: A Revelation.* New York: Harper & Bros., 1954.

Blake, Caesar R., and Wells, Carlton F., eds. *The Recognition of Emily Dickinson: Selected Criticism Since 1890.* Ann Arbor: University of Michigan Press, 1964.

Buckingham, Willis J. *Emily Dickinson: An Annotated Bibliography.* Bloomington: Indiana University Press, 1970.

Capps, Jack Lee. *Emily Dickinson's Reading: 1836–86.* Cambridge, Mass.: Harvard University Press, 1966.

Chase, Richard. *Emily Dickinson.* American Men of Letters Series. New York: William Sloane Associates, 1951.

Clendenning, Sheila T. *Emily Dickinson: A Bibliography 1850–1966.* Kent, Ohio: Kent State University Press, 1968.

Cody, John. *After Great Pain: The Inner Life of Emily Dickinson.* Cambridge, Mass.: Harvard University Press, Belknap Press, 1971.

Davis, Thomas M., ed. *14 by Emily Dickinson: With Selected Criticism.* Chicago: Scott, Foresman, & Co., 1964.

Duncan, Douglas. *Emily Dickinson.* Edinburgh and London: Oliver and Boyd, 1965.

Ford, Thomas W. *Heaven Beguiles the Tired: Death in the Poetry of Emily Dickinson.* Alabama: University of Alabama Press, 1966.

Franklin, R. W. *The Editing of Emily Dickinson: A Reconsideration.* Madison: University of Wisconsin Press, 1967.

Gelpi, Albert J. *Emily Dickinson: The Mind of the Poet.* Cambridge, Mass.: Harvard University Press, 1965.

Griffith, Clark. *The Long Shadow: Emily Dickinson's Tragic Poetry.* Princeton: Princeton University Press, 1964.

Higgins, David James Monroe. *Portrait of Emily Dickinson: The Poet and Her Prose.* New Brunswick: Rutgers University Press, 1967.

Johnson, Thomas H. *Emily Dickinson: An Interpretive Biography.* Cambridge, Mass.: Harvard University Press, Belknap Press, 1955.
Leyda, Jay. *The Years and Hours of Emily Dickinson.* 2 vols. New Haven: Yale University Press, 1960.
Lindberg-Seyersted, Brita. *The Voice of the Poet: Aspects of Style in the Poetry of Emily Dickinson.* Cambridge, Mass.: Harvard University Press, 1968.
Longworth, Polly. *Emily Dickinson: Her Letter to the World.* New York: Thomas Y. Crowell Co., 1965.
Lubbers, Klaus. *Emily Dickinson: The Critical Revolution.* Ann Arbor: University of Michigan Press, 1968.
MacLeish, Archibald; Bogan, Louise; and Wilbur, Richard. *Emily Dickinson: Three Views.* Foreword by Reginald F. French. Amherst: Amherst College Press, 1960.
McNaughton, Ruth Flanders. *The Imagery of Emily Dickinson.* University of Nebraska Studies, new series, no. 4. Lincoln: University of Nebraska Press, 1949.
Miller, Ruth. *The Poetry of Emily Dickinson.* Middletown, Conn.: Wesleyan University Press, 1968.
Patterson, Rebecca. *The Riddle of Emily Dickinson.* Boston: Houghton Mifflin Co., 1951.
Pickard, J. B. *Emily Dickinson: An Introduction and Interpretation.* New York: Holt, Rinehart, and Winston, 1967.
Pollitt, Josephine. *Emily Dickinson: The Human Background of Her Poetry.* New York: Harper & Bros., 1930.
Porter, David Thomas. *The Art of Emily Dickinson's Early Poetry.* Cambridge, Mass.: Harvard University Press, 1966.
Power, Sister Mary James. *In the Name of the Bee: The Significance of Emily Dickinson.* New York: Sheed & Ward, 1944.
Rosenbaum, S. P., ed. *A Concordance to the Poems of Emily Dickinson.* Ithaca: Cornell University Press, 1964.
Sewall, Richard B., ed. *Emily Dickinson: A Collection of Critical Essays.* Englewood Cliffs, New Jersey: Prentice-Hall, 1963.
———. *The Lyman Letters: New Light on Emily Dickinson and Her Family.* Amherst: University of Massachusetts Press, 1965.
Sherwood, William R. *Circumference and Circumstance: Stages in the Mind and Art of Emily Dickinson.* New York: Columbia University Press, 1968.
Taggard, Genevieve. *The Life and Mind of Emily Dickinson.* New York: Alfred A. Knopf, 1930.
Thackrey, Donald E. *Emily Dickinson's Approach to Poetry.* University of Nebraska Studies, new series, no. 13. Lincoln: University of Nebraska Press, 1954.
Walsh, John Evangelist. *The Hidden Life of Emily Dickinson.* New York: Simon and Schuster, 1971.

Ward, Theodora. *The Capsule of the Mind: Chapters in the Life of Emily Dickinson.* Cambridge, Mass.: Harvard University Press, Belknap Press, 1961.

Wells, Henry W. *Introduction to Emily Dickinson.* Chicago: Packard and Co., 1947.

Whicher, George Frisbie. *This Was a Poet: A Critical Biography of Emily Dickinson.* New York: Charles Scribner's Sons, 1938.

Parts of Books, Articles, Parts of Articles, and Explications

Adams, Richard P. "Pure Poetry: Emily Dickinson." *Tulane Studies in English,* 7 (1957): 133–52.

———. "Dickinson Concrete." *Emerson Society Quarterly,* no. 44 (1966), pp. 31–35.

Agrawal, I.N. "Emily Dickinson and the Living Word." *The Literary Criterion,* 6 (Summer, 1964): 52–55.

Aiken, Conrad. "Emily Dickinson." In *Emily Dickinson: A Collection of Critical Essays,* edited by Richard B. Sewall, pp. 9–15. Englewood Cliffs, N.J.: Prentice-Hall, 1963.

Allen, Gay W. "Emily Dickinson." In *American Prosody,* pp. 307–21. New York: American Book Co., 1935.

Anderson, Charles R. "The Conscious Self in Emily Dickinson's Poetry." *American Literature,* 31 (1959): 290–308.

———. "The Trap of Time in Emily Dickinson's Poetry." *Journal of English Literary History,* 26 (1959): 402–24.

Birdsall, Virginia Ogden. "Emily Dickinson's Intruder in the Soul." *American Literature,* 37 (1965): 54–64.

Blackmur, R. P. "Emily Dickinson: Notes on Prejudice and Fact." In *Language As Gesture,* pp. 25–50. New York: Harcourt, Brace, and Co., 1952.

Cambon, Glauco. "Violence and Abstraction in Emily Dickinson." *Sewanee Review,* 68 (1960): 450–64.

———. "Dickinson: Confrontation of the Self with Otherness in the Inner Space." In *The Inclusive Flame: Studies in American Poetry,* pp. 27–52. Bloomington: Indiana University Press, 1963.

———. "Emily Dickinson and the Crisis of Self-Reliance." In *Transcendentalism and Its Legacy,* edited by Myron Simon and Thornton H. Parsons, pp. 123–33. Ann Arbor: University of Michigan Press, 1966.

Davidson, Frank. " 'This Consciousness': Emerson and Dickinson." *Emerson Society Quarterly,* no. 44 (1966), pp. 2–7.

Davidson, J. "Emily Dickinson and Isaac Watts." *Boston Public Library Quarterly,* 6 (1954), pp. 141–49.

Donoghue, D. "Emily Dickinson." In *Connoisseurs of Chaos: Ideas of Order in Modern American Poetry,* pp. 100–28. New York: Macmillan Co., 1965.

Fasel, Ida. "Emily Dickinson's Walden." *Iowa English Yearbook,* no. 7 (1962), pp. 22–28.

Frohock, Wilbur M. "Emily Dickinson: God's Little Girl." In *Strangers to this Ground: Cultural Diversity in Contemporary American Writing,* pp. 98–110. Dallas: Southern Methodist University Press, 1961.

Frye, Northrop. "Emily Dickinson." In *Fables of Identity: Studies in Poetic Mythology,* pp. 193–217. New York: Harcourt, Brace, & World, 1963.

Gohdes, C. L. F. "New Voices in Verse." In *Literature of the American People,* edited by A. H. Quinn, pp. 729–36. New York: Appleton-Century-Crofts, 1951.

Higginson, T. W. "Emily Dickinson." In *Carlyle's Laugh and Other Surprises,* pp. 247–83. Boston: Houghton Mifflin and Co., 1909.

Hirsch, David H. "Emily Dickinson's 'Presentiment.'" *American Notes and Queries,* 1 (1962): 36–37.

Hogue, Caroline. "Dickinson's 'I Heard a Fly Buzz When I Died.'" *The Explicator,* 20 (November, 1961): item 26.

Howard, William. "Dickinson's 'I Can Wade Grief.'" *The Explicator,* 14 (December, 1955): item 17.

Jennings, Elizabeth. "Emily Dickinson and the Poetry of the Inner Life." *Review of English Literature,* 3 (1962): 78–87.

Johnson, Thomas H. "The Poet and the Muse: Poetry as Art." In *Emily Dickinson: A Collection of Critical Essays,* edited by Richard B. Sewall, pp. 70–77. Englewood Cliffs, N.J.: Prentice-Hall, 1963.

Kazin, Alfred. "Called Back." *The Griffin,* 9, no. 11 (1960): 2–9.

Khan, Salamatullah. "The Love Poetry of Emily Dickinson." *The Literary Criterion,* 6 (Summer, 1964): 37–51.

Kher, Inder Nath. " 'An Abyss's Face': The Structure of Emily Dickinson's Poem." *Emily Dickinson Bulletin,* no. 9 (June, 1969), pp. 52–55.

Leyda, Jay. "Late Thaw of a Frozen Image." *New Republic,* 132 (February, 1955): 22–24.

Lindberg, Brita. "The Theme of Death in Emily Dickinson's Poetry." *Studia Neophilologica,* 34 (1962): 269–81.

Lowell, Amy. "Emily Dickinson." In *Poetry and Poets,* pp. 88–108. Boston: Houghton Mifflin Co., 1930.

Lynen, John F. "Three Uses of the Present: The Historian's, the Critic's, and Emily Dickinson's." *College English* 28 (1966): 126–36.

MacLeish, Archibald. "The Private World: Poems of Emily Dickinson." In *Poetry and Experience,* pp. 91–114. Boston: Houghton, Mifflin Co., Riverside Press, 1961.

Marcus, Mordecai. "Walt Whitman and Emily Dickinson." *Personalist,* 43 (1962): 497–514.

Martin, Jay. "Emily Dickinson." In *Harvests of Change: American Literature 1865–1914,* pp. 285–96. New Jersey: Prentice-Hall, 1967.

Matthiessen, F. O. "The Problem of the Private Poet." *Kenyon Review,* 7 (1945): 584–97.

McCarthy, Paul. "An Approach to Dickinson's Poetry." *Emerson Society Quarterly,* 44 (1966): 22–31.

McElderry, B. R., Jr. "Emily Dickinson: Viable Transcendentalist." *Emerson Society Quarterly,* 44 (1966): 17–21.

Miller, James E., Jr. "Emily Dickinson: The Thunder's Tongue." *Minnesota Review,* 2 (1962): 289–304.

Moore, Marianne. "Emily Dickinson." *Poetry,* 41 (January, 1933): 219–26.

Ochshorn, Myron. "In Search of Emily Dickinson." *New Mexico Quarterly,* 23 (1953): 94–106.

O'Connor, W. V. "Emily Dickinson: The Domestication of Terror." In *The Grotesque: An American Genre, and Other Essays,* pp. 98–108. Carbondale: Southern Illinois University Press, 1962.

Pearce, Roy Harvey. "Emily Dickinson." In *The Continuity of American Poetry,* pp. 174–191. Princeton: Princeton University Press, 1961.

Perrine, Laurence. "Dickinson's 'There is a Certain Slant of Light.' " *The Explicator,* 11 (May, 1953): item 50.

———. "Dickinson's 'A Clock Stopped – Not The Mantel's.' " *The Explicator,* 14 (October, 1955): item 4.

Pommer, Henry F. "Dickinson's 'The Soul Selects Its Own Society.' " *The Explicator,* 3 (February, 1945): item 32.

Rabe, Olive H. "Emily Dickinson as Mystic." *Colorado Quarterly,* 14 (1966): 280–88.

Ransom, John Crowe. "Emily Dickinson: A Poet Restored." *Perspectives USA,* 15 (1956): 5–20.

Reiss, Edmund. "Recent Scholarship on Whitman and Dickinson." In *The Teacher and American Literature,* edited by L. G. Leary, pp. 115–27. Illinois: National Council of Teachers of English, 1965.

Rose, E. J. " 'The Ship? Great God, Where Is the Ship?' An Editorial Critique of American Literature." *The English Teacher,* 2, no. 1 (February, 1962): 5–20.

Scott, Wilbur. "Dickinson's 'I'll Tell You How the Sun Rose.' " *The Explicator,* 7 (November, 1948): item 14.

Sewall, Richard B. "Dickinson's 'To Undertake Is to Achieve.' " *The Explicator,* 6 (June, 1948): item 51.

———. "Emily Dickinson: The Problem of the Biographer." *Occasional Stiles* (Yale University), 5 (April, 1968): 120–28.

Spencer, Benjamin T. "Criticism: Centrifugal and Centripetal." *Criticism,* 8 (1966): 139–54.

Tate, Allen. "Emily Dickinson." In *Interpretations of American Literature,* edited by Charles Feidelson Jr. and Paul Brodtkorb Jr., pp. 197–211. New York: Oxford University Press, 1959.

Untermeyer, L. "Emily Dickinson." In *Makers of the Modern World,* pp. 132–38. New York: Simon & Schuster, 1955.

Voigt, Gilbert P. "The Inner Life of Emily Dickinson." *College English,* 3 (November, 1941): 192–96.

Waggoner, Hyatt H. "Emily Dickinson: The Transcendent Self." *Criticism,* 7 (September, 1965): 297–334.

Ward, Theodora V. W. "Emily Dickinson and T. W. Higginson." *Boston Public Library Quarterly,* 5 (1953): 3–18.

Warren, Austin. "Emily Dickinson." *Sewanee Review,* 65 (Autumn, 1957): 565–86.

Wheatcroft, J. S. "Emily Dickinson's White Robes." *Criticism,* 5 (1963): 135–47.

Wilson, Suzanne M. "Structural Patterns in the Poetry of Emily Dickinson." *American Literature,* 35 (1963): 53–59.

———. "Emily Dickinson and Twentieth-Century Poetry of Sensibility." *American Literature,* 36 (1964): 349–58.

Winters, Yvor. "Emily Dickinson and the Limits of Judgment." In *Maule's Curse: Seven Studies in the History of American Obscurantism,* pp. 149–65. Norfolk, Connecticut: New Directions, 1938.

Unpublished Doctoral Dissertations

Anselmo, Sister Peter Marie, R. S. M. "Renunciation in the Poems and Letters of Emily Dickinson." University of Notre Dame, 1965.

Arp, Thomas Roscoe. "Dramatic Poses in the Poetry of Emily Dickinson." Stanford University, 1962.

Chaliff, Cynthia. "Emily Dickinson against the World: An Interpretation of the Poet's Life and Works." New York University, 1967.

Copple, Lee B. "Three Related Themes of Hunger and Thirst, Homelessness, and Obscurity as Symbols of Privation, Renunciation, and Compensation in the Poems of Emily Dickinson." University of Michigan, 1954.

Davis, William Faber, Jr. "The Moral Vision of Emily Dickinson." Yale University, 1964.

Di Salvo, Leta Perry. "The Arrested Syllable: A Study of the Death Poetry of Emily Dickinson." University of Denver, 1965.

Frank, Bernhard. "The Wiles of Words: Ambiguity in Emily Dickinson's Poetry." University of Pittsburgh, 1965.

Gregor, Norman. "The Luxury of Doubt: A Study of the Relationship between Imagery and Theme in Emily Dickinson's Poetry." University of New Mexico, 1955.

Jones, Rowena Revis. "Emily Dickinson's 'Flood Subject': Immortality." Northwestern University, 1960.

Keller, Karl. "The Metaphysical Strain in Nineteenth-Century American Poetry," pp. 175–213. University of Minnesota, 1964.

Marcus, Mordecai. "Nature Symbolism in the Poetry of Emily Dickinson." University of Kansas, 1958.

Molson, Francis Joseph. "The 'Forms' of God: A Study of Emily Dickinson's Search for and Test of God." University of Notre Dame, 1965.

Phillips, Emma J. "Mysticism in the Poetry of Emily Dickinson." Indiana University, 1967.

Thomas, Owen Paul, Jr. "The Very Press of Imagery: A Reading of Emily Dickinson." University of California at Los Angeles, 1959.

Todd, John Emerson. "Emily Dickinson's Use of the Persona." University of Wisconsin, 1965.

Wheatcroft, John Stewart. "Emily Dickinson and the Orthodox Tradition." Rutgers University, 1960.

Wilson, Suzanne Marie. "Structure and Imagery Patterns in the Poetry of Emily Dickinson." University of Southern California, 1959.

OTHER WORKS AND BACKGROUND STUDIES

Abrams, M. H. *The Mirror and the Lamp: Romantic Theory and Critical Tradition.* New York: W. W. Norton and Co., 1958 [1953].

————. "Structure and Style in Greater Romantic Lyric." In *From Sensibility to Romanticism,* edited by Frederick W. Hilles and Harold Bloom, pp. 527–60. New York: Oxford University Press, 1965.

————, ed. *Literature and Belief: English Institute Essays, 1957.* New York: Columbia University Press, 1958.

Allen, Gay Wilson; Rideout, Walter B.; and Robinson, James K., eds. *American Poetry.* New York: Harper & Row, 1965.

Anderson, Charles R. *The Magic Circle of Walden.* New York: Holt, Rinehart, & Winston, 1968.

Aurobindo, Sri. *Letters of Sri Aurobindo: On Poetry and Literature,* 3rd ser. Pondicherry: Sri Aurobindo Ashram, 1949.

————. *Life, Literature, Yoga: Some New Letters of Sri Aurobindo.* Pondicherry: Sri Aurobindo Ashram, 1952.

————. *The Future Poetry.* Pondicherry: Sri Aurobindo Ashram, 1953.

Barnes, Hazel E. *Humanistic Existentialism: The Literature of Possibility.* Lincoln: University of Nebraska Press, 1959.

Barrett, William. *Irrational Man: A Study in Existential Philosophy.* Garden City, New York: Doubleday and Co., Anchor Books, 1962 [1958].

Beardsley, Monroe C. *Aesthetics from Classical Greece to the Present: A Short History.* New York: Macmillan Co., 1966.

Beauvoir, Simone de. *The Ethics of Ambiguity.* Translated by Bernard Frechtman. 3rd paperbound ed. New York: Citadel Press, 1967 [1948].

Benziger, James. *Images of Eternity: Studies in the Poetry of Religious Vision from*

Wordsworth to T. S. Eliot. Carbondale: Southern Illinois University Press, 1962.

Berdyaev, Nicolai. *Christian Existentialism: A Berdyaev Synthesis.* Selected and translated by Donald A. Lowrie. New York: Harper and Row, Harper Torchbooks, 1965

Bergson, Henri. *Time and Free Will: An Essay on the Immediate Data of Consciousness.* New York: Harper & Row, Harper Torchbooks, 1960 [1910].

Blake, William. *Poetry And Prose.* Edited by David Erdman; commentary by Harold Bloom. New York: Doubleday & Co., 1965.

Bodkin, Maud. *Archetypal Patterns in Poetry: Psychological Studies of Imagination.* London: Oxford University Press, Oxford Paperbacks, 1963 [1934].

Brandon, S. G. F. *History, Time, and Deity: A Historical and Comparative Study of the Conception of Time in Religious Thought and Practice.* New York: Barnes and Noble, 1965.

Brontë, Emily. *Poems. The Shakespeare Head Brontë,* vol. 18. Oxford: Shakespeare Head Press, 1931.

———. *Wuthering Heights.* Edited, with an introduction, by V. S. Pritchett. Boston: Houghton Mifflin Co., Riverside Press, 1956.

Brooks, Cleanth. *The Well Wrought Urn: Studies in the Structure of Poetry.* New York: Harcourt, Brace, & World, 1947.

Browne, Sir Thomas. *Religio Medici.* Edited by James Winny. Cambridge: Cambridge University Press, 1963.

Buber, Martin. *I and Thou.* Translated by Ronald Gregor Smith. New York: Charles Scribner's Sons, 1958.

———. *Between Man and Man.* Translated and introduced by Ronald Gregor Smith. 4th impression of the Fontana Library edition. London: Collins, 1966 [1947].

Cambon, Glauco. *The Inclusive Flame: Studies in American Poetry.* Bloomington: Indiana University Press, 1963.

Campbell, Joseph. *The Hero with a Thousand Faces.* New York: Pantheon Books, 1961 [1949].

———. *The Masks of God: Oriental Mythology.* New York: Viking Press, 1962.

———. *The Masks of God: Creative Mythology.* New York: Viking Press, 1968.

Cassirer, Ernst. *Language and Myth.* Translated by Susanne K. Langer. New York: Dover Publications, 1953 [1946].

Choron, Jacques. *Death and Western Thought.* New York: Collier Books, 1963.

Cirlot, J. E. *A Dictionary of Symbols.* Translated by Jack Sage. Foreword by Herbert Read. New York: Philosophical Library, 1962.

Clive, Geoffrey, ed. *The Philosophy of Nietzsche.* Toronto: New American Library of Canada, 1965.

Coleridge, S. T. *Biographia Literaria.* Introduction by Arthur Symons. London: J. M. Dent & Sons, Everyman Library, 1952.

———. *The Poems.* Edited with Textual and Bibliographical Notes by Ernest Hartley Coleridge. London: Oxford University Press, 1960.

Collingwood, R. G. *Essays in the Philosophy of Art.* Edited by Alan Donagan. Bloomington: Indiana University Press, 1964.

———. *The Principles of Art.* Oxford: Clarendon Press, 1965 [1938].

Copleston, Frederick S. J. *A History of Philosophy, Volume 5, Modern Philosophy: The British Philosophers,* Part 1, Hobbes to Paley. New York: Doubleday & Co., Image Books, 1964.

Crane, Hart. *The Complete Poems.* Edited by Waldo Frank. Garden City, New York: Doubleday & Co., 1958.

Crews, Frederick C. "Literature and Psychology." In *Relations of Literary Study,* edited by James Thorpe, pp. 73–87. New York: Modern Language Association of America, 1967.

D'Arcy, Martin C. *The Mind and Heart of Love.* New York: World Publishing Co., 1964 [1945].

Dostoevsky, Fyodor. *The Brothers Karamazov.* Translated by Constance Garnett; introduction by Marc Slonim. New York: Random House, 1950.

Eliade, Mircea. *The Myth of the Eternal Return.* New York: Pantheon, 1954.

———. *Myth and Reality.* New York: Harper & Row, 1968 [1963].

Eliot, T. S. *Collected Poems: 1909–35.* London: Faber & Faber, 1958.

———. *Four Quartets.* London: Faber & Faber, 1959.

Emerson, Ralph Waldo. *Essays,* 1st and 2nd series. With an introduction by Shiv Kumar. New Delhi: Eurasia Publishing House, 1965.

Empson, William. *Seven Types of Ambiguity.* Middlesex, England: Penguin Books, Peregrine Books, 1961 [1930].

Fallico, Arturo B. *The Quest for Authentic Existence.* Stockton, Cal.: College of the Pacific Publications in Philosophy, 1958.

———. *Art and Existentialism.* Englewood Cliffs, N. J.: Prentice-Hall, 1962.

Faust, Clarence H., and Johnson, Thomas H., eds. *Jonathan Edwards: Representative Selections.* New York: American Book Co., 1935.

Feidelson, Charles, Jr. *Symbolism and American Literature.* Chicago: University of Chicago Press, 1953.

———, and Brodtkorb, Paul, Jr., eds. *Interpretations of American Literature.* New York: Oxford University Press, 1959.

Fiedler, Leslie A. *Love and Death in the American Novel.* New York: Criterion Books, 1960.

Fordham, Frieda. *An Introduction to Jung's Psychology.* Middlesex, England: Penguin Books, 1966 [1953].

Frank, Joseph. *The Widening Gyre: Crisis and Mastery in Modern Literature.* New Brunswick, N. J.: Rutgers University Press, 1963.

Frazer, J. G. *The Golden Bough: A Study in Magic and Religion.* London: Macmillan & Co., 1963 [1922].

Freedman, Ralph. "Wallace Stevens and Rainer Maria Rilke: Two Versions of a Poetic." In *The Poet as Critic,* edited by Frederick P. W. McDowell, pp. 60–80. Evanston: Northwestern University Press, 1967.

Fromm, Erich. *The Art of Loving.* Toronto: Bantam Books of Canada, 1967 [1956].

Frost, Robert. *Complete Poems.* New York: Holt, Rinehart, and Winston, 1949.

Frye, Northrop. *Anatomy of Criticism: Four Essays.* New York: Atheneum, 1966 [Originally published by Princeton University Press, 1957].

———. "The Realistic Oriole: A Study of Wallace Stevens." In *Fables of Identity: Studies in Poetic Mythology,* pp. 238–55. New York: Harcourt, Brace, & World, 1963.

———. "The Knowledge of Good and Evil." In *The Morality of Scholarship,* edited by Max Black, pp. 3–28. Ithaca: Cornell University Press, 1967.

———. *A Study of English Romanticism.* New York: Random House, 1968.

———, ed. *Romanticism Reconsidered: Selected Papers from the English Institute.* New York: Columbia University Press, 1963.

———; Hampshire, Stuart; and O'Brien, Conor Cruise. *The Morality of Scholarship.* Edited by Max Black. Ithaca: Cornell University Press, 1967.

Gardner, W. H. *Gerard Manley Hopkins (1844–89): A Study of Poetic Idiosyncrasy in Relation to Poetic Tradition.* 2 vols. New Haven: Yale University Press, 1948 and 1949 [vol. 1, 1944].

Ghiselin, Brewster. "The Birth of a Poem." In *The Creative Process,* pp. 125–34. Toronto: New American Library of Canada, 1967 [1965].

Glicksberg, Charles I. *The Tragic Vision in Twentieth-Century Literature.* With a preface by Harry T. Moore. Carbondale: Southern Illinois University Press, 1963.

Goethe. *Faust,* part 2. Translated, with an introduction, by Philip Wayne. Middlesex, England: Penguin Books, 1962 [1959].

Happold, F. C. *Religious Faith and Twentieth-Century Man.* Middlesex, England: Penguin Books, 1966.

Hawthorne, Nathaniel. *Complete Novels and Selected Tales.* Edited, with an introduction, by Norman Holmes Pearson. New York: Modern Library, 1937.

Head, Joseph, and Cranston, S. L. *Reincarnation in World Thought.* New York: Julian Press, 1967.

Heidegger, Martin. *An Introduction to Metaphysics.* Translated by Ralph Manheim. Garden City, New York: Doubleday & Co., Anchor Books, 1961.

———. *Existence and Being.* With an introduction by Werner Brock. Chicago: Henry Regnery Company, 1965 [1949].

Heinemann, F. H. *Existentialism and the Modern Predicament.* New York: Harper & Row, Harper Torchbooks, 1965 [1953].

Heller, Erich. *The Disinherited Mind: Essays in Modern German Literature and Thought.* Middlesex, England: Penguin Books, 1961 [1952].

———. *The Artist's Journey into the Interior and Other Essays.* New York: Random House, Vintage Books, 1968.

Henderson, Joseph L. and Maud Oakes. *The Wisdom of the Serpent: The Myths of Death, Rebirth, and Resurrection.* New York, George Braziller, 1963.

Hesse, Hermann. *Demian: The Story of Emil Sinclair's Youth.* Introduction by Thomas Mann; translated by Michael Roloff and Michael Lebeck. New York: Bantam Books, 1966.

Hirst, R. J., ed. *Perception and the External World.* New York: Macmillan Co., 1965.

Hoffman, Daniel G., ed. *American Poetry and Poetics: Poems and Critical Documents from the Puritans to Robert Frost.* Garden City, New York: Doubleday & Co., Anchor Books, 1962.

Hoffman, Frederick J. *The Mortal No: Death and the Modern Imagination.* Princeton: Princeton University Press, 1964.

———. *The 20's: American Writing in the Postwar Decade.* Rev. ed. New York: Free Pres, 1966.

Hofstadter, Albert, and Kuhns, Richard, eds. *Philosophies of Art and Beauty: Selected Readings in Aesthetics from Plato to Heidegger.* New York: Modern Library, 1964.

Hopkins, Gerard Manley. "No Worst, There Is None." In *The Mentor Book of Major British Poets,* edited by Oscar Williams, with an introduction by Julian Symons. Toronto: New American Library of Canada, 1963.

Hopkins, Vivian C. *Spires of Form: A Study of Emerson's Aesthetic Theory.* Cambridge, Mass.: Harvard University Press, 1951.

Hopper, Stanley Romaine, ed. *Spiritual Problems in Contemporary Literature.* New York: Harper & Row, 1957.

Jaspers, Karl. *Truth and Symbol.* Translated, with an introduction, by Jean T. Wilde, William Kluback, and William Kimmel. New York: Twayne Publishers, 1959 [originally published in 1947, in Germany].

———. *Way to Wisdom: An Introduction to Philosophy.* Translated by Ralph Manheim. New Haven: Yale University Press, 1966 [1954].

Jung, C. G. "Psychology and Literature." In *Modern Man in Search of a Soul,* translated by W. S. Dell and Cary F. Baynes, pp. 152–72. New York: Harcourt, Brace, & World, 1933.

———. *Psyche and Symbol: A Selection from the Writings.* Edited by Violet S. de Laszlo. Garden City, New York: Doubleday and Co., Anchor Books, 1958.

———. *Psychological Reflections: Selections.* Edited by Jolande Jacobi. New York: Harper & Row, Harper Torchbooks, 1961.

———. *Symbols of Transformation.* 2 vols. Translated by R. F. C. Hull. New York: Harper & Brothers, 1962 [1956].

————. *The Undiscovered Self.* Translated by R. F. C. Hull. Fifth printing. New York: New American Library, 1964.

Kant, Immanuel. *Analytic of the Beautiful,* from *The Critique of Judgment.* Translated, with an introduction, comments, and notes, by Walter Cerf. New York: Bobbs-Merrill Co., 1963 [originally published in 1790].

Karl, Frederick R., and Hamalian, Leo, eds. *The Existential Imagination.* New York: Fawcett Publications, 1965 [1963].

Kaufmann, Walter. *From Shakespeare to Existentialism.* Garden City, New York: Doubleday & Co. 1960 [1959].

————, ed. and trans. *The Portable Nietzsche.* New York: Viking Press, 1968 [1954].

————, ed. and trans. *Existentialism from Dostoevsky to Sartre.* New translation, with an introduction and prefaces. New York: World Publishing Co., 1965 [1956].

Kaul, A. N. *The American Vision: Actual and Ideal Society in Nineteenth-Century Fiction.* New Haven: Yale University Press, 1963.

Kazin, Alfred, ed. *The Portable Blake.* New York: Viking Press, 1966 [1946].

Keats, John. *Complete Poetry and Selected Prose.* Edited, with an introduction, by Harold E. Briggs. New York: Modern Library, 1951.

Kermode, Frank. *Wallace Stevens.* Edinburgh and London: Oliver and Boyd, 1960.

Kher, Inder Nath. "Hinduism and Hippies." *Pluck,* 1, no. 1 (January, 1968): 29–32.

Kierkegaard, Søren. *Fear and Trembling and the Sickness unto Death.* Translated, with introduction and notes, by Walter Lowrie. Garden City, New York: Doubleday & Co. 1954 [1941].

————. *Concluding Unscientific Postscript.* Translated by David F. Swenson; introduction and notes by Walter Lowrie. Princeton: Princeton University Press, 1964 [1941].

————. *Either/Or.* Vol. 1. Translated by David F. Swenson and Lillian Marvin Swenson, with revisions and a foreword by Howard A. Johnson. Garden City, New York: Doubleday & Co., 1959 [1944].

————. *Edifying Discourses: A Selection.* Edited, with an introduction, by Paul L. Holmer. Translated by David F. Swenson and Lillian Marvin Swenson. New York: Harper & Bros., 1958.

————. *Works of Love.* Translated by Howard and Edna Hory. New York: Harper & Row, 1964.

Kockelmans, Joseph J., ed. *Phenomenology: The Philosophy of Edmund Husserl and Its Interpretations.* Garden City, New York: Doubleday & Co., Anchor Books, 1967.

Koestler, Arthur. *The Act of Creation.* London: Pan Books, 1966 [1964].

Krieger, Murray. "The Existential Basis of Contextual Criticism." *Criticism,* 8 (1966): 305–17.

Krutch, Joseph Wood. *Experience and Art.* New York: Collier Books, 1962.

Langan, Thomas. *The Meaning of Heidegger: A Critical Study of an Existentialist Phenomenology.* New York: Columbia University Press, 1961 [1959].

Langer, Susanne K. *Philosophy in a New Key: A Study in the Symbolism of Reason, Rite, and Art.* New York: New American Library, 1951.

————. *Feeling and Form.* New York: Charles Scribner's Sons, 1953.

————. *Philosophical Sketches: A Study of the Human Mind in Relation to Feeling, Explored through Art, Language, and Symbol.* New York: New American Library, 1964 [1962].

Lawrence, D. H. *Selected Poems.* Edited by Kenneth Rexroth. New York: New Directions, 1947.

Lessing. Gotthold Ephraim. *Laocoön: An Essay on the Limits of Painting and Poetry.* Translated, with an introduction and notes, by Edward Allen McCormick. New York: Bobbs-Merrill Co., 1962 [originally published in 1766].

Lewis, C. S. *The Four Loves.* London: Geoffrey Bles, 1960.

Lewis, R. W. B. *The American Adam: Innocence, Tragedy, and Tradition in the Nineteenth Century.* Chicago: University of Chicago Press, 1955.

Lowell, Amy. "The Process of Making Poetry." In *The Creative Process,* edited by Brewster Ghiselin, pp. 109–12. Toronto: New American Library of Canada, 1967 [1965].

Lynch, William F. S. J. *Christ and Apollo: The Dimensions of the Literary Imagination.* Toronto: New American Library of Canada, 1963 [1960].

MacLeish, Archibald. *Poetry and Experience.* Boston: Houghton, Mifflin Co., Riverside Press, 1961.

Mandel, Eli. *Criticism: The Silent-Speaking Words.* Toronto: CBC Publications, 1966.

Marcel, Gabriel. *Being and Having: An Existentialist Diary.* Introduction by James Collins. New York: Harper & Row, Harper Torchbooks, 1965.

————. *The Philosophy of Existentialism.* Translated by Manya Harari. 8th paperbound ed. New York: Citadel Press, 1967.

Maritain, Jacques. *Art and Scholasticism and the Frontiers of Poetry.* Translated by Joseph W. Evans. New York: Charles Scribner's Sons, 1962.

————. *Creative Intuition in Art and Poetry.* New York: World Publishing Co., Meridian Books, 1966 [1953].

Martz, Louis L. *The Poetry of Meditation.* New Haven: Yale University Press, 1954.

————. "Wallace Stevens: The World as Meditation." In *Literature and Belief: English Institute Essays, 1957,* edited, with a foreword, by M. H. Abrams. New York: Columbia University Press, 1958.

Maslow, Abraham H. *Toward a Psychology of Being.* New York: D. Van Nostrand Co., 1962.

Mason, Eudo C. *Rilke.* Edinburgh and London: Oliver and Boyd, 1963.

Matthiessen, F. O. *American Renaissance: Art and Expression in the Age of Emerson and Whitman.* New York: Oxford University Press, 1968 [1941].

May, Rollo. "Creativity and Encounter." In *The Creative Imagination: Psychoanalysis and the Genius of Inspiration,* edited, with an introduction, by Hendrik M. Ruitenbeek, pp. 283–91. Chicago: Quadrangle Books, 1965.

———. *Man's Search for Himself.* New York: New American Library, Signet Books, 1967.

McClelland, David C. *The Roots of Consciousness.* New York: D. Van Nostrand Co., 1964.

McDowell, Frederick P. W., ed. *The Poet as Critic.* Evanston: Northwestern University Press, 1967.

Melville, Herman. *Collected Poems.* Edited by Howard P. Vincent. Chicago: Packard and Co., 1947.

———. *The Works.* Standard edition in 16 vols. New York: Russel & Russel, 1963.

Merleau-Ponty, Maurice. *The Primacy of Perception and Other Essays on Phenomenological Psychology, the Philosophy of Art, History, and Politics.* Edited, with an introduction, by James M. Edie. Evanston: Northwestern University Press, 1964.

Miller, Perry. "From Edwards to Emerson." *The New England Quarterly,* 13 (1940): 589–617.

Monk, Samuel H. *The Sublime.* Ann Arbor: University of Michigan Press, 1960 [1935].

Moore, Marianne. *Collected Poems.* New York: Macmillan Co., 1955.

Mora, José Ferrater. *Being and Death: An Outline of Integrationist Philosophy.* Berkeley and Los Angeles: University of California Press, 1965.

Mordell, Albert. *The Erotic Motive in Literature.* New York: Collier Books, 1962.

Munro, Thomas. *Oriental Aesthetics.* Cleveland: Western Reserve University Press, 1965.

Neumann, Erich. *The Origins and History of Consciousness: The Psychological Stages in the Development of Personality.* 2 vols. New York: Harper & Bros., 1962.

Nietzsche, Friedrich. *The Birth of Tragedy and the Genealogy of Morals.* New translation by Francis Golffing. Garden City, New York: Doubleday & Co., 1956.

———. "Composition of *Thus Spake Zarathustra.*" In *The Creative Process,* edited by Brewster Ghiselin, pp. 201–3. Toronto: New American Library of Canada, 1967 [1965].

Nostrand, Albert D. Van, ed. *Literary Criticism in America.* New York: Liberal Arts Press, 1957.

Nygren, Anders. *Agape and Eros: A Study of the Christian Idea of Love,* part 1. Translated by A. G. Herbert. New York: Macmillan Co., 1937 [1932].

O'Brien, Elmer, trans. *The Essential Plotinus*. Toronto: New American Library of Canada, 1964.

O'Connor, William Van. *Sense and Sensibility in Modern Poetry*. Chicago: University of Chicago Press, 1948.

Olson, Robert G. *An Introduction to Existentialism*. New York: Dover Publications, 1962.

Organ, Troy W. *The Self in Indian Philosophy*. The Hague: Mouton & Co., 1964.

Ortega y Gasset, José. *The Dehumanization of Art and Other Writings on Art and Culture*. Garden City, New York: Doubleday & Co., Anchor Books, 1956.

————. *On Love: Aspects of a Single Theme*. Translated by Toby Tolbot. New York: World Publishing Co., 1967 [1957].

Ostroff, Anthony, ed. *The Contemporary Poet as Artist and Critic: Eight Symposia*. Boston: Little, Brown, and Co., 1964.

Otto, Rudolph. *Mysticism East and West*. Translated by Bertha L. Bracey and Richenda C. Payne. New York: Collier Books, 1962 [1932].

Paul, Sherman. *Emerson's Angle of Vision: Man and Nature in American Experience*. Cambridge, Mass.: Harvard University Press, 1952.

Pearce, Roy Harvey. *The Continuity of American Poetry*. Princeton: Princeton University Press, 1961.

Phillipson, Moris, ed. *Aesthetics Today*. New York: World Publishing Co., Meridian Books, 1966.

Plantinga, Alvin, ed. *The Ontological Argument from St. Anselm to Contemporary Philosophers*. Introduction by Richard Taylor. Garden City, New York: Doubleday & Co., 1965.

Plato. *Great Dialogues*. Complete texts of *The Republic, Apology, Crito, Phaedo, Ion, Meno,* and *Symposium*. Modern translation by W. H. D. Rouse. Edited by Erich H. Warmington and Philip G. Rouse. New York: New American Library, 1956.

Plutarch. *Selected Essays on Love, the Family, and the Good Life*. A new translation by Moses Hadas. New York: New American Library, Mentor Books, 1957.

Poe, Edgar A. *Complete Works*. Edited by James A. Harrison. 17 vols. New York: Crowell, 1902.

Porte, Joel. *Emerson and Thoreau: Transcendentalists in Conflict*. Middletown, Conn.: Wesleyan University Press, 1966.

Prabhavananda, Swami, and Isherwood, Christopher, trans. *The Song of God: Bhagavad-Gita*. With an introduction by Aldous Huxley. New York: New American Library, 1956 [1944].

————, and Manchester, Frederick, trans. *The Upanishads: Breath of the Eternal*. New York: New American Library, 1957 [1948].

Prall, D. W. *Aesthetic Judgment.* With an introduction by Ralph Ross. New York: Thomas Y. Crowell Co., 1967.

Price, George. *The Narrow Pass: A Study of Kierkegaard's Concept of Man.* London: Hutchinson & Co., 1963.

Rank, Otto. *The Myth of the Birth of the Hero and Other Writings.* Edited by Philip Freund. New York: Random House, Vintage Books, 1964.

Rans, Geoffrey. *Edgar Allan Poe.* Edinburgh and London: Oliver and Boyd, 1965.

Read, Herbert. *The Meaning of Art.* Middlesex, England: Penguin Books, 1956 [1931].

———. *The Forms of Things Unknown.* New York: World Publishing Co., Meridian Books, 1963.

———. *The True Voice of Feeling: Studies in English Romantic Poetry.* London: Faber & Faber, 1968.

Reik, Theodor. *Listening with the Third Ear.* New York: Pyramid Books, 1965 [1948].

Richards, I. A. *Principles of Literary Criticism.* London: Routledge & Kegan Paul, 1955 [1924].

Rilke, Rainer Maria. *Sonnets to Orpheus.* Translated by M. D. Herter Norton. New York: W. W. Norton & Co., 1942.

———. *Letters to a Young Poet.* Translated by M. D. Herter Norton. Rev. ed. New York: W. W. Norton & Co., 1954.

———. *Selected Letters.* Edited, with an introduction, by Harry T. Moore. Garden City, New York: Doubleday & Co., Anchor Books, 1960.

———. *The Notebooks of Malte Laurids Brigge.* Translated by M. D. Herter Norton. New York: W. W. Norton & Co., 1964.

Rose, Edward J. " 'A World With Full and Fair Proportions': The Aesthetics and Politics of Vision." *Thoreau Society Bulletin 19,* 10, no. 1 (1963): 45–53.

———. "Blake's Hand: Symbol and Design in JERUSALEM." *The University of Texas Studies in Literature and Language,* 6, no. 1 (Spring, 1964): 47–58.

———. "Blake's Milton: The Poet as Poem." *Blake Studies,* 1, no. 1 (1968): 16–38.

Ross, Nancy Wilson. *Three Ways of Asian Wisdom: Hinduism, Buddhism, and Zen, and Their Significance for the West.* New York: Simon and Schuster, 1966.

Rougemont, Denis de. *Passion and Society.* Translated by Montgomery Belgion. Rev. ed. London: Faber and Faber, 1956 [first appeared in 1941].

Royce, Joseph R., ed. *Psychology and the Symbol: An Interdisciplinary Symposium.* New York: Random House, 1965.

Ruitenbeek, Hendrik M., ed. *Psychoanalysis and Literature.* New York: E. P. Dutton & Co., 1964.

————, ed. *The Creative Imagination: Psychoanalysis and the Genius of Inspira-tion.* Chicago: Quadrangle Books, 1965.

Santayana, George. *The Sense of Beauty: Being the Outline of Aesthetic Theory.* New York: Dover Publications, 1955 [1896].

Sartre, Jean-Paul. *The Psychology of Imagination.* New York: Citadel Press, 1966 [1948].

————. *Existential Psychoanalysis.* Translated by Hazel E. Barnes; introduction by Rollo May. Chicago: Henry Regnery Co., 1966.

————. *Being and Nothingness: An Essay in Phenomenological Ontology.* Special abridged edition; translated and with an introduction by Hazel E. Barnes. New York: Citadel Press, 1966 [1956].

Schiller, Friedrich. *On the Aesthetic Education of Man: In a Series of Letters.* Translated, with an introduction, by Reginald Snell. New York: Frederick Unger Publishing Co., 1965.

Schneider, Herbert W. *A History of American Philosophy.* New York: Forum Books, 1957.

————. "American Transcendentalism's Escape from Phenomenology." In *Transcendentalism and Its Legacy,* edited by Simon Myron and Thornton H. Parsons, pp. 215–28. Ann Arbor: University of Michigan Press, 1966.

Sewall, Richard B. *The Vision of Tragedy.* New Haven: Yale University Press, 1959.

Shakespeare, William. *The Complete Works.* Edited, with an introduction and glossary, by Peter Alexander. Tudor Edition. London and Glasgow: Collins, 1954 [first published in 1951].

Shapiro, Karl. *Beyond Criticism.* Lincoln: University of Nebraska Press, 1953.

Shelley, P. B. *The Complete Poetical Works.* Edited by Thomas Hutchinson. London: Oxford University Press, 1965.

————. *Selected Poetry and Prose.* Edited, with an introduction, by Harold Bloom. Toronto: New American Library of Canada, 1966.

Slote, Bernice. *Keats and the Dramatic Principle.* Lincoln: University of Nebraska Press, 1958.

Spender, Stephen. "The Making of a Poem." In *The Creative Process,* edited by Brewster Ghiselin, pp. 112–25. Toronto: New American Library of Canada, 1967 [1965].

Steiner, George. *Language and Silence: Essays on Language, Literature, and the Inhuman.* New York: Atheneum, 1967.

Stevens, Wallace. *The Collected Poems.* New York: Alfred A. Knopf, 1954.

Stone, Edward. *Voices of Despair: Four Motifs in American Literature.* Athens, Ohio: Ohio University Press, 1966.

Suzuki, D. T. *Mysticism: Christian and Buddhist—The Eastern and Western Way.* New York: Collier Books, 1962 [1957].

Swartz, Robert J., ed. *Perceiving, Sensing, and Knowing.* Garden City, New York: Doubleday & Co., Anchor Books, 1965.

Symons, Arthur. *The Symbolist Movement in Literature.* Introduction by Richard Ellmann. New York: E. P. Dutton and Co., 1958.

Tagore, Rabindranath. *Creative Unity.* London: Macmillan & Co., 1922.

Tate, Allen. *Reactionary Essays on Poetry and Ideas.* New York: Charles Scribner's Sons, 1936.

———. "Narcissus As Narcissus." In *The Creative Process,* edited by Brewster Ghiselin, pp. 134–45. Toronto: New American Library of Canada, 1967 [1965].

Thoreau, Henry David. *Walden and Other Writings.* Edited, with a biographical introduction, by Brooks Atkinson; foreword by Townsend Scuddey. New York: Modern Library, 1950.

———. *Collected Poems.* Edited by Carl Bode. Baltimore: Johns Hopkins Press, 1964.

Thorpe, James, ed. *The Aims and Methods of Scholarship in Modern Languages and Literature.* New York: Modern Language Association of America, 1963.

———. *Relations of Literary Study: Essays on Interdisciplinary Contributions.* New York: Modern Language Association of America, 1967.

Tillich, Paul. *The Shaking of the Foundations.* New York: Charles Scribner's Sons, 1948.

———. *The New Being.* New York: Charles Scribner's Sons, 1955.

———. *Love, Power, and Justice.* New York: Oxford University Press, 1960 [1954].

———. *The Courage to Be.* New Haven: Yale University Press, 1966 [1952].

Trilling, Lionel. *The Liberal Imagination: Essays on Literature and Society.* Garden City, New York: Doubleday & Co., Anchor Books, 1953.

———, ed. *The Selected Letters of John Keats.* Garden City, New York: Doubleday & Co., 1956.

Unamuno, Miguel de. *Tragic Sense of Life.* Translated by J. E. Crawford Flitch. New York: Dover Publications, 1954.

Underhill, Evelyn. *Mysticism: A Study in the Nature and Development of Man's Spiritual Consciousness.* New York: E. P. Dutton & Co., 1961 [1911].

Vatsyayana. *The Kama Sutra.* Translated by Sir Richard Burton and F. F. Arbuthnot; edited, with a preface, by W. G. Archer; introduction by K. M. Panikkar. New York: Capricorn Books, 1963 [1883].

Walzel, Oskar. *German Romanticism.* New York: Capricorn Books, 1966 [1932].

Watts, Alan W. *The Two Hands of God: The Myths of Polarity.* New York: George Braziller, 1963.

———. *The Supreme Identity: An Essay on Oriental Metaphysics and the Christian Religion.* New York: Noonday Press, 1966.

Wellek, Réné, and Warren, Austin. *Theory of Literature.* Rev. ed. New York: Harcourt, Brace, & World, 1956.

Westbrook, Perry D. *The Greatness of Man: An Essay on Dostoyevsky and Whitman.* New York: Thomas Yoseloff, 1961.

Weston, Jessie L. *From Ritual to Romance.* Garden City, New York: Doubleday & Co. 1957 [1920].

Whalley, George. *Poetic Process.* London: Routledge & Kegan Paul, 1953.

Wheelwright, Philip. *Heraclitus.* New York: Atheneum, 1964 [originally published by Princeton University Press in 1959].

Whitehead, Alfred North, *Adventures of Ideas.* New York: New American Library, 1933.

————. *Process and Reality: An Essay in Cosmology.* New York: Harper & Row, Harper Torchbooks, 1960.

Whitman, Walt. *Leaves of Grass.* With an introduction by Gay Wilson Allen. New York: New American Library, 1959.

Wild, John. *The Challenge of Existentialism.* Bloomington: Indiana University Press, 1966 [1955].

Wilde, Jean T., and Kimmel, William, eds. and trans. *The Search for Being: Essays from Kierkegaard to Sartre on the Problem of Existence.* New York: Twayne Publishers, 1962.

Williams, Oscar, ed. *The Mentor Book of Major British Poets.* With an introduction by Julian Symons. Toronto: New American Library of Canada, 1963.

Wordsworth, William. *Poetical Works.* Edited with introduction and notes by Thomas Hutchinson; a new edition, revised by Ernest de Selincourt. London: Oxford University Press, 1960 [1936].

Zabel, Morton Dauwen, ed. *The Portable Henry James.* New York: Viking Press, 1965 [1951].

Zweig, Arnold. *The Living Thoughts of Spinoza.* New York: David McKay Company, 1963.

INDEX OF POEMS ACCORDING
TO FIRST LINES

Poems are quoted in full or in part; numbers within parentheses refer to the Harvard Edition of *The Poems of Emily Dickinson.*

GENERAL INDEX

Abrams, M. H., 289–90*n*8, 291*n*13, 291*n*15

Absence, 38, 43, 100, 136, 271–72, 285*n*19; landscape of, 46–47, 249; as intense presence, 48; as mystery, 49; as experience, 50–54; as being, 55–56; as distance, 57–62; as withdrawal, 63–66; as deception, 67–69; as perception, 70–72; as love, 73–77; as death, 78–82; as time, 83–84. *See also* Presence

Aesthetic(s), 2, 28, 32, 43, 47, 49–50 passim, 51, 52, 54, 57, 62, 64, 65, 66, 70, 82, 85–87 passim, 100, 117, 120, 126, 160, 217, 230, 249, 261, 273; of terror, 7, 18, 271; strategy, 37, 114; vision, 58, 129, 159; of love, 136, 138, 170; of marriage, 159, 163; of continuity, 180, 228

Agape, 136, 153, 166, 272, 302*n*13, 303*n*15

American culture, 4–5

Amherst, 62, 131, 275

Anderson, Charles R., 1, 5, 74, 200, 277*n*1, 286*n*27, 290*n*11, 296–97*n*42, 298*n*46, 308*n*10, 311*n*8; on Dickinson's Biblical language, 31, 34; on Attar and India, 118–19

Anguish, 10, 12, 54, 56, 102, 103, 165, 197, 210, 231, 234; existential, 11, 55, 232; of dying, 195, 206; of existence, 225, 235

Art, 1, 11, 16, 18, 20, 39, 46, 51, 62, 65, 66, 102, 103, 118, 121, 122, 126, 130, 132, 158, 176, 208, 234, 242, 244, 257, 262, 270, 274, 275, 288–89*n*4, 293*n*27, 313*n*14; as process, 2, 125, 296–97*n*42; Dickinson's, 5, 8, 29, 38, 49, 75, 123, 125, 127, 129, 153, 163, 225, 227, 232, 243, 259, 265; as "haunted house," 43–44, 101, 108

Aurobindo, Sri, 110

Awe (awful), 11, 12, 16, 20, 41, 52, 56, 60, 106, 109, 110, 133, 161, 178, 179, 187, 202, 234, 259, 295*n*34; of creation, 39, 46, 107

Baptism: theme of, 33–34; mark of, 159; Kierkegaard on, 281*n*21

Beauvoir, Simone de, 56

Being, 5, 14, 22, 26–32 passim, 34, 43–44 passim, 46–47 passim, 51, 57, 69, 95, 100, 103, 106, 111, 113, 126, 129, 135, 139, 147, 150, 156, 159, 165–67 passim, 175, 176, 178, 184, 203, 204, 207, 209, 218, 221, 231, 239–41, 243, 249, 250, 264–65 passim, 267–68 passim, 269, 271, 273, 284*n*5; mystery of, 9, 29, 37, 49, 254; terror of, 16, 55, 210, 230; the here and now of, 23, 170, 179; as nonbeing, 54, 80, 283–84*n*4; as becoming, 54, 56; of the existent, 56, 260–61; sense of, 77, 99, 229; the abyss of, 172, 230, 239, 254; the awareness of, 215, 233, 251, 253, 256; body as the container of, 245–47; phenomenology of, 251–53. *See also* Identity; Self

347

62, 71, 78, 80, 100, 136, 229, 271. *See also*
Absence
Process, 4, 7–9 passim, 14, 23, 39, 59, 62,
72, 83, 90, 95, 98, 99, 106, 132, 143, 148,
152, 159, 169, 230, 246, 252, 253, 261–
63, 266, 293*n*25; of life and art, 2, 76,
101, 179, 180, 210; poetic and creative,
2, 7, 29, 38, 69, 85, 92, 93, 97, 107, 109,
111, 112, 114–19, 123–25, 129–30, 133,
234, 271, 272, 294*n*29; of being and becoming, 54, 76, 117, 135, 261; of life
and death, 79, 113, 201, 204, 211, 213,
219, 221, 223, 225, 293*n*25; of love, 140,
142, 146, 149, 151, 164, 300–01*n*4; of
self and identity, 231, 237, 245, 267
Psychoanalysis (psychologize), 3, 105
Psychology (psychologist), 15, 105,
293–94*n*27

Quest, 7, 39, 76, 229–31 passim, 244, 273

Read, Herbert, 105, 284*n*13, 289*n*6,
291*n*13, 293–94*n*27, 296*n*38
Reality, 12, 16, 30, 40–42 passim, 50, 52,
53, 57, 58, 60, 62, 72, 80, 82, 118, 122,
129, 133, 143, 152, 178, 180, 182, 191,
198, 199, 204, 206, 225, 237, 262, 271,
272, 307*n*8; primal and spiritual, 2, 28,
37, 38, 46, 68, 87, 93, 103, 243; existential, 7, 67, 85, 86, 98, 180; external and
objective, 26, 28, 58, 67, 76, 91–97 passim, 156, 177, 241; poetic and creative,
86, 90, 114, 164, 254, 255
Rebirth, 8, 61, 76, 114, 115, 131, 159, 179,
215, 217, 223, 236, 304*n*19
Rilke, Rainer Maria, 5, 59, 64, 97,
279–80*n*3, 284*n*7, 291*n*13, 304–05*n*1
Romantic(ist), 5, 76, 85, 92, 95, 289–90*n*8,
291*n*13
Rose, Edward J., 221, 296*n*39, 296–97*n*42,
298*n*45
Rougemont, Denis de, 302*n*13

Schiller, Friedrich, 66, 284*n*13, 291*n*13
Self, 2, 19, 22, 30, 38, 50, 66, 83, 98, 99,
106, 134, 149, 151, 162, 166, 169, 190,
203, 229–69, 273, 286*n*26, 310–11*n*7,

312*n*12; essential or regenerated, 9, 26,
41, 43, 76, 110, 138, 143, 229, 230, 236,
239, 241, 249, 254, 256, 257–59, 263,
264, 267, 268, 269; narrow or egocentric, 26, 41, 80, 193, 208, 230, 235, 237,
239, 240, 241, 261; discovery or realization of, 75, 76, 128, 136, 230, 231,
234–38, 242, 249, 251, 254, 271; as integral to the other or nonself, 147, 156,
157, 231, 259–61. *See also* Being; Identity
Sewall, Richard B., 30, 273–74, 279*n*13,
279*n*14, 279*n*15, 282*n*25, 309–10*n*2,
313–14*n*3
Shakespeare, William, 2; *Hamlet,* 53, 212;
Romeo and Juliet, 283*n*3, 295*n*35; *King
Lear,* 304*n*18; *Othello,* 309*n*12
Shelley, Percy Bysshe, "A Defence of Poetry," 28, 281*n*12, 282*n*29, 295*n*35
Silence, 8, 15, 41–43 passim, 46, 49–54
passim, 57, 73, 91, 109, 116, 125, 133,
136, 151, 152, 164, 175, 179, 180, 182,
183, 204, 209, 220, 229, 230, 235, 238,
242, 243, 271, 273, 282–83*n*29, 310*n*6
Solitude, 53, 62–64, 99, 110, 204, 230, 238,
239, 312–13*n*13
Soul (spirit). *See* Being; Identity; Self
Spencer, Benjamin T., 278*n*11
Spender, Stephen, 293*n*24
Steiner, George, "Silence and the Poet,"
282–83*n*29
Stevens, Wallace, 97–99, 275, 291*n*13,
292*n*21; "The World as Meditation," 97;
"Credences of Summer," 97–98; "The
Man with the Blue Guitar," 98; "The
Snow Man," 98–99
Stillness, 7, 8, 49, 50, 54, 57, 150, 229, 271
Suffering, 7, 8, 11–14 passim, 23, 30–32
passim, 38, 103, 106, 110, 117, 123, 125,
132, 140–42 passim, 149, 163, 166, 168,
176, 192, 230–34 passim, 248, 267,
271–73 passim, 309–10*n*2
Symbol(s), 2, 9, 23, 31, 54, 58, 69, 70, 104,
106, 108, 120, 121, 131, 142, 161, 162,
163, 170, 175, 178, 206, 217, 223, 227,
239, 247, 252, 257, 271; of life and
death, 9, 70, 161, 170, 178, 217, 223. *See
also* Symbolic; Symbolism